TALKING LEADERSHIP

LEEDS

TALKING LEADERSHIP

CONVERSATIONS
WITH
POWERFUL
WOMEN

■

EDITED BY

MARY S. HARTMAN

RUTGERS UNIVERSITY PRESS
NEW BRUNSWICK, NEW JERSEY, AND LONDON

Photo Credits:
Peggy Antrobus – courtesy of DAWN
Susan Berresford – photo © Ben Russell
Mildred Dresselhaus – photo © Mark Ostow, Boston, Mass.
Antonia Hernandez – photo by George Rodriguez
bell hooks – photography by Pinderhughes
Lois Juliber – courtesy of Colgate-Palmolive
Karen Nussbaum – photo by Rick Reinhard
Jacqueline Pitanguy – photo by Nick Romanenko
Anna Quindlen – photo by Royce Carlton, Inc.
Nafis Sadik – courtesy of UNFPA
Patricia Schroeder – courtesy of Patricia Schroeder
Ruth J. Simmons – photo by Jim Gite
Christine Todd Whitman – Linz Photography, Toms River, N.J.

Library of Congress Cataloging-in-publication Data
Talking leadership : conversations with powerful women / edited by
  Mary Hartman.
      p.   cm.
   Includes bibliographical references.
   ISBN 0-8135-2559-4 (cloth : alk. paper). — ISBN 0-8135-2560-8
(pbk.)
     1. Leadership in women. 2. Women in development—Interviews.
3. Women in politics—Interviews. 4. Women in public life—
Interviews. 5. Women politicians—Interviews.   I. Hartman, Mary,
1941–   .
HQ1233.T35 1999
305.4—dc21   98-17574
                                                        CIP

British Cataloging-in-Publication data for this book is available from
the British Library.

Composition by Colophon Typesetting

Manufactured in the United States of America

CONTENTS

■

ACKNOWLEDGMENTS

■

First, the interviewers wish to express their thanks to the special women who agreed to participate in these conversations about their lives in leadership. They have made this inaugural book of the Institute for Women's Leadership a joy to produce as well as a lively record of the ways women are leading at the dawn of a new century.

Support that made this book possible has come from many places. A grant from the Beneficial Corporation enabled the institute to bring several of these leaders to campus for public presentations and interviews. A gift from Albert and Ruth Morgan Kurtz (Douglass College '45), who were among the early benefactors of the institute and its programs, covered many of the expenses of the project. Students who expressed enthusiasm for these particular leaders, often after hearing their presentations in one of our programs, deserve thanks for helping us to decide whom to include in the interviews.

At every state of this project, from selecting and contacting interviewees to correcting final copy of the transcribed conversations, we have been blessed by the help of committed and creative people. Special thanks go to Randy Bergman, Finn Caspersen, Jill Ker Conway, Ann Dwyer, Beth Hutchison, Gretchen W. Johnson, Richard Keller, Jane Kenny, Eileen McGinnis, Janet S. Mais, Joseph J. Seneca, Marlie Wasserman, and Virginia Yans-McLaughlin.

TALKING LEADERSHIP

INTRODUCTION

■

Margaret Mead once said, "Never doubt that a small group of thought-ful, committed citizens can change the world: Indeed, it's the only thing that ever has."[1] *Talking Leadership: Conversations with Powerful Women* is a set of conversations with thirteen women. All of them came to the conclusion that the world needed to change and that part of the job was up to them. Some of these women were conscious from the beginning that leading was what they were all about. Others came late, and with strong misgivings, to that awareness. In the end, however, all would agree that, at the least, small groups of committed persons have played a crit-ical role in changing the world and will doubtless continue to do so. Yet although each would call herself an optimist, none has illusions about the challenges remaining, no matter which part of the world she has cho-sen to change.

The comfort level with the term *leader* varies widely here among the thirteen women interviewed—as it does among their interlocutors, all of whom are affiliated with the Institute for Women's Leadership at Douglass College of Rutgers University. Some of these women not only readily em-brace the term *leader* but admit being energized by the chance to exercise the power that such recognition confers. Others are uncomfortable or im-patient with the term, citing negative associations with traditional leader-ship systems or styles. Some note distaste for a media culture that thrives on manufacturing—and then demolishing—superstar "leaders," a practice they say eclipses a far larger number of at least equally worthy persons. Several women think we need to overhaul both the theory and practice of leadership. Just as important, each offers, in her reflections on leadership as well as in the example of her remarkable life, visions of what such a new theory and practice might look like.

Regardless of their different reactions to the label *leader,* these women are united in a commitment to positive change—change that includes im-proving women's lives and options. Some have made the enhancement of women's lives the main focus of their work; others treat it as a significant if not central objective. Without necessarily agreeing on which specific changes are most needed or should happen first, they all, it is fair to say, welcome evidence that women everywhere are emerging as more visible and vocal players in every social arena. As Charlotte Bunch, who currently directs Rutgers's Center for Women's Global Leadership, puts it in her preface to a recent study of women leaders in higher education:

> *During the past three decades, women have taken a leadership role in redefining fundamental aspects of our lives—work, family, sexuality, equality, and justice. Women have influenced how we define reality, conceive of knowledge, and exercise leadership. This has happened both through the collective leadership of women as a social force and through the efforts of many individual women giving shape to this movement in its diverse forms.[2]*

For people accustomed to recognizing as leaders only those who hold formal or "positional" slots on an organizational grid—elected officials or corporate officers, for example—some of the women interviewed here will appear to be peculiar choices. The president of a college will make sense, to be sure, as will the governor of a state or the president of a large corporation. But the inclusion of journalists and writers, or exemplary scholars, not to mention activists working outside the formal structures of power altogether, is likely to raise questions. What is more, to the extent that a model of the leader as a male figure remains rooted in our collective consciousness, even high elected officials and corporate officers who are women will continue to seem anomalous, never quite fitting the image of a real leader despite having attained formal leadership positions. (Many still refer to such women in the grating but still prevalent phraseology of "lady" governors or "lady" presidents—imposters, that is, not the genuine article.)

It is true enough that women remain scarce at the uppermost levels of formal leadership hierarchies. At this writing, for example, fewer than 1 percent of Fortune 500 companies in the United States are headed by women; and only two states, New Jersey and New Hampshire, have elected female governors. Although for the first time in history more than half of the world's governments are declared democracies, women have very low representation in most elected bodies, averaging under 12 percent worldwide. (The U.S. congressional figure in 1997 stood at 11 percent.)[3] Even the Nordic parliaments, where quotas in some places now help to ensure higher female representation, typically average just over one-third women, whereas the lowest representation of women, in the Arabic states, is just over 3 percent. Of the 179 states with parliaments in 1997 (59 of them with bicameral structures), only 17 had one elective body that was headed by a woman; and ironically, most of the handful of women who are actual heads of state come from countries where women's overall economic and political participation rates are among the lowest in the world.[4]

The participants in this book's conversations endorse the view, more readily accepted in developing societies than in fully industrialized ones, that the term "leader" properly encompasses not only the occupants of formal positions in the upper rungs of major institutions but also those whose ability to influence and move people has been demonstrated through teaching, writing, or being effective actors on a whole variety of less prominent stages—regional sites, neighborhood communities, even family households. Most people, in fact, are scarcely aware that throughout the long span of human history, men and women alike have done most of their leading from the base of their immediate households and extended kinship networks, rather than from the many religious, political, economic, and cultural institutions that have come to be erected outside those networks.

Overlooking this fact has allowed us to imagine, quite mistakenly, that women only lately have begun to emerge as leaders, whereas they, like men, have always led. As societies shifted more of their critical economic and social functions to places beyond households and local communities— "public" places that men, for various reasons, came to occupy sooner than women—leadership itself, along with the most prestigious social rewards, came to be associated ever more tightly with whatever it was that men were doing in such places, whether praying, making money, waging international warfare, or passing trade legislation. In recent years, of course, growing numbers of women have left their households daily for paid work in such places. The more educated and privileged among them, once confined to extradomestic employment in a restricted choice of fields, such as teaching and nursing, have increasingly entered a broad range of professional arenas. In the process, the leadership women used to exercise almost exclusively within their households and communities has at last begun to be felt in union halls, legislative assemblies, faculty meetings, and boardrooms. The transition is far from complete, however, and has produced challenges of its own—at work sites and within the families and neighborhoods back home.

Women's comparatively longer history of leadership in their homes and communities is likely to be discounted or completely overlooked in industrialized societies such as the United States, in which most adult married women since World War II have shifted quite rapidly into paid employment outside their homes. Critics remarking on the disintegrating infrastructure of neighborhoods, for example, or the dwindling quality of leadership in schools, fail to recognize that it was the confinement of most women's contributions to these arenas that actually forestalled even swifter decline. Meanwhile, for the same achievements in an expanded public realm that have brought leadership recognition to their brothers, husbands, and sons, women have often met with a chorus of blame from men and women alike, at least in the U.S. context. Senator Barbara Mikulski captures the classic double bind of one type of would-be leader, the female political candidate, in a wry account of what happens to any American woman with the audacity to run for public office: If she's married with children, according to Mikulski, she's clearly neglecting them. If she's married and without children, then it's her husband who is being neglected. If she's single, she's probably a little "funny," as they say. And if she's a widow, it's obvious that she killed the poor guy.

Some societies have been less critical of their aspiring female leaders, as these interviews suggest. One woman, an economist and a leader in promoting global development policies more attentive to women's needs, points out that throughout the Caribbean region, where she was raised, the minority of women fortunate enough to receive an advanced education have not been made to feel guilty about pursuing an ambitious public career while being married with children. Indeed it is expected of such privileged women that they use their education well, which helps to explain why the region has produced more than average numbers of women leaders in so many fields. Another enabling factor there, as she notes, is the continued strength of extended families that can temporarily absorb the children of mothers working outside the home.

Nuclear families, in contrast, hardly offer the same child-care flexibility, with only two adults normally residing in each household. The "solutions" to child-care needs in such cases continue to feature stressful and expensive individual arrangements. In a recent survey of the career paths of almost five hundred senior U.S. women executives (in which one-fifth stated that they decided not to have children at all and more than one-quarter that they had postponed having them), the nearly two-thirds with children reported that they purchased child care and made drastic accommodations in their personal lives, including forgoing sleep and—in more than half the cases—eliminating most outside interests. It is worth noting, too, that whereas fewer than two-thirds of these senior female executives had children, 85 percent of American women overall have children, as do more than 90 percent of senior *male* executives.[5]

Social context, supporting or impeding women's ability to assume leadership roles, then, is one of many topics addressed in these dialogues. But before turning to some of the others, it makes sense to place *Talking*

Leadership in a broader context, first by saying something about the current interest in the topic of leadership—and women's leadership in particular—and then by noting how this book came to be and whom its collaborators see as its audience.

During the last third of the twentieth century, women's advance into leadership positions, particularly formal ones, has hardly kept pace with other advances that many—though hardly all—women throughout the world have experienced. Those advances include not only a raised awareness of their rights and needs but an expansion of organizations serving women's concerns, increased employment opportunities, improved access to education, greater availability of health care, and expanded legal protection against sexual violence and abuse. At the 1995 Non-Governmental Organization Forum of the United Nations Fourth Conference on Women in Beijing, a gathering of established groups working worldwide in these and related areas, the two stated goals were to influence the official conference proceedings and "to consolidate women's global leadership at the Forum itself, through a broadly inclusive, substantive and visionary celebration of women's diversity, common ground and universal aspirations."[6]

The strategy was effective. In addition to addressing issues of poverty, education, human rights, and more, the formal Beijing Declaration and Platform for Action explicitly affirmed the objective of expanding women's leadership roles, which some participating national delegations had already endorsed before the conference. Madeleine K. Albright, then U.S. ambassador to the United Nations and head of the U.S. delegation, cited, for example, "expanding the participation of women in political and economic decision making" as one of the five U.S. goals for the conference.[7] The resulting action objective, "Women in Power and Decision Making," was one of twelve strategic objectives in the Platform for Action passed by the participating nations in Beijing. It featured two specific recommendations: (1) "Take measures to ensure women's equal access and full participation in power structures and decision making," and (2) "increase women's capacity to participate in decision making and leadership."[8]

Before this formal and highly visible United Nations affirmation of the need for more women in leadership positions, the dearth of women leaders had attracted little attention, even within women's movements around the world. Some limited if important efforts had, however, been undertaken. For example, in the education, foundation, corporate, and nonprofit communities in the United States, a few programs had been launched for the purpose of understanding and promoting women's leadership. These efforts owe something to periodic concerns about strengthening the overall quality of leadership nationally, especially in the business and political sectors. A far more important impetus came from the awareness that as opportunities for women and other underrepresented groups expanded, their continuing absence in positions of real authority became ever more glaring and awkward to explain and defend.

The goals of these initiatives included understanding women's status and performance in particular leadership settings, examining the causes of their underrepresentation, and preparing them—as students, as volunteers, or as participants in the workforce—for leadership and advancement. The purpose was also to help society benefit more fully from the untapped talents and leadership potential of more than half the population. Although most of these initiatives are rather recent, a handful, including programs to research leadership and to promote women's advancement in higher education administration, in the corporate world, and in elective and appointive office, date back to the 1960s and 1970s.[9]

It is noteworthy, however, that despite this activity, and despite clear evidence that women *are* emerging in increasing numbers as "positional" as well as "nonpositional" leaders, our understanding of what leadership is all about, and whether women's leadership is different—as some have argued—has not deepened a great deal. Anne Firth Murray, founder and first director of the Global Fund for Women, remarked at a conference on women's leadership at Mills College in California in 1993, "Our common sense about leadership leads us to paraphrase former Supreme Court Justice Potter Stewart: leadership, like obscenity, is impossible to define, but *we know it when we see it!* Or do we?" she asks. Murray stresses that whatever we think about it, ever more women are being elected and put forward as leaders:

> *Who cares? Are their styles different? Does it make a difference that women are in these positions? Will this trend last? Should it? In the meantime, we see thousands of women's groups emerging around the world, in all countries, with visions of a different future for women and society. These groups are taking the lead to change their societies; the so-called leaders of their societies and in this society are often indecisive, lacking in vision, ineffective, lacking in compassion, and maybe even corrupt. People—especially women, I believe—are taking matters into their own hands. They are changing their worlds.[10]*

The women's movement has itself shown ambivalence toward leadership and proved better at providing critiques of established authority than at either supporting its own leaders or devising more effective alternative models of leadership. Most of the nearly six hundred women's studies programs in the United States, moreover, have neither singled out leadership as a major issue nor targeted it as a significant new research field. Nonetheless, among scholars and activists focusing on women's lives, a consensus has begun to emerge that there is a need to reimagine leadership, to think in new ways about what it is and what it might be, and to articulate more forcefully why it matters that women in far larger numbers be supported in seeking and securing decision-making positions.

It is not that we lack a scholarly literature that grapples with broad issues of theory and practice. Although women's leadership as a research field is still new, leadership studies more generally have been a minor but growing research area throughout the twentieth century. Between the mid-eighties and the late nineties, well over a thousand books and articles were published in English alone on the topic of leadership. What is more, approximately five hundred colleges and universities in the United States instituted programs on leadership and leadership development over the same time frame.[11]

It is is no coincidence, though, that a preoccupation with leadership has been and remains most intense in the business community, especially among corporations and business schools newly concerned about international competitiveness. Joseph Rost, who wrote the comprehensive and controversial *Leadership for the Twenty-First Century* (1991),[12] complains that a major problem with leadership studies is that too much of the research has been done from within the single discipline of business and rests on a corporate paradigm that too simply equates good leadership with good management.[13] He adds that despite the promising direction for future research in James MacGregor Burns's *Leadership* (1978), still the most widely read and respected book in the field, and despite Burns's singling out a so-called transformational mode of leadership that appeals to more elevated human needs and values, leadership studies have failed to undergo the analytical paradigm shift that might have been predicted from such a compelling formulation. Instead, Rost says, the concept of transformational leadership was cheapened in the eighties by popularizers in the business field who hijacked it to serve the bottom-line needs of downsizing corporate managers.[14]

Rost is especially troubled by the lack of clarity in the literature on the activity of leadership, as well as on its goals. In his examination of close to six hundred books and articles on leadership written since 1900, he found that only one-third even bothers to offer a definition of leadership. The other two-thirds, he suggests, appear to take a common understanding of leadership for granted. After a lengthy bibliographic foray, Rost offers the following terse definition of his own: "Leadership is an influence relationship among leaders and followers who intend real changes that reflect their mutual purposes."[15]

Though it raises obvious questions about the qualities and values of both leaders and followers—questions to which Rost does devote a good deal of time in his discussion—this rather elegant, brief definition has the real merit of acknowledging that leadership is a goal-oriented activity that always involves a relationship. It does not reside exclusively in the leader, as traditional versions of the "great man" theory of leadership tend to do. Rost explains, moreover, why leadership must not be approached from the vantage point of a single discipline, such as business. His stirring call for a multi- and interdisciplinary approach to the subject "leadership" is reminiscent, in fact, of earlier calls for the complete reenvisioning of the subject "woman," which continues to be the ongoing passion of the rich, interdisciplinary field that is women's studies:

> *Leadership studies as an academic discipline needs to come out of the woodwork of management science in all of its guises (business, education, health, public, nonprofit) and out of such disciplines as social psychology, political science, and sociology wherein academics have developed an interest in leadership as a subspecialty. Leadership scholars need to develop an academic presence as an interdisciplinary area of studies serving both undergraduate and graduate students in specialized programs that deal with the study and practice of leadership in organizations and in societies.*[16]

Neither Rost's nor most other studies of leadership—the majority of which are summarized in the massive *Bass & Stogdill's Handbook of Leadership*,[17] a 900-plus–page tome that analyzes some 4,725 studies of leadership—spend much time on the topic of women's leadership, or on the growing literature devoted to women as leaders. A few book-length studies on women in particular fields do address more theoretical issues of women and leadership, typically in the fields of business, politics, and education,[18] but the bulk of the material on women and leadership consists of articles in specialized journals, mostly in the disciplines just cited and often by persons in these fields whose professional training includes psychology.

My own simple computer search for materials—including dissertations in progress from the mid-1980s to the mid-1990s in what might be called the subspecialty of leadership and women—confirms that we are far from approaching genuinely interdisciplinary research as yet. Leadership studies focusing on women remain confined to specialties within a few disciplines that use traditional methodologies drawn from those disciplines. The bulk of such research is in management; a significant body of work is, however, being done in education administration and, to a lesser extent, in politics and political behavior. In addition, in the professional student life journals, there is a growing and often engaging literature on leadership programs for students.

It must be noted that in the 1970s, there was a brief but intense focus on issues of leadership and organization in some women's liberation movement writings. Such attention owed much to the mixed results when early consciousness-raising groups and other women's forums sought to eliminate altogether the formal hierarchies and standard organizational structures negatively associated with traditional, male leadership styles. These initiatives often brought about the emergence of informal or "hidden" leadership hierarchies that many women realized were undercutting the stated aims of their movement. Efforts were then made to reaffirm leadership but to devise more suitable and workable feminist approaches. Many of the insights about leadership from this era remain fresh and relevant today—see, for example, discussions in feminist journals, notably *Quest*, which in 1976 devoted an entire issue to different perspectives on women's leadership.[19]

In the seventies, too, the remarkable, pioneering *Men and Women of the Corporation* by Rosabeth Moss Kanter challenged the view that male models of leadership were the most effective and that women needed to become more like men.[20] Kanter argued that women's problems in the corporation had more to do with the unequal distribution of power and resources than with any biological or psychological imperative. Women managers encountered difficulties not because they were women, she said, but because they were "tokens" and isolated; and women bosses were unpopular because they usually lacked power comparable to that of their male counterparts in an organization. Yet the feminist conversation on leadership was interrupted in the eighties—or at least the public portion of that conversation—as other issues claimed the attention of theorists. After nearly two decades, the interrupted dialogue is resuming among theorists, practitioners, and a wider world that has become increasingly curious about women's leadership.

In the meantime, the mainstream leadership literature discovered women as subjects, although it began not by asking what was wrong with leadership that so few women were singled out as leaders, but rather what was wrong with women that they had not achieved more leadership positions. It then provided different versions of the same bleak answer: certain rooted female behaviors are antithetical to successful leadership. It now appears that some of these early studies of female traits were merely feeding back preconceived views about women's lack of leadership ability;[21] but for some time, would-be experts solemnly informed would-be female leaders, especially those in business, that the single thing they needed to do to be more effective leaders was to act (and, of course, to dress) more like men. This was precisely what women managers in corporate contexts in the pre– and post–World War II generations had been doing right along, without benefit of condescending outside advice. The tactic was adopted as a survival measure by career women who felt constrained not only to "pass" as men—insofar as this can be done—but to abandon any thought of marriage and children. By the time the new generation of the 1970s began to be urged to "dress for success," it was no longer mandatory to blend in with the men. It was merely wise.

Finally, both the research questions about women and leadership and the answers brought forward began to be more sophisticated, and some of the early findings that fixed on women's stubborn, if not innate, psychological deficiencies as leaders have been revisited. A study by Carol Watson from 1988, for example, directly tested the "a-woman-should-be-more-like-a-man" approach to leadership by encouraging female subjects in structured "boss/employee" encounters consciously to adopt a dominant, stereotypically male style. Those who did so, it turned out, were actually less effective overall than those adopting a more considerate, problem-solving, stereotypically female style, and *significantly* less effective when supervising all-male rather than mixed-sex groups of employees. Equally interesting, though, was that women in the employee groups gave these "dominant" female supervisors higher effectiveness ratings than they gave the "considerate" female supervisors. All women employees, however, reported a dislike for the female bosses greater than the men's, judging them more negatively regardless of whether they were consciously dominant or considerate.[22]

Using such research to advise would-be women managers contains practical perils, not to mention ethical dilemmas, even assuming that the results will be replicated over time in real-life situations—which is itself doubtful given that sex-role stereotypes not only are in flux but vary widely across generations as well as within racial and ethnic groups. In fact, other much-touted research, again in corporate contexts, is already arguing that the hierarchical, dominance style of leadership no longer is so effective in today's business contexts, especially in international market environments. According to these studies, women's "difference" needs to be seen in such settings as an asset rather than a liability. In short, women can be effective leaders not in spite but because of being women—or more precisely, because of the experiences they are likely to have shared as women and the sensibilities they are likely to have developed.[23]

The point here is *not* that one or the other of these theories about women's leadership is right or wrong. It is instead that as leadership research on women has begun to appear, it is forcing to the surface appropriate and important issues concerning the role of leadership in social change which ought to concern everyone. These include questions about the influence of varied social contexts—local, national, and global—that provide the "stages" on which leadership is played out. They involve hard questions about what "good" leadership really is and how important it is not only for making positive change but for guarding valued social and political structures, including democracy itself. They also include questions about which qualities leaders have exhibited that may have worked in the past but no longer work now, about whether so-called charismatic leadership by visionary individuals will or should continue to matter in the future. They raise new questions, too, about whether our institutions, educational ones in particular, should be more consciously preparing the next generation for the responsibilities of leadership.

In other words, focusing on the perceived aberrant position of women as leaders invites us to reenvision our entire view of leaders and leadership—past, present, and future. In tracking recent studies on women and leadership, in fact, the parallel that suggested itself to me, as a historian, was with the recognition of women as historical subjects. Trained in the field before women were imagined to have had a history of their own worth recording and taking seriously, I have been fortunate to participate with growing numbers of colleagues of several generations now in helping to recover women's past. In the early stages of that extraordinary collaborative adventure, the object was the straightforward one of showing that women were there too, that they were part of the story, and that they made some noteworthy contributions.

In time, practitioners came to see that what they were up to was something rather more grand than merely justifying a proposition that ought to have been self-evident, that is, that women have a past that is worth knowing. They showed that introducing women into historical accounts does not simply enrich those accounts, it changes them. In some cases, it changes them beyond recognition. Introducing women into leadership studies has the potential to do the same for that field. It can help us understand leaders and leadership in new and more complete ways, to see that people of both sexes from a whole range of past and current social contexts have long been engaged as actors making consequential change. Looking at the supposed "anomaly" that is women's leadership, in short, can animate that expansive multi- and interdisciplinary vision for "leadership studies" articulated above.

As to how this book came into being, as well as to its intended purposes and audience, it should be said first that *Talking Leadership* is the inaugural publication of the Institute for Women's Leadership, established in 1993 as a consortium of six units located on the campus of Douglass College of Rutgers University. Each member unit has its own distinctive mission and each engages in appropriate teaching, research, and public service associated with that mission. Consortium members, in the order of their founding, are Douglass College, the college for women at Rutgers University (1918); the Center for the American Woman and Politics (1971); the Rutgers/New Brunswick Women's Studies program (1971); the Institute for Research on Women (1976); the Center for Women's Global Leadership (1990); and the Center for Women and Work (1993). Directors and affiliated members of each unit not only participated in the interviews here but were involved in every stage of the project. (More information on each unit is included in the biographical notes on interviewers.)

Building on a history of cooperation, representatives of the units have been meeting regularly since the late eighties to discuss a closer working relationship around a theme and a set of projects of mutual interest. The group determined that understanding and encouraging women's participation in leadership and policymaking in all arenas was the single most pressing issue on the agenda for all women's advancement in the coming century as well as being the issue that our individual units were best prepared to address. Although just two of the units in the new institute—the Center for the American Woman and Politics and the Center for Women's Global Leadership—devote "full time" to issues of women's leadership, all units are critically engaged in research and programs addressing that topic, directly or indirectly, from a variety of perspectives.

The aim reflected in this collection of conversations has less to do, however, with the harmony that has emerged among institute member units on the theme of women's leadership than it does with the ongoing debates among us—and out there in the wider world—about what women's leadership (and leadership more generally) really is, why it matters, and what should be done about it. If there were genuine consensus on any of these issues, it would have made more sense for our Institute for Women's Leadership to present a blueprint of recommended research, teaching, and public service programs for interested parties to consider. Yet even the long experience of those of us most fully involved with women's leadership suggested another course for this "signature" publication of the new Institute— namely, a set of conversations with outstanding women practitioners of leadership from a variety of fields. As interviewers, representatives of the member units do not hesitate to express their own viewpoints or draw on their own varied experience, which makes these encounters more like informal exchanges than many published interviews. The focus throughout is nonetheless on the women subjects themselves.

There has been no attempt here to present a comprehensive or inclusive selection of women leaders, an impossible task in any case. In most instances, one or more of our units had had prior acquaintance with a woman chosen; in a few cases, we had recommendations from friends who kindly offered to vouch for us. Emphasis in the selection was not only on the women's impressive achievements but also on their willingness to offer candid and thoughtful assessments of their experiences in leadership— the costs as well as the rewards, the strategies that worked and those that did not. We also sought subjects who were willing to offer advice to new generations of prospective women leaders.

These thirteen women ultimately achieved recognition as "positional" leaders in a variety of fields, although most of them, at different stages in their careers, were also "nonpositional" leaders whose personal qualities were critical in motivating and inspiring thought and action on issues they championed. Some worked to change minds and hearts through their words; others sought to change aspects of how the world works through their deeds. But the two activities overlap; and as all the women would say, there is no single formula for effective leadership anyway. A necessary ingredient does emerge here, however, and that is the willingness to invest countless hours in pursuing issues or projects that may seem hopeless to anyone but the most indefatigable optimist—which each of these women is.

What do these encounters have to tell us about women as leaders at the turn of the twenty-first century? Most of those interviewed would concur that women often lead differently than men do, although none would cite innate biological or psychological reasons. What they point to are shared female experiences that often cut across socioeconomic, racial, and national boundaries. Women's more exclusive responsibility for early child nurture and education, for example, is seen as contributing to their more consistent focus, as leaders, on support for children and families.

The women also resist the idea that as a sex, they are any more pure or moral than men, although several suggest that women's relative newness to power structures encourages them to behave in more inclusive ways and to be less tied to hallowed "top-down" models of leadership. Again and again, too, they emphasize that women's distinctive experience has to be represented in all decision-making contexts, that as more women leaders move up, they need to guard a critical perspective on all the traditional ways that organizations function. Several worry, indeed, that the very advances of recent years have made younger women less likely to engage in risk taking, which is still badly needed. They urge would-be women leaders not to be afraid to put out their own visions, to speak up on someone else's issues as well as their own, to learn from criticism, and to keep a focus on positive change. They never suggest that any of these things will be easy.

These women have drawn strength from many places, some of which keep reappearing in these accounts. They cite supportive families, especially fathers but mothers as well, who constantly prodded them to achieve. In a couple of cases there were no sons competing for a father's attention; in others there was an overriding belief in education for daughters as well as sons. Family dinner tables—whether in the household of a "colored" colonial administrator in the West Indies, a liberal Jewish family in Chicago "where reading distressing novels about social injustice earned high marks," an immigrant Mexican-American family where the children sold tamales, or a privileged, Republican WASP family in the hills of New Jersey—were sites where daughters were exposed daily to lively give-and-take with parents and siblings about issues in the news.

Vivid vignettes of youthful experiences are recalled as contributing to later achievements. A language teacher at an elite eastern college in the sixties is supremely confident that a discouraged exchange student from a historically black southern college *will* succeed in his class, which he teaches entirely in French. In time and with his confidence to boost hers, she does; and throughout her distinguished academic career, she will tout multiculturalism, most recently as the first African-American president of Smith College. The chance to take violin lessons opens doors to new social and cultural worlds for a poor, working-class mathematics prodigy from Depression-era Brooklyn, who will later become the first tenured woman engineer at Massachusetts Institute of Technology. Regular athletic competition, from her earliest memories of a devastating loss in a sack race at age four, helps a superbly talented, self-admittedly headstrong future corporate executive, also from Brooklyn, learn useful lessons from losing as well as winning.

A school library's enticing collection of slim, orange-bound biographies of famous Americans, systematically read from A to Z during mandatory daily library periods, convinces a grammar school student (and future president of the Ford Foundation) that individual people really do make a difference in the world. A teacher in a southern California public elementary school invests extra time with the daughter of agricultural workers from Mexico (a future lawyer and Hispanic rights leader), convincing the eight-year-old that her achievement in mathematics proves that she will succeed and should ignore classmates' taunts over her poor English. A supportive church and school community in racially segregated rural Kentucky nurtures the budding rhetorical talents of one of its daughters through Scripture reading, poetry presentations, and talent contests. Her church follows her every achievement as she goes on to become a major feminist writer and speaker. Proud to have retained ties with the rural Appalachian coal-mining community of her birth, she says that when she goes back to her home church, the deacon is likely to stand up to welcome her and announce: "-She's written another of these feministic books, and I think the whole church should rise at the end of the service and shake her hand, because she belongs to us."

This group bears out prior and more systematic findings that a disproportionate number of women leaders attended female-only schools, women's colleges, or both. Eight of the thirteen here did so, and most cite the experience as helping to develop their leadership talents—giving them a space of their own that promoted a sense of sisterhood along with examples, among their teachers, of powerful and often unconventional women. The account by a Brazilian human rights leader of her early experiences in a school run by a strict French order of nuns reveals that the leadership qualities fostered in such environments might also prove awkward for school administrations. When a new nun became head of her school and instituted a regime of spying on students for supposed sins and rule infractions, she and a few of her fourteen-year-old friends led a protest that united their class, condemning the atmosphere of suspicion and the failure to respect students. In the end, the entire class withdrew at midyear, with full approval from their parents.

As adults in positions of influence, the women here continue to cite the importance of support from families, friends, and community to their ability to function as leaders; and most acknowledge as well the obstacles, challenges, and compromises with which they coped along the way. The married women and the women living with partners admit that family life regularly takes a beating—even with planning and rules to protect privacy. One woman, currently single, wants young women to understand that time is a precious thing and that she, at least, has decided to put up with some loneliness for now in order to have the time she needs to think, to write, and also to participate in public life as a speaker and an activist. About half the women here currently have husbands or partners, a smaller proportion than among women as a whole; and ten of the thirteen have children. One says she and her husband made a "tough decision" to have no children, a decision she says younger women with similar aspirations are now less likely to have to confront. Another says she was disappointed when she failed to become pregnant in her late thirties, having postponed the decision until then for career and financial reasons.

Even the women blessed with supportive partners, however, admit to the frustrations of living in uncharted territory, where people still deal clumsily with the spouses and significant others of well-known women, often assigning them traditional, quasi-wifely roles and assuming that any opinions they express are not really their own. As for those with unsupportive partners, the pain is recounted here in a situation in which a husband who resented his wife's success became increasingly contemptuous of her, regularly trivializing her work. Until the marriage became too brittle to last and she decided to leave, this woman says she coped by leading a totally schizophrenic life, acting the role of doormat at home, where she occupied herself with domestic chores and showy indifference to her career, while being recognized everywhere else as a competent, powerful, and committed leader. "In the privacy of my household I came to understand, through therapy, that I was actually quite intimidated, that I colluded in my powerlessness even as I was perceived as powerful in my public life."

For most of those interviewed, however, including that brave woman, there is little desire to dwell on challenges that are often more daunting for female than male leaders. New Jersey's governor swiftly dismisses complaints that as more young women become interested in public life, they are being told that little can be changed anyway. "I don't have a lot of tolerance for that. . . . It's never been easy to get things done. . . . People always say that you have to compromise, and that's bad since they don't like to compromise. But we all compromise every day. . . . I believe, deep down, 'Yes, a lot of the tough stuff may be because I'm a woman; but I'm not going to spend my whole time thinking and complaining about it, because then I won't get anything done.' "

The distinguished MIT professor says that owing to more objective performance standards in science, she has probably confronted less knee-jerk discrimation than other women who are leaders. She acknowledges that some of that discrimination persists even now but notes that the number of women in science has increased much faster than she would have predicted in the sixties; that the real problem now, in her view, is that basic structures that should be in place—such as decent child care and consistently good K–12 education—are not there; and that these things continue to have greater power to derail women's careers than men's. Still, she insists, the future is "pretty bright for woman in the sciences, especially if we keep working on all those other areas that still make it hard for women to take advantage of opportunities."

While they are working on longer-term solutions in some of those areas, many of these women manage to be not only optimistic but funny, often using humor to get tough points across. The veteran congresswoman from Colorado found a chilly climate in 1972 for a new member with a two- and a six-year-old. When reporters asked after the election about whether the family would be coming to Washington, she replied, "I notice you never ask the *men* what they're going to do with their families. What do you think I'm going to do, freeze them?" (This is the same woman who admits she mortified her own mother when, exasperated by being asked for the umpteenth time about being a congresswoman *and* a mother, replied tersely, "I have a brain and a uterus, and they both work.")

Another example, among many, of the use of humor to make a point comes from the senior United Nations officer from Pakistan, who was astonished to find more acceptance in Pakistan than in the United States for women in high-level positions. "You come to a western country and you think that everybody accepts women, but that's not the case," she says, adding that even senior-level women are often "just sort of ignored" by European and American men, "as if they don't exist." One of many strategies

for neutralizing such women, namely, complimenting them on their ap-
pearance, became clear to her in the late 1980s when she became the only
woman on the U.N. committee consisting of heads of all the agencies.
Each week there were elaborate assurances that all the men looked forward
to seeing the sari she would be wearing to the next meeting.

At first she just joked that whereas they might look forward to seeing
her saris, they were unlikely to be looking forward to what she had to say.
But then she hit on the idea of returning the compliments, with effusive
exclamations on the men's suits or ties, or comments on their youthful ap-
pearance. "I must say I didn't at first do it deliberately, but rather just as a
way of saying something nice back to them. But to men, it comes as a great
shock when they're complimented on their looks or their clothes, and it
doesn't come as a shock to me; I'm quite happy." She adds: "These compliments and joking about how we looked actually helped me in introducing
more serious gender perspectives on many issues, including family planning and the rights of women."

What is most valuable in these interchanges, well beyond the undeniable
pleasures of personal details and entertaining anecdotes, is the variety of
images, experiences, approaches, strategies, and insights that these women
have to offer about what it is like, in these waning years of the twentieth
century, to be a woman and a leader. Each of the women here is fully aware
that though she may not be a first-generation pioneer in her field, she still
occupies space in her work life that remains gendered as "male," space in
which her very womanhood sets her apart—and more often in uncomfortable ways than in comfortable ones. "I don't look at the place [the U.S.
Congress] with this warm, wonderful feeling," says the congresswoman
from Colorado. "I look at it as a place that constantly needs to be hammered at."

Their awareness of their own difference is infused, too, with the sense
that ongoing change is already so profound that usable and appropriate advice for the next generation of women is bound to be different from what
has worked for this one, as women as well as men are changing so fast. In
many places, indeed, the experiences of the sexes are converging more rapidly than ever before. To take a simple example, few younger men—in developed societies, anyway—would be thrown by a compliment from a
woman on a tie or a suit, although more of them than their counterparts in
the older generation would be likely to mull over whether such a compliment was intended as a sexual overture.

As the women here would be among the first to note, moreover, a welcoming response to a compliment on clothes has little to do with a welcoming response to a wish to share power in places still controlled by men. It is not surprising that the eager desire of some female newcomers to Congress to be "insiders" and "players" is greeted skeptically by the congresswoman with long experience there. "Why do you want to be a player?" she asks them. "What tune are they playing that you want to be part of that band?"

Which brings me to the evidence in these interviews for the quieter but often more radical work that these women leaders have been performing, even in very high places, to bring about positive change. Asked to describe what made her proudest in twenty-four years in office, the congresswoman from Colorado answered swiftly and simply: "Survival. I mean it. When I think of the people that I have seen that came there and got hammered, chewed up, and spit out—the people that lost their families, and all the other things that happened—just surviving looks like an amazing thing."

The comment may sound strange, even shocking; but if you read and ponder the daily papers, it is finally profound. Some commentators who are making the case for more women in leadership are in fact arguing that as newcomers to many of these rather creaky institutions, women are in a unique position to challenge them and show how they have become dysfunctional for men and women alike. One, Constance Buchanan, says:

> *The key to generating effective new public vision lies in systematically revising fundamental aspects of our traditional way of thinking about society, especially the minimal degrees of responsibility for families and communities assigned to the public world. . . . Woman especially possess the will to take the initiative in this social reorganization. They are most acutely aware that the unpaid labor of family and community welfare, caught as it is between new realities and old cultural beliefs, is an endangered social value. . . . Still on the threshold of the public world, pressed to rearrange the meaning and structure of their own lives, they can more easily notice and question the institutional and work norms to which most men have become habituated. As many struggle to maintain family and community commitments in the face of a workplace structured for an ideal worker who delegates both, women can call attention to the personal costs that employed men have been paying for years and to the social implications of these costs. But women too are subject to the socializing power*

of mainstream values and many soon may be sidetracked in their effort to lead, either by being installed as second-class citizens in the workplace or by having their own values reshaped.[24]

Not only do our institutions continue to embody assumptions that the maintenance of family and commmunity are appropriately delegated to an unpaid and largely female workforce, our visions of those we elevate to leadership are equally distorted. While according them an often ephemeral but glamorous "star" quality, we deny them the very privacy and contemplation they need to perform their public roles well. In the words of one of the interviewees here, we "work our leaders to an intellectual and emotional death." In offering advice to young women, she cautions that untold harm has been done to progressive social movements by the self-destructive behavior of charismatic leaders with unresolved personal dilemmas. "We are better able to lead if we have also chosen the path of mental and emotional well-being for ourselves. . . . This would mean that a different sort of person would come into leadership, one who is truly capable of representing communal interest, not someone who is driven by ego-centered needs for stardom, authority, and power." She warns, too, that people are little aware of what she calls "the gendered nature of fame," namely, that for women singled out as leaders, and especially women of color among them, the formal and informal support structures that make it possible for men to function well in such roles are far less likely to be in place.

Pressed further to name the legacy that gave her most pride in her years in Washington, the congresswoman acknowledged, "I suppose I'm proud that I tackled all sorts of things in Armed Services which you weren't supposed to do. I did an awful lot on women, children, and family issues, although those were not seen as big power issues. I did a lot of challenging the institution, trying to bring it into the twentieth century. It didn't want to come." The corporation is another institution that has not wanted to come into this century, at least insofar as that means advancing women into management. Yet a few highly placed women are now working with like-minded male corporate leaders to make it happen: "I think the competent women who exhibit strong leadership throughout their careers will eventually ascend," says the corporate executive here. "What we've got to do is increase the level of security or confidence that if they do something a little bit different, they can eventually get where they want to go. We need to increase their risk orientation."

A willingness to take risks, a major thread in these conversations, is part of the larger rejection of "business as usual" that runs through these women's lives and approaches to leadership. One, whose friends advised her not to typecast herself, and possibly derail a career as a mainstream player in high academic administrative circles, went ahead anyway and accepted a position as the head of Afro-American studies at Princeton University. There she worked quietly toward a hardly modest goal of recruiting the best, succeeding against all the naysayers in attracting extraordinary talents such as Nell Painter, Cornel West, Toni Morrison, and more. Her goal, as she said, was not just to transform Afro-American studies but to transform Princeton. "I was working for transformation on a much broader scale. . . . One is not always seeking to play a visible leadership role, because sometimes the best leader is acting invisibly to bring about change. What I did in Afro-American studies was to unify a lot of people in a common effort."

Another of these leaders, who is quite prepared to engage in compromise to achieve even limited goals for women's reproductive rights in a global context, speaks out frankly about why women need to be more involved in policymaking at every level. "I think that control over fertility by society, by religion, by imposition of authority of all kinds—especially by men—is one of the chief ways in which women are controlled and kept powerless. Motherhood may be, what you call it, idealized, but women are not really supported in that role either." This leader defines her role as preparing governments to recognize women's needs and issues as part of the mainstream agendas of their societies, but at the same time she regularly challenges male leaders everywhere around the globe, asking them whether they are speaking out publicly against rape and sexual violence, and whether they are actively promoting women's education.

There are other conceptions of leadership in these interviews that are equally subversive of the status quo. The founder of "9 to 5," a U.S. organization for clerical workers, says that she was interested in expanding the women's movement to women workers in the 1970s, when there was no organized union movement appealing successfully to women. She created one, and says that she never worried about leadership. The main thing, she said, is to attract the women and talk about the issues. Once that happens, leaders emerge of their own. "You can find leadership in anybody," she insists. Similarly, on the global scene, an economist describes her growing awareness of the need for those who would enhance women's status in underdeveloped societies to engage women directly in the process of development. They should devote their attention, she says, to giving women in these countries "the skills, resources, and access to decision making which would enable them to have more power to make a difference in their own communities."

Collectively, these interviews suggest several critical directions for future work, not only in women's leadership studies but in leadership studies generally, as these seek to understand and evaluate the role of human agency in major social change. By placing women, who have been marginal to traditional notions of leadership, at the center of the inquiry, it becomes easier to recognize the shortcomings of current approaches and to "denaturalize" leadership as a presumed exclusively male activity. Even now that many functions—such as productive work, education, health, and elder care—that used to be performed in the household have been moved outside of it, the interviews repeatedly point to the family household as a site where leadership remains vitally important. One subject, who gave up a brilliant career as a columnist to write novels and spend more time with her family, describes her new (and equally brilliant) career as a novelist as one that explores issues of leadership and power in a variety of ideal and less than ideal domestic contexts:

> So we have to broaden the idea of leadership and acknowledge the extent to which leadership takes place on a micro level every day in our own homes. To the extent that leadership on a macro level is more like that of families, it is better, I think. It can take us more places that we need to go. I feel that a good family is the kind of model that can teach us everything we need to know about life and that a good organization works on the same principles as a good family. People have roles to play, various roles are accepted, and it's not necessarily hierarchical although people have different amounts of power at different times. Two purposes are served here. One is that those exclusively involved with families do not feel as though they're doing devalued work, and those doing the supposed great work of the world will do it better if they take families more often as a model.

In addition to offering critiques of current models of leadership which are worth pursuing, critiques that in different ways challenge accustomed divisions between public and private spheres, these interviews present a multitude of other routes to explore. Most obviously, they display the richness of individual biography for teasing out complex leadership issues. One reason so many attempts to define leadership and to categorize its features have foundered, often turning into brain-numbing mush, is that they are not grounded in the messy but momentous details of everyday experience and happenings, contexts that alone can give life and meaning to abstractions. To take just one ingredient in the making of leaders, at once obvious and elusive, the critical role of expectation and affirmation in nurturing future leaders is cited repeatedly in these accounts. It is no accident that the tiny Kentucky town of Hopkinsville produced many black leaders, including several Rhodes scholars. But it is also no accident that the multiply reinforcing mechanisms of family, church, and school consistently worked more smoothly for boys than for girls. Girls continue to receive mixed messages, at best, about their own individual value as well as about the value of becoming leaders.

Accustomed as we are to the concept of the leader as a "lone ranger," we are startled by the contrary views of several of these women. Leadership needs to be a "collaborative project," declares one. We think of it unidimensionally, she says, in terms of public activism; but it makes more sense to conceptualize leadership around a task that needs to be done, with people of varied talents supplying leadership in different areas. Another interviewee, asked to identify ways for women to enhance their leadership potential, points to the on-line world of the Internet. Acknowledging that men dominate there now, she notes the possibilities for enhancing leadership if women take more advantage of this tool. "Networks on the Internet are the easiest way for busy people to communicate about subjects of substance," she says, "not only as themselves but anonymously; and they're wonderful ways to share scholarship. I think women really have to move full speed ahead into the world of the new technology."

Candor about a still-uneven playing field is easier to come by from those who have at least temporarily withdrawn to the sidelines, so it is all the more remarkable that so many of the women interviewed are willing to speak out. One says that she thinks an important part of women's leadership right now is the willingness of women in secure positions to take every opportunity to be open about the special challenges women face and to help others, both women and men, who are still making their way:

> *If you are in a safe place, if you are secure in your job or in your personality, if they need you more than you need them, you have almost a moral obligation to rub their faces in the realpolitik of what women's lives are like and what they need to be like. When you have somebody like me who's not going to get busted down to private anytime soon, you've got to say to them, "Presence doesn't equal productivity, and I'm walking out of this meeting because I've*

got to relieve the baby-sitter." You can't say, "I have another meet-
ing," because telling the truth makes it easier for women who are
not in as safe a place. It also makes it easier for a male colleague
to say, "I'm with her. We've been talking about this for two hours,
and I've got a daughter with a soccer game."

The multitalented scientist here notes that until recently, men students
at one of the nation's most competitive institutions in the sciences systematically harassed the then-small numbers of women students. The
women's performance dramatically improved when this woman took the
initiative to start an informal support group, helping the women students
to feel less isolated. The president of the Ford Foundation, describing her
efforts to ensure the access of female and male employees alike to leadership roles throughout the organization, warns that putting a single woman
at the head of an organization does not of itself guarantee anything, but
she adds, "The more women you have who get into leadership positions,
the more likely it is that the common experiences of women and the common interests of women are going to be represented in policy decisions."
The high corporate leader, similarly, warns against practices, however
well-meaning, that introduce single "token" women or minority officers
into corporate settings, a practice that too often has set these lone individuals
up for failure.

The governor complains that she does not receive enough women or
minority nominees for important appointive posts and that unqualified
women are cynically thrown onto lists of submitted nominees. In addition
to returning such lists with a request for more qualified women and minority candidates, she cites the importance of making appointments that
carry significant hiring or appointment authority of their own. The woman
she named chief justice of the state supreme court, for example, can name
and has named other women to the bench. This is one way to ensure a legacy
of leadership that includes more women.

The advice these women offer to girls and young women presents possibilities not only for new research but for leadership courses and programs.
One global leader urges that young women be formally encouraged to become directly involved in addressing all issues. She says that they should be
urged not only to speak out themselves but to press their countries' leaders
to speak out on behalf of the young women and men of the rising generation. In those many societies where girls receive less formal education, she
says, those who enjoy that privilege should be relentless in insisting that ways
be found to get all girls as well as boys into school and keep them there.

Women everywhere simply must gain more formal political power, she says; and others here echo that sentiment. The congresswoman expresses astonishment that so few students, women or men, are learning how to be effective citizens. "What people need to be aware of, finally, is that in our system, they are the ones who have power, if they will only use it and use it well. One way to use it well is to use your head when you choose the people you call your leaders. . . . Americans need to understand that the core principles of the people they elect are more important than anything else." Which brings us back to the theme of the need for more self-conscious leadership in the home and in the community.

The president of Smith College often stresses the importance, for leaders, of a truly multicultural education; but when it comes down to basics, that is not the answer she gives to young women who ask her what they must do to become leaders. "I think they are often surprised by the answer, because I always say that you have to have regard for other people first if you want to be a good leader. That is one of the things women bring to leadership, I think—an intensity of feeling about the people for whom they are responsible." Though formal education can surely help, in this woman's experience what usually matters most is the example of a caring parent—in her own case, a mother who:

> *was very wise in her understanding of the human character and of human possibilities. What she was able to teach us was about the challenges we would face in life. She would tell us stories about the past, about my grandmother and her experiences as a woman trying to survive; for her husband died when the children were very young. Her education of her children was in a sense the gift my mother gave us, because she taught us about life, about wisdom, about respect for people, about how to place a value on what we encountered, about what mattered in life and what didn't. Without her knowing it, her life inspired us and fueled our independence. Every time we saw her have to take a back seat, or have to serve or to do all the things that women of her generation did, we were angry for her, because we knew that it was not just.*

The theme of more self-conscious leadership in the home and the community is perceived as an intensely personal as well as professional challenge by several of the women here, who, far from compartmentalizing their public and private lives, see them as a continuum informed by common challenges. "How," asks the leader of the Mexican American Legal

Defense and Education Fund, "do I tell my community that to be successful, we have to be collaborative . . . how do I help to get my community to go from the mental state of a minority to the mental state of a majority?" And as change accelerates, she asks, how do we name and pass on those things that must not change?

> *How do you provide "constants" in an ever-changing world? To me, that is the biggest challenge of my life. How do I provide the values for my children that my parents did while at the same time helping them to adapt to rapid change? When I die, it's not finally what I did as president of MALDEF that will matter most. It's what I did to shape these three human beings whom I brought into the world. Did I give them the values to be good human beings? Did I give them values to guide their lives well?*

For those coming to this book from the land of generic "leadership studies," and especially those who have not included women as a serious subject in the field, the introductions may be awkward for a while before common ground can be established with some of the women in these dialogues. There are, after all, good and painful reasons why many women, at least, might be suspicious of an academic field that has taken so long to present women as an untapped leadership resource, rather than as defective leadership material whose best hope is to slip under the leadership tent in heavy male disguise.

At the same time, it would be foolish to deny that the paucity of research on women and leadership in many appropriate fields—not just in the interdisciplinary one of women's studies but in history, sociology, and even political science—has had much to do with the familiar midcentury revulsion in academe toward traditional theories of great individuals (male, in most cases) as the ones who make things happen and move history forward. For long, social thinkers of all stripes embraced theories of change in human affairs that dramatically diminish meaningful roles for individual agents, a habit they have only lately begun to query. Ironically, the very rescue work that has been conducted in the century's last quarter in women's history and women's studies more generally has brought onto the historical stage countless examples of female actors making change— women who were demonstrable agents of social transformation. Reform movements, suffrage initiatives, labor organization, and more have been presented in ways that show again and again the critical involvement of particular individuals.

We have hesitated to call them leaders, undoubtedly for good reason. But now it is time to renew the dialogue on the subject, however awkward it may be at first to bring the parties to the table. It is a dialogue in many ways overdue, for, as Anne Firth Murray has already reminded us, the world's women did not have to wait for academics to tell them that they can be leaders. Thousands of them are already out there leading, with "visions of a different future for women and society."[25]

Thirteen of these women are here in this book to share their experiences and their visions for the future. These are women who have long been engaged in meeting the mandate of the world conference on women in Beijing to advance women's equal access and full participation in power structures and decision making. They are also women whose lives of reflection and action offer an abundance of fruitful ways to think about and practice leadership. We dedicate this book to the young women we hope will be inspired by these conversations and learn something from them about leading. We direct the book as well to the women and men of older generations, academics and nonacademics alike, who may be persuaded through these examples that leadership is worth another look.

PEGGY ANTROBUS

■

IN CONVERSATION WITH CHARLOTTE BUNCH
AND MARIANNE DEKOVEN

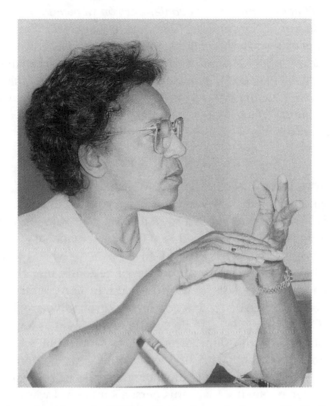

Peggy Antrobus, born in 1935 in Grenada and educated in St. Lucia, St. Vincent, and the United Kingdom, is an economist who has worked in several Caribbean countries with both governmental and non-governmental organizations. Since 1974 when she was appointed by the Jamaican government to establish their Women's Bureau, her work has focused on enhancing women's role in development. In 1978 she established the Women and Development unit (WAND) within the School of Continuing Studies of the University of the West Indies in Barbados, and she was its director until her retirement in 1995.

In 1984, Peggy Antrobus was one of the initiators of the network of third world feminists promoting Development Alternatives with Women for a New Era (DAWN), and from 1990 to 1996, she was DAWN's general coordinator. In her work with both WAND and DAWN, she has been one of the preeminent leaders of global feminism, speaking at nu-

merous regional and global meetings and playing a key role in devel-
opment activities. She was among the most prominent leaders shap-
ing women's nongovernmental presence for the second, third, and
fourth United Nations world conferences on women in, respectively,
Copenhagen, 1980; Nairobi, 1985; and Beijing, 1995. She is the re-
cipient of many awards, including the Paul G. Hoffman Award (1982)
from the Society for International Development, for "outstandingly sig-
nificant work in national and international development"; the Women
Who Dared Award (1994) from the National Black Women's Health
Project in the United States; and a UNIFEM Twentieth Anniversary
Award (1995).

CHARLOTTE BUNCH: We'd like to start with some questions about your background, including how you came to see yourself as both a leader and a feminist. We're interested in how you began your work on women's issues at the community level, and then on the international level.

PEGGY ANTROBUS: It's difficult to say exactly when I first thought of myself as a leader. In my school days I certainly thought of myself as somebody with a contribution to make to her country—not as a woman, but as a person from a certain background where that was expected. That's why I chose to do economics, I saw it as a way to make a contribution. I didn't think of myself as a woman until I was breastfeeding my second child (my first was adopted), well before I knew the word *feminist*. I suddenly had this consciousness of being an "object." I was this person's wife, I was this person's mother, I was this person's source of food. I clearly remember thinking about that and not knowing who I was. Only later on did I realize this was my first moment of feminist consciousness.

I think consciousness of myself as a leader came first when I began to be defined that way by women in the movement. I remember the first time this happened: I had been director of the Jamaican Women's Bureau [the governmental mechanism set up within the U.N. framework for the decade on women, sometimes referred to as "national machinery"] for about a year. Someone came to do a film on the bureau's operation and wanted to interview me. It was the first time I realized that what I was doing for advancing women's status had some significance, and that somebody else saw me as a leader.

CB: Were you working as a professional throughout the sixties and seventies?

PA: Yes, although I was in and out of the labor force. In the Caribbean most women have jobs, even those who are married and have children. Maybe it has something to do with living in a developing country. If you have a profession, if you're university trained, then you are expected to work. When I got married I planned to take off time only when the children were very young. I had received a government scholarship and felt obligated to return something to the community and country that supported my education. Not all women had the luxury of taking time off when children were young, of course.

MARIANNE DEKOVEN: How many children do you have?

PA: Two. I also recognized that as a wife I would be moving around wherever my husband's work took him. So there has been a lot of discontinuity in my career.

MDK: You mentioned that your first moment of feminist consciousness came when you were breast-feeding your second child. Can you fill in the gaps between that moment of self-realization and your consciousness of becoming a feminist leader?

PA: At first, I was just preoccupied with being a good mother. There were not too many moments for that kind of insight or resentment, because there was nothing else I wanted to do. Then when my daughter was two and ready for a play group, I decided to train as a teacher. I thought that would be a good career to combine with motherhood since I'd get the same school holidays as my children.

It was at that point, however, that Lucille Mair [a Jamaican leader, later secretary-general for the 1980 U.N. World Conference of Women and ambassador to the U.N.] asked me to apply for the post of adviser on women's affairs to the Jamaican government, which she was about to vacate. She chose me because she thought I was a good administrator, not because I was a feminist, since to that point I'd never been associated with the women's movement. Mair was also in charge of the women's hall of residence at the University of the West Indies, and she had known me as somebody who worked within the university to define a new program, as someone she thought could take initiatives, conceptualize them, and translate them into action. My job then was assistant registrar of buildings; and I was liaison between the architects, the departments, and the administration, making sure money allocated for the building program was spent on schedule. This administrative job gave me valuable experience for all the work I've done subsequently.

CB: Staff and budgets! At a recent party to celebrate your work, somebody said that what they remembered from a long way back is that you always came into women's movement circles with the same questions: "What is the staff and what is the budget?"

PA: It proves that what I brought to my women's movement work was experience as a project manager. My feminist consciousness came later. In fact, I may have been appointed to the post of adviser on women's affairs *because* I was not associated with the women's movement and feminism—that is, because I was considered to be conventional and "safe," someone who was married with children and unlikely to make waves. If so, they had not reckoned with the power of feminism to transform the lives of women.

MDK: How quickly did you move from there to the kind of work you're doing now?

PA: It was a long process, and in fact meeting Charlotte Bunch was a critical point in the process. In 1979, I went to an international workshop in Bangkok entitled "Feminist Ideologies and Structures in the First Half of the Decade for Women." I remember leaving Jamaica very uncomfortable with the word *feminist* and telling everybody I was going to a workshop on "national machinery," the term we used for the governmental units set up to address women's status. At the meeting Charlotte gave a presentation on how she became involved in the women's rights movement as a result of earlier involvement in the U.S. civil rights movement. Her experience helped me to see the connections: the common issues of power and domination and internalized oppression. I realized a feminist analysis was relevant to an understanding of relations between other social groups.

What was even more fascinating was that I could also see how a feminist understanding of structured power could help our understanding of the relations between countries. In 1979 there was a lively international debate on the need for a New International Economic Order (NIEO)—for more equitable relations between countries of the industrialized North and the developing South. I came away from that workshop with the determination to use the word *feminist* as often as possible, but since it was so alienating to people, I wanted to find ways to discuss and define it that would make it more acceptable. That is why I thought up the idea of having a videotaped discussion on international feminism. I asked Charlotte to organize a global workshop in less that a year so we could have it in time for the 1980 World Conference on Women in Copenhagen. That videotape, *World Feminists,* which was filmed and produced by Martha Stewart Communications, was shown daily followed by discussion at the NGO [nongovernment organization] forum in Copenhagen. Charlotte reminded me recently that I had said to her, "You're going to do this, and here is how you're going to do it." I did not know that I was such a directive person!

CB: I think I saw something similar to what Lucille Mair saw in you. From the first, I realized you were a person who could take an idea and figure out an action plan to make it happen. But let me tell my side of the story. The meeting with you in 1979 was also a turning point for me. I was a feminist from the USA trying to figure out a way to do work internationally. When this dynamic woman from the Caribbean said to me, "You should organize a workshop and help us produce a videotape for the 1980 mid-decade conference," it was very enabling for me. It was permission and encouragement from a woman from the third world to work internationally. You offered me a context for starting to do global feminist organizing—a specific project that made sense and used my organizing skills. You identified the desired outcome and the people to do it: potential funders, participants, a filmmaker, and an organizer. You knew how to bring them together and make it happen.

PA: Bringing things together is one of my skills, and I don't know where it comes from! But when I think about it, all the work I've done has been about creating new programs, going back to my first job as a social worker with the Save the Children Fund in St. Vincent, and later setting up the government's community program there.

CB: You used those skills in 1978 to set up WAND [the Women and Development unit at the University of the West Indies], one of the early women's regional organizations. Talk a bit about what led you to do this, even before you saw yourself as a feminist.

PA: The idea of setting up a women's program there came out of a regional meeting sponsored by the Jamaica Women's Bureau. When I worked in Jamaica, I realized that as Caribbean women meeting at Latin American conferences during the early years of the first U.N. Decade on Women [1976–1985], we were all new to the work. Each meeting involved a different set of women, so we were never able to formulate a specific Caribbean position, even though our priorities were often different from those set out by the Latin American women. Before leaving Jamaica, I wanted to have our own regional meeting and got support from the university. Together with the person who ran a regional program in which I had taught, we organized a workshop entitled the "Integration of Women in Caribbean Development." Out of this meeting, a steering committee was formed to follow up on recommendations, including setting up the special program that became WAND.

I was on the steering committee and had some time, since I had not taken a job after we left Jamaica. In fact, when I left Jamaica I was quite burnt out and thought I would be a proper housewife again. But since I still had contacts with funders, I began to talk to them about funding the proposed regional program at the university. I did not see myself heading it, but they were not prepared to fund the program without a director. That was when I learned you need to know who's going to run a program, that leadership is often more important than just the quality of the proposal. Ultimately I said I might go back to work, as I missed my work. I was lucky to have funders whose philosophy of leadership development was identifying people with some kind of vision and supporting them.

CB: I have noticed over the years how many strong women leaders have come out of the Caribbean region, including yourself, Lucille Mair, and Dame Nita Barrow [a Barbadian whose public roles have included president of the World Council of Churches, convener for the NGO Forum in Nairobi in 1985, and ambassador from her country to the U.N.]. Can you explain why the Caribbean has nurtured so many global women leaders?

PA: Yes. I think it has something to do with the particular historical moment. My father was a senior public servant at a time when adult suffrage was being introduced and there was a lot of political discussion in our household: about colonialism, the relationship with Britain, Caribbean development, the different roles of policymakers and the executive branch. It wasn't surprising that I chose to read for a degree in economics. I think the other women you mentioned had similar experiences. We all grew up in an era when our countries were moving from colonial status to independence, and we were all exposed to the notion of public service and contributing to the development of our countries.

MDK: And you were included in all those discussions, regardless of your gender?

PA: Yes, my father encouraged me. I remember sitting at the dinner table when I was quite young, and too shy to say anything; but I absorbed the conversations and the values.

MDK: Boy, I identify with that. I wonder for how many of us that's true.

PA: I was shy, but I didn't mind sitting around listening. I remember reading things my father had, like official reports from the Colonial Office on Caribbean development, and on social and economic issues. I learned much more from those reports and conversations in my home than from school. In those days there were not many textbooks on the Caribbean in our schools; the ones we had were mostly about Britain. I knew every cornfield and river in England, but very little about my own country's history or geography. It was a good colonial education!

MDK: Did you go to Britain for higher education?

PA: Yes, to Bristol University. The then newly established University of the West Indies had no faculty of economics at that time. Going to Bristol was a strange experience, since apart from the cultural differences I was also doing a course in which there were not many women. In addition, it was my first awareness of racism; for growing up in the Caribbean I felt nothing strange about being black, or "colored" as we called ourselves. It was when I went to Britain and read a book about slavery that I had my first encounter with that history, and I was quite traumatized by it. Fortunately, within university circles there wasn't much discrimination. In my second year I was put in change of a residence hall annex with all white students. I recall somebody asking how these women felt about being supervised by a black person. I said it had never occurred to me that there was anything strange about it and that none of the women made me feel there was anything unusual.

This was the mid-fifties and a fascinating time for me, with a new awareness of things I had not thought about, like race and gender. It was also a time when I found my own voice, and when my confidence began to develop. I grew up in the shadow of a younger sister who was as extroverted and sociable as I was introverted and shy. Sitting around the table with my father's associates, I didn't have to exert myself in part because she was there. When I was in England, however, I no longer had the option of hiding behind my sister's social graces. The other thing that promoted confidence was being sought after by the student leaders of the political parties on campus. I guess I was thought a membership asset, being black and female!

CB: So you were political very early?

PA: Not really. Although I was involved in student branches of the major parties, I was more related to their social than political functions. People who knew me thought me very conservative then, and in fact I was more attracted to the Young Conservatives because they gave better parties than the Labour Party people, who tended to be very earnest!

The first incident that excited me politically was when the British government invaded Egypt in response to Nasser's nationalization of the Suez Canal. In my first public political stand, I became involved in the protest against the invasion. The other thing that energized me was when the British Parliament introduced their first Immigration Act to restrict the

migration of black people. I did research showing that the amount of re-
mittance money from Jamaicans working in England in one year was
more than the Colonial Development and Welfare grants for the entire region for four years. I wrote a letter to *The Times* of London, which published it. It was a big thing to get a letter in *The Times*!

MDK: Did you go directly from your degree in economics to that social work position?

PA: No. That came afterwards as a choice I thought would be com-
patible with being a wife and mother. After getting my degree, I returned
to Jamaica for what I hoped would be a career in public finance. When I
realized public finance was not a good choice to combine with motherhood, I never questioned the idea that my first priority was marriage and
children, that my career choice had to fit with my husband's needs. (No
feminist consciousness there!) It was not until I began work in the women's
movement that I realized what was involved in these choices.

CB: When Lucille asked you to head the Women's Bureau in Jamaica,
why did you take the job? Did you have any interest in women then?

PA: No. What attracted me was that it was a part-time job that would
not interfere with my responsibilites as a mother. For several months I maintained the myth that I was doing part-time work, although almost from the
beginning it was more than full time. Almost immediately I found myself
caught up in work that would completely change my life. I began to see
my life in a different way—to reinterpret all the things that had happened
to me in the context of a new understanding of what it meant to be a woman.
Two years earlier, while breast-feeding, I had asked, "Who am I?" but I
didn't pursue it then. Once I started working with women, that question
and all the politics began to come together.

MDK: Was it a struggle to admit that you were doing more than full-
time work?

PA: No, because I was enjoying it so much. Also, in the Caribbean,
domestic help is widely available, so it wasn't as though I was a single parent or had no help. If you can afford such help, it is not difficult to combine the roles of wife, mother, and professional.

MDK: Easier than here in the United States?

PA: Much easier. Furthermore, since it is expected that you will work,
you're not made to feel guilty about it, and you have a lot of support if
you're middle class or professional. I wasn't aware of any role conflicts
and didn't feel any "feminist" guilt about employing another woman to
help me. At that time, I didn't have any class consciousness either.

So why didn't I take the job full time? I don't know. But there was something else that became more obvious to me as I got more into this work: my husband felt very uneasy about it. I think the more that I got into it, the more alienated he became. As my work began to absorb more and more of my energy, it was a source of conflict between us. Sometimes I pretended that what I was doing was not important.

MDK: So the conflict was with your marriage, not with working and being a mother?

PA: Yes, it was my husband's disapproval of my commitment to my work. His weapon was to trivialize my commitment.

CB: After you came to see yourself as a feminist, how did that change the way you saw the work that you were doing and the way you saw yourself as a woman doing it?

PA: Discovering feminism was a turning point in my life. It helped me to understand the structure of power relations, as I said earlier, not only in terms of the social relations between men and women but in terms of class, race, and even the relations between countries. I had never dealt with the issue of power before. Feminism changed my analysis and you can see this in my writing. I've often said that I won't be held accountable for anything I wrote before 1980, or before 1984 for that matter.

There are discrete stages in my development that actually fall into decades. The decade of my twenties, 1955 to 1965, was the beginning of my professional life and my marriage: I went to university in 1955, married in 1959, and had my first professional job as a social worker in 1963. In 1967, I adopted our first child, and in 1972 had my second, so in my thirties I was mostly occupied with being a good wife and mother. The U.N. Decade for Women was the decade of my forties, and it was when I discovered feminism. In my fifties my life changed quite fundamentally: I remember standing in the courtyard of the University of Nairobi, the site of the NGO Forum for the third World Conference on Women, in July 1985. I decided then that I would take a year's sabbatical to reflect and write about my work. It was a decision that led to the end of my marriage, and also to the beginning of my work at an international level with DAWN.

A deepening feminist consciousness led me to question assumptions I had never confronted before. For example, I began to question why I always had to move from one country to another just because my husband had made the choice to take another job. I began to wonder why I had to pretend that what I was doing was not important. I didn't challenge my husband, but I became increasingly conscious of the imbalance in power between us. Years later I talked about the walls I had built to protect my marriage, walls separating the private and public spheres of my life, so that

I could deny the contradictions in the two. In the privacy of my household I came to understand, through therapy, that I was actually quite intimidated by my husband, that I colluded in my powerlessness even as I was perceived as powerful in my public life. This contradiction between the private and the public ultimately had to be confronted, but in the first instance there was only a consciousness of the difference between the way I was behaving privately and the way I was acting publicly. I realize now that it was easier to challenge patriarchy in public than at home. In fact, the more I challenged it publicly, the more more careful I was not to challenge my husband's authority at home.

MDK: Why was it easier for you to challenge male power publicly?

PA: It seemed more threatening to deal with it privately. I must have realized that it would implicate my relationship with my husband, my children, my marriage, everything. For a long time, I wasn't ready to place all of that in jeopardy. When I understood more about power, I was finally able to confront the contradictions. The age of my children had something to do with it too. I could not have raised these issues when they were younger.

MDK: Was it therapy that made you ready?

PA: No, it was reflection on my own, in addition to my relationships with other women—their friendship and support, but *not* their encouragement. No one encouraged me to leave my marriage, unlike what some people believed at the time. My husband once observed that it was my associating with single women in the movement that was driving me from my marriage, but the fact is that the decision to leave was much more influenced by the unhappiness of the married women I knew.

MDK: Did you see yourself reflected in these unhappy marriages?

PA: Yes. I could see in other people what I didn't want to see in myself.

CB: You've talked about how feminism changed your life. Can you reflect on how it changed your work and your leadership style?

PA: It changed my work by helping me see the central importance of women's empowerment and leadership. It was soon after the meeting in Bangkok, where I first saw the relevance of feminism to my work, that I recognized the need to empower women to change things, rather than to "integrate" them into existing patterns of development. I had been invited by the Society for International Development (SID) to write a paper on the theme of development for the NGO Forum at the mid-decade conference in Copenhagen in 1980. My research showed that women were actually worse off on almost every indicator—social, economic, political—than they were at the beginning of the decade. This was a startling conclusion, and many NGOs were upset by it. I didn't realize at the time that this was related to the global economic recession, the beginning of the debt crisis, and the macroeconomic policies of adjustment that were being adopted to deal with the repayment of international debt. At that time, our analysis still tended to focus on women without relating their condition to what was happening in the larger society, and certainly not to macroeconomic policies.

For myself and many others, what came out of the 1980 NGO Forum was the recognition of the need to work differently, to experiment with new strategies, to work to change things in a more basic way. I saw the need to work at two levels: first, building women's self-esteem in order to strengthen their leadership, and second, giving women the skills, resources, and access to decision making which would enable them to have more power to make a difference in their own communities. In other words, leadership for change. We didn't use the word *empowerment* at that time, but this is what our strategies were intended to achieve. All this was reinforced in 1984, following the founding meeting of DAWN in Bangalore, India, when I had a better grasp of the structures that would need to be changed by women in order to realize a more equitable and humane society.

What is involved is a dynamic process in which my own thinking changed as a result of insights from discussions with women from other countries, which I integrated into my own action and ongoing analyses. These in turn led to new insights which I shared with women from other countries, starting a new cycle of action and reflection. This is the methodology of applied behavioral science—action, reflection, analysis, generalization, and internalization, or implementation. In 1988, as a result of my clearer understanding of the structures that needed to be changed, I actually changed the objectives of WAND from "integrating women in development" to "empowering women for social change."

CB: When you talk about the empowerment of women's leadership, do you see that leadership as something distinct, or is it just empowering women to be leaders like any other leaders?

PA: At first I wasn't looking for something different, but as I have worked in this field, I have seen quite strong differences between the ways in which men and women operate. Not all of course, but there is something different about the leadership of many women, especially those who are feminist and conscious of women's position and condition in patriarchal society. Maybe it has to do with being outside the power structure. Being on the outside of the arenas of power allows you to see things differently, to be more critical. The interesting thing for me is that in the

Caribbean, I may be part of the elite because of my class and color, but because of my gender I'm not part of the power structure. Of course, the Caribbean itself is marginal in the global power structure.

Women seem more aware of complexity, and more willing to see the relevance of personal things to job performance. I read a novel once in which a woman reflects on the fact that women have one room into which they bring all the elements of their lives, while men have many rooms that they move through, shutting the door on each as they go from one to the next. For example, a friend of mine, the deputy governor of a bank who chose not to be governor because of her commitment to her family, told me that when she goes to work each morning, she brings a list of things related to what her husband and children are doing that need her help, which she then asks her secretary to remind her to take care of.

MDK: Do you see that as a liability? Is that positive or negative?

PA: Well, it's both. It's negative when you think of how stressful it is, because you are caught in the tension of trying to perform all these roles at once. On the other hand, it's positive because it keeps you in touch with reality. I think that if people are more conscious about the realities of other people's lives, they make better decisions. The trouble with the men who rule the world is that they haven't had to deal with the family laundry, or with a sick child when they have a job to do. . . .

MDK: Does it also seem to you that the usual things one reads about women's leadership styles are true, that they are less hierarchical and more cooperative?

PA: Sometimes yes and sometimes no. One of the things that I've been criticized about is the fact that while I try to be nonhierarchical in my leadership style, there are times when I believe I have to take responsibility, to make decisions alone. I think that there is a tension between being nonhierarchical and taking responsibility. I don't know whether men experience this tension. Most women are ambivalent about power, even with the feminist distinction between power to act and power to empower. For example, I find myself very uncomfortable when people want to give me awards and so on. I don't see myself in that way, as a person with that kind of status. I don't know whether other women feel like that, but I suspect many do. That has not stopped me from claiming power; it's the fame and recognition that make me uncomfortable, not the exercise of power.

MDK: I'd like to ask you more about the kinds of connections you make between your commitment to the Caribbean and your global work as a feminist leader.

PA: Obviously, I love the Caribbean! I cannot imagine living anywhere else. I come from a family of public servants who worked in many of the islands, so my identification is with the region, rather than with a particular country there. I grew up at a time when Caribbean identity and destiny was a strong motivational force. It was a time when the countries of the English-speaking Caribbean were trying to form a West Indian Federation, a time when regionalism was seen as an important force for the development of our countries. Even though the federation only lasted two years, it made an indelible impression on my generation. In the fifties and sixties we had a different type of political leadership. There was no money to be made if you were in leadership, so people entered politics with a sense of service, unlike today when most people expect to make a lot of money through political office. I also have a strong sense of the beauty and diversity of the islands, with a mixture of every culture and ethnic group— the Africans, Europeans, Indians, Chinese, and more.

MDK: How do you connect that regional feeling with the global?

PA: I don't know if it's because we're small countries, but it's very clear to me that there's a limit to what we can do to change internationally conditioned factors in our own countries. Maybe it is also because I am conscious of the fact that we come out of a history of colonialism, but I have a strong understanding that what happens in our own country is connected to decisions people are taking in the power centers of the world, in London or in Washington. So, long before globalization, there was that understanding that part of the struggle would have to take place in those centers of power. It's a consciousness of the powerlessness and the marginality of the colonial experience. I think that this is what gives me an awareness of the importance of linking the local (or regional, in our case) with the global. This was true of Nita Barrow too. For us, working for justice in our own country *requires* that we also act globally. So for me it was never a matter of either/or.

MDK: To move into the present, I understand that you're working on a Ph.D. in economics. How does the academy appear to you as an activist; what are your views of the state of feminist scholarship now? What do you see as the most fruitful kinds of interactions between activism and research or scholarship?

PA: Some of my friends think it's a bad idea for me to do a dissertation and they say, "Don't get trapped by the narrow requirements of a doctoral study." But I have to say that I have not come across a lot of feminist scholarship that is not concerned about these things, that is not activist. I suppose it is because a lot of feminist scholars are also activists; they don't see these as contradictory roles.

There is nevertheless a recognition among feminist activist scholars that new methodologies are needed which are more interdisciplinary and which reduce the distance between the researcher and the researched. There is also increasing sensitivity to the fact that academic research can sometimes be exploitative of the communities being studied, that there are power imbalances between academia and the community. There is also an understanding in some institutions that activists need to be directly involved in research if the research is intended to lead to social change. This is not always easy to do, as academics are not good at giving up their power to nonacademic activists. Perhaps it is easier when the initiative comes from activists, when control of the research is in their hands, and when the research has a political purpose. DAWN's work attempts to do this. The network links the work of activists and researchers both by using the experience and knowledge of activists and by subjecting the research to the critique of activists. This is a very different process from the one normally used in the production of academic knowledge or studies.

CB: Scholars working on women internationally are more likely to combine activism and research, I think. Can you describe how you go about preparing a DAWN book?

PA: DAWN's analyses come out of a collective process that starts with the production of an outline of the issues to be covered, prepared by our research coordinator, and then proceeds through a series of regional consultations that elaborate and enrich the work from the perspective of the women in that region. Although the research coordinator takes major responsibility for production of the document and may be named as the author, we acknowledge the contribution of those who attended the regional consultations and commented on the document. Our steering committee must then approve it before release.

Getting back to my doctorate, I'm hoping to do it in such a way as to validate my own experience. If there are those who challenge it and want to know where I read this, or what I can cite in defense of my arguments, I will point out that many books come from people's experiences. All my life, other people have used my own and others' experiences as the basis for their books and doctorates, so why shouldn't I use my own experience as the basis for my own doctorate?

CB: I think that's what people were saying when they questioned whether you need to write a dissertation at this point in your life. You have so much that needs to be said, it is important that it not be locked into someone else's Ph.D. box. But if you can write what you want to say and make it your dissertation, maybe that will help to break down the division between activism and what is validated by the academy as legitimate research.

PA: We are speaking about the legitimacy of knowledge, and this sometimes has to do with how it is produced. I don't want to criticize more formal research methodologies, but the choice of methodology must be determined by what you want the research to do. If you want it to sit on a shelf where people may or may not consult it, that's one thing. If you want to inform and shape the world and reflect the reality of people, then you need a methodology that is more participatory and action oriented, one that raises the consciousness of the "subjects-objects" of research even as it proceeds. If you are an activist and want your research to contribute to social change or to a better understanding of the way the world works, then you would do well to use this latter methodology.

Feminist research must also be different in content. DAWN's research and analysis attempts to be holistic. We feel that you cannot look at economic issues purely from an economic point of view—similarly with so-called political issues. You need the integrated approaches that are at the heart of interdisciplinary studies. I think that women's studies brings that to scholarship. When we introduced women's studies into the University of the West Indies, those were the principles that were emphasized.

MDK: Was there resistance to that? I'm speaking out of our experience here in Rutgers in women's studies, where issues come up regularly about the difficulties people have with methodologies from disciplines other than their own.

PA: Again, it is the complexity that makes it difficult. It's much more difficult to do multidisciplinary work, and much easier to do research in a linear, one-dimensional way. I'm not saying that there is no place for a single focus—for economists to look at economic parameters, for example. But I think it is important to acknowledge the limitations of working purely within narrow disciplinary boundaries.

CB: One final question: what would you like to pass on to others and particularly to younger women who are reading this and thinking about how they can contribute effectively to change as women?

PA: I think it's a combination of things on the personal as well as professional levels. First of all, it's very important for young women to do some work on themselves, to find their own center, to become aware of themselves, to relate the personal to the political and the professional, to ground themselves in who they are. This is an ongoing process that is never finished, of course. I am talking about a lifelong commitment to learn and to grow. It is important to be open to change, to taking risks. You should not be afraid to try something new, to go a little further than you think you can actually manage. You should try to understand the larger picture even though what you can actually do is work on the small things within your own area of experience. You do not have to do everything. You can't. It's not healthy. You need to take care of yourself; you should not imitate people who are self-confessed workaholics!

MDK: Do you put yourself in this category?

PA: Completely, but let me go on giving advice to these young women! Don't feel guilty if you take time off to go on vacation, or take a walk in the park, or smell the flowers. Everyone needs something that helps them to relax; for me, it's gardening and music. Music helps the creative imagination that makes my work flow. I do those things even though I'm a workaholic; I take time to relax.

Also, don't let anybody tell you that you have to choose between relationships and work. You don't have to make such a terrible choice. Don't abandon relationships for the sake of the work. I think that's one of the most important things about women's leadership. It was one of the things that made Nita Barrow's leadership special. Although she held the highest offices of state, she never behaved like a man or like a machine. She always paid attention to little things when we worked together. It doesn't take a lot of time just to be considerate, to be thoughtful. I can hear her voice yet saying, "We'd better get Peggy some food!"

CB: Thank you, Peggy. That's a good note on which to conclude this formal interchange and invite you to lunch!

SUSAN BERRESFORD

■

IN CONVERSATION WITH RUTH B. MANDEL
AND MARY S. HARTMAN

In 1994 when then-president Franklin Thomas announced his decision to resign, the board of trustees at the Ford Foundation, the venerable New York–based philanthropic organization, named Susan Berresford his successor and the first woman president of the foundation. Berresford was born in New York in 1943 and educated at the Brearley School in New York City before attending Vassar College. After two years, she transferred to Radcliffe, where she graduated with a B.A. in American history in 1965. After several years working in federal and city antipoverty programs, Berresford took a position at the Ford Foundation in 1970, as a research assistant for national affairs. She then spent twenty-four years in various posts of increasing responsibility at the foundation, working as a program officer, vice president of the program division, and then executive vice president.

> *Since becoming president in 1996, Susan Berresford has paid particular attention to the changing global context for philanthropic work. After surveying the entire staff of the foundation at its New York headquarters and its branches around the world, she determined to make some administrative changes to strengthen the communications capacities of the organization, both internally and externally. She is using input from all levels of the organization to uphold the foundation's tradition of innovative projects in philanthropic work, to ensure a broad diversity of staff at all levels, and to give all foundation personnel an understanding of program operations. Berresford hopes that these initiatives will help to dissolve boundaries between innovators worldwide and encourage many more talented grant seekers to bring their ideas to the foundation and enhance global partnerships for a new millennium of international problem solving.*

RUTH MANDEL: As the head of a powerful institution by anyone's standards, you are a leader from whom we would like to know how it all came about! We'll be asking what you see as the most important features of your rise to power here, and how you would describe the circumstances, skills, and visions that played a role in that rise.

MARY HARTMAN: Perhaps we can begin by talking about the people who inspired you along the way, your family background, your education, and so forth.

SUSAN BERRESFORD: I'd enjoy starting out that way. The first thing I would say is that I think I was very lucky in being born into a family that supported me in doing a tremendous variety of things. It was not a family that said, "Let's figure out the one thing you're good at and try and make you the best at that." They were very encouraging in a huge range of things. I took lessons in the banjo, the piano, singing—all kinds of different things—and I never really mastered any of them, which some people would feel is a disappointment. When I look back on it, though, one of the things that impresses me is the support I felt to explore a lot of different things and the confidence that gave me. Later on, I kept surprising myself by being able to draw upon my early exposure to so many areas, all of which gave me assurance in dealing with new experiences.

Not that I could knock the ball out of the park every time, but I was ready to try! I found it fun to try things and to put myself into new situations. It was very liberating to be encouraged to pursue whatever appealed to me, for however long it appealed to me, without being told, "Now you must become the best pianist in the family."

MH: Did this exposure to different things include travel?

SB: No, I mostly stayed in the New York area as I was growing up. Yet that also prepared me for a job like this. Your question prompted me to think about something very specific, namely, travel to other places and times through books. I went to a school where students spent a lot of time reading. We had "Library" as a special part of the daily schedule. It was not to do your homework but to take out a book and read. The books I was especially drawn to—I was very little and I've never seen them since—were small, thin biographies, all of them bound in orange. I remember them sitting on a long library shelf at school. One was about Abe Lincoln and another Thomas Jefferson—some of the heroes of American history. There were few women; but it was a seemingly endless series, and I think the appeal of those books was partly learning about a person and partly the challenge of completing the series.

The series fascinated me and I kept pushing through it. The books made me think more about individuals and their roles in society, although I don't think I was much aware of that as I was reading them. As I look back, though, individual heroes and heroines made a great impression on me, and I think those orange books and all that time in the library started that. My school also showed a lot of current events films. You know, they'd darken the room and we'd all look at Eleanor Roosevelt or at the president. My parents also took us to the newsreel show in Grand Central Station. It wasn't particular women or men that I remember, but I do recall being very touched by the heroism and the courage of people trying to change something. I think that experience with news films extended the orange book ideas into real life, into something more contemporary. So for me that was an important part of my preparation.

I was also very lucky in my teachers. I went to the Brearley School, a private girls' school here in New York, and the teachers—most of them women—were extraordinary. A lot were very unconventional people by their history, by the things they chose to do, and by their style. I think that was another model that slowly and in a very indirect way began to seep into my consciousness. I was exposed to this interesting group of women leaders who had been trained and educated in different ways. One, for example, had been in the Women's Army Corps. This was an unusual person for me to meet when I was in sixth grade.

RM: If I'm remembering correctly, you had a single-sex education all the way through.

SB: Yes. I went on to Vassar for the first two years and then I transferred to Radcliffe and got married at the end of my second year of college. My husband was at the Harvard Business School. By then, Radcliffe and Harvard were integrated, so we went to the Harvard classes.

RM: What about Radcliffe in those days? Do you remember it as a place that talked about pouring tea, or were the images there very different?

SB: First of all, I wasn't a typical Radcliffe student in the sense that I lived off campus, and I was married. The campus atmosphere meant very little to me. What was important to me were the challenge and distinction of the incredible people who taught our classes, and of course the size of the place. I'd gone to Vassar for two years and had very small classes and wonderfully individualized instruction. You knew the professors, and they knew you very well. Anything you wanted to pursue individually was provided in the most supportive, intimate, and challenging setting. To go at the end of two years to a huge university, where you were one of five hundred people in a lecture hall, was for me a wonderful combination. What I remember about the Radcliffe-Harvard experience was this opening up of a world, becoming part of a great, complex university.

MH: What was your major, and what effect did that have on your subsequent intellectual development and career choices?

SB: I majored in American History, and I think again of the orange books and the grounding they gave me in questions such as, What is this country about, where did it come from, and where is it going? All that was very compelling to me. Since I hadn't traveled, what I knew of the rest of the world was still very superficial. I was most interested in understanding my own country, and I studied colonial history right up through contemporary history. I was lucky to have some truly wonderful people as instructors. I think studying history allowed me to place myself in the periods that I was studying, and to think about what I would have done, how I would have acted. I constructed a sort of personal adventure for myself in the larger historical and political framework.

RM: It is intriguing to me to hear you talk about the importance of this series of biographies in your intellectual development, because what used to be called the "great man" view of history is out of favor. Today we're not inclined to credit individuals, male or female, with being responsible for bringing about major change. Our students are taught to understand historical change as rooted primarily in broad social, political, and economic forces. I incline to your school of thought, though. I also think individuals matter a great deal; and I especially like to introduce students to inspiring individuals!

SB: This prompts me to remember a disappointment along those exact lines. I was always interested in heroic figures and what they did, male or female. But I remember at some point in either junior high or high school, we were studying the French Revolution and we each had to do a special project. I wanted to make up a diary of an ordinary person in this period, because we had been studying only the leadership group. I remember the school not letting me do it, saying, "That's not the right kind of a project." Now I think probably today—

MH: Right. You were far ahead of your time with that idea!

RM: Today you'd be encouraged to do the diary of the ordinary person and not encouraged to study the so-called extraordinary person. I think more balance makes sense.

SB: I think the other thing about the school I went to, which was very important in the long run but I didn't understand it then, was that although it was what people call an elite private school, it had an enormous range of people. They came from very different backgrounds and had very different talents—talents that were recognized and nurtured. For example, there was a fabulous pianist in my class who is world famous today. Another classmate now heads a major art museum, and both had fabulous artistic gifts that the school treated with as much respect and interest as gifts in writing or math. That was a good lesson, since talent takes so many forms. I worry now when I see schools taking the arts out of the regular program. That is saying, "We don't care about a whole reservoir of important talent." That talent is then far less likely to emerge and be developed.

RM: You said you had a family that encouraged lots of different activities. What was your family life like? Do you have siblings?

SB: I'm one of four children. I'm the second, with one older sister and two younger brothers. My mother and father raised us. My father died when I was about twelve and my mother remarried a few years later. I grew up in a busy family, with lots of people and lots of things going on all the time.

I have a son. I was divorced a few years after he was born and continued as a single parent for another few years. For the last twenty-some years, I have lived with a man to whom I'm not married; but we live as a married couple. He's a judge in the criminal court here in the city. My son also lives in New York. He went to college, worked for a year, and then went to the Yale Drama School for three years. Having him here now—in theater and movie work—is great. He's married to a woman who's just starting out in the business world. I think the greatest invention since all of us had children is e-mail. We're constantly in touch.

MH: Everyone tells me this. My son is going off to college and they say, "Don't worry, you'll talk to him more on e-mail than you've talked to him for years."

RM: It's absolutely true. My daughter and I talk on e-mail all the time. Let's jump ahead to the Ford Foundation, to a description of your work here and your position of leadership. Why did you want this job?

SB: Why did I want this job? Well, I can't think of anyone who wouldn't.

RM: It's a very nice office!

SB: It *is* a nice office. Seriously, though, it has been almost like a blessing to get this job, because it enables me to pursue things that I care deeply about with significant resources and a wonderfully talented staff and group of colleagues. Most people's jobs do not allow them to do what they care about most deeply, besides their families. They have to make extra time for those things. I'm the lucky person who gets to work at the head of this noble institution while pursuing values the foundation stands for and that I personally embrace. I feel terribly lucky to have had this chance.

I started here as a research assistant twenty-six–plus years ago and never thought at that time that I would end up as the president. I loved what I did every stage of the way, and at each one I thought, "Well, this is the last stage, now I'll go and do something else." Then I would be offered another step! So it's been a fascinating progression. I began on the U.S. side of the foundation, on issues of community development and poverty. I also worked on women's issues, particularly those involving employment, welfare, and family well-being. Then after many years—it must have been nine or ten—I was asked if I wanted to explore the international part of the foundation's work, to which I had had very little exposure. Again it was a great gift to me to be able to go to countries where the foundation had worked and meet the extraordinary people who get the grants—a new group of true heroes and heroines. I appreciated being able to explore the problems I had worked on in the U.S. through another optic, and that changes how you think about things. This was before the Internet and the other easier means of communication we have now. Going to these places was very important and reinforced my need to continue learning, which I do every day here.

The people the foundation supports are pushing the edges of questions, developing new kinds of knowledge, and building new types of institutions. I have had the great luck to learn what they want to do and then to try to be helpful to them. It makes me look forward to work every day, and to going home each night knowing that I've been able to support extraordinary people. We have a motto here that the foundation is a resource for innovative people and institutions worldwide. You hear it on NPR [National Public Radio], and we're beginning to use it more. The word *resource* is very important to me, because this is an institution that has grant money, but much more. It has a voice it can use when it wishes. It has a convening power, a bridge-building power, and it has publications capacity. All those things are resources. It's just fun to think about how to use those resources to support people with good ideas. There is a huge flow of such people here.

MH: Something that occurred to me in looking at your background along with Ruth's and mine is that we're kind of unusual—though perhaps less so for women of our generation—in that each of us has spent most of her career at a single institution. You've already spoken to some of the advantages to having been so long at Ford. I am interested in your discussing this further in terms of both advantages and drawbacks, seeing the organization over time and from different angles. I can imagine one thing, which is that when you achieved this position, you might well have said to yourself, "Now I've got the levers, I know what's working and what's not working in the place. Now I think I can fix some things." That could be very exciting!

SB: Right, right. The pluses of being here a long time are that you feel that you understand to some degree how the institution actually functions. Of course there's always the daily discovery that you don't *quite* understand it, and there are new things you always learn, which is fun. That's the nice part of ignorance. But I do feel I have a sense of the institution. I also think I have a pretty good historical sense of what some of the great accomplishments have been and why they occurred. Of course, there are many things you can't control that have to do with the world outside the foundation; but looking back over twenty years, you can still say, "Here was what we did about this thing that turned it into a big success."

The most extraordinary work of the foundation falls into three categories: one is when there's a powerful social movement that emerges in the world, such as the civil rights movement in America, the international human rights movement, or the women's rights movement. The movement's leaders come to us and ask for help in building institutions that will enable the movement to advance values it stands for and which the foundation shares. We don't start the social movement. It's out there, and it comes to us. That's a wonderful kind of work we can do.

A second is when the foundation's work begins to support people who are developing a new field of knowledge. You mentioned women's studies, and I think that's a very good example. Another is demography, a field the foundation helped create with a new analytical approach. If you look at those histories, we usually support one or two scholars in the beginning and then a group of scholars and then the institutes and centers in which they're housed. After that, there is the publication of their work, and seeing it become part of the mainstream. There's a natural progression for that kind of effort. Sometimes the new field of knowledge is not an intellectual field. Instead, it may be a field of practice. We're working in a field right now called development finance—how banking and banklike institutions can be structured and used to advance urban and rural low-income community development. There is a set of practical, on-the-ground experiments, then building new institutions, followed by development of a body of knowledge that comes out of those experiments and institutions.

The third category of the foundation's work is inventing a totally new kind of institution. Part of some community comes to us and says, "Our field needs a new kind of institution; will you help us build it?" Over a ten- or twenty-year period we do that. So knowing those three major arenas of activity, having a point of view about how these developments occurred, was a great advantage for me. It came from being in the institution for a considerable period of time. Although I think there are other ways you could have developed this knowledge, for me the experience felt like an advantage.

The disadvantage is that you may not set your sights high enough. You may take things for granted, as the way to do things because that is how they've always been done. I again feel blessed that when the board selected me, knowing I had been here for a really long time, they offered me a sabbatical. They gave me a number of months to leave the foundation and just go away, wherever I wanted to go, to talk to whomever I wanted to talk to, to rethink. I spent three months not coming in here, having almost nothing to do with the place, just talking to people and trying to frame some new ideas. What was very important for me was encountering some truly visionary people who reminded me that there were times in history when people set their sights to do something that no one thought could be done.

My favorite example from one of these conversations was someone who said, "Remember there was a time when people started to try to abolish slavery, and no one could imagine a world without slavery. It was a part of so many cultures in history that it was hard to imagine that it could be done, even though there were powerful desires to do it." Watching my son's generation look back at the civil rights movement and talk about it, I've often had similar conversations with people, saying, "It's amazing that there were courageous individuals who thought they could change things that seemed so ingrained and evil, with such brutality behind them. It's amazing that they could do it."

So I am most grateful that the board gave me a chance to reset my own compass and be sure that I talked with people from different parts of the world who have had new and interesting visions. The board didn't assume that things had to be the way they are. I also went and looked at a number of other institutions—not just nonprofits, but also for-profit institutions—to see how some of the best of them are run, what's new, and how people are reforming institutions. Again our motto, "innovative people and institutions," expresses what was happening. I think some institutions encourage innovation because of the way they are run and set up. Institutions have to keep reinventing themselves, so this period of exploration with different models was a great help in overcoming what could have been a constraint from being in the institution for so long.

MH: Let's talk a bit about some of the things that you're beginning to implement. I also want to get into questions of agenda and how you order priorities, but let's hear first about some of those ideas that you picked up when you were on your sabbatical and some of the ideas that I assume you brought to the presidency before you ever went on sabbatical.

SB: Let me mention just three, or maybe four, and I could talk forever about them! The first has to do with the internationalization of our staff here. We are an international organization with offices in fifteen countries; but our program staff for the most part has been American, with slowly increasing numbers from Africa, Asia, and Latin America, where our offices are. I think increasing those numbers more quickly than we have is critically important. I am convinced more than ever of what Frank Thomas brought to the foundation when he became president—that there is a tremendous value in cross-national learning and comparative analysis. We need, for example, to have in this headquarters in New York people from Africa who have worked on problems of democracy there, or on education or rural poverty. We need to understand what their experiences have been, and they will help us think differently about what we do here or what we do in Poland or somewhere else. So that is a very important first objective for me.

Having been a woman who came in here when there were very few women, I also know that these are not easy transformations. New people come in with new perspectives and new ways of thinking about what the point of the work is. These newcomers—in my case, women, and before that, American minorities, but now, more people from all over the world—are going to bring new ways of talking about the foundation's values, new ways of understanding our objectives, new suggestions for how we work and operate. I believe they will transform our current thinking in positive ways, but people don't give up their old ways of thinking and working easily, so it is going to be very interesting.

A second area of change has to do with learning. Foundations really are of two types, I think. One is a charitable sort of foundation that feeds the hungry and clothes the poor. The other is a developmental type that tries to get at the root causes of problems. The categories do overlap, but Ford is certainly at the developmental end of that spectrum. We're an institution devoted to practice and learning, and the people who come to foundations like this are very problem driven. They want to get on with the change process, they want to help something move forward. I know this was true of me.

The very minute I began to gain some traction on something, I was always looking at the next hurdle to get over. I didn't spend as much time as I now think I should have on saying what we had accomplished, what our grantees had accomplished, and celebrating that. We work on difficult problems like poverty or educational reform or human rights; and we don't often enough celebrate how far we've come, or try to enunciate clearly what we've learned so that others can either challenge it or gain from it. Learning is not something foundation people should do in isolation, but rather in groups with grantees. A group of grantees and a group of our staff working on a particular topic need to meet together in a structured way over a period of time and keep refining the sense of what we're learning together. You have to make it possible for people to set out time to do that. Because of the problem-driven dynamic and the fact there's always the requirement to make grants, it seems as though too many of the rewards can go to people who come up with fresh new things all the time rather than to those who consolidate and express what they've done and learned. So that's another reform area for us.

A third one is communications. If you're going to spend all this time on what you've learned, you really ought to disseminate it in an effective way. Today the potential for communication is so much more powerful and varied than in the past. In the old days you'd have a conference and you'd get out a publication, that was the mode. Now we have loads of other ways to do this. The world is cluttered with communication efforts, and I think we need to spend a lot more time thinking strategically about what it is we want to communicate, how well we do it, and how we can most effectively use the resources that the foundation has, along with our grantees, to carry this off.

The fourth and last reform I'll comment on has to do with the institution reinventing itself. I was here for nine years or so before Frank [Thomas] became the president. I watched him and hope I helped him reinvent the foundation—not because it was broken, but because the times had changed and new demands were being placed on the institution. Also, new capacities were available to us. He totally transformed the way we were structured, what our assumptions were, and how we operated. I feel a desire now, and an opportunity, to do the same thing, because there's a new frontier out there all the time.

One of the things I have experimented with in the last few years is trying to be very explicit about the value of hearing from people about what they want to try and reinvent, and then creating a staff capacity to back them up to do that. We have some experiments going all the time that we talk about internally. I think if we continue to do that we'll be better grant makers. All organizations need renewal.

For example, we have a new function here now, an office of organizational development. It will operate within the program division and help us experiment with new ways of running the grant-making division and getting better at what we're doing. Some of this has to do with how to improve the working relationship among three categories of people: grant makers, grant administrators who track the payment and reporting side, and the secretary or administrative person who works with the program officer. The goal is helping that team work coherently together, because they've actually been thought of as people in three different worlds. So I want to be very explicit about such experiments here. We'll learn from them and we'll move on; but it is very important to be explicit about the capacity to reinvent yourself.

RM: The way that you describe your own experience is remarkable. It's wonderful to hear someone talk about being blessed in her work, about joy in coming to work every single day.

MH: Yes, you can disregard that question we raised before we started taping about whether you are having fun!

RM: I'm struck that you describe all these things as if they just sort of happened to you. In other words, you were here, and the board came along and elevated you. Did you not have a role in the transition to becoming president; did you play no active part in that advancement? You moved into a very powerful position. Is it something that really is almost a unique experience, in which someone with real merit who's demonstrated her value was recognized for that and was promoted for it? Were you not involved more actively as a part of that process?

SB: Well, I was a part of it to the extent that I love this institution and I worked my heart out for it because I believe in it. I love my colleagues here, I love the people we work with, and I am energized by that every day. I think I contributed good things in that process. But quite honestly, I thought that at the end of Frank's tenure here, I would leave the foundation. I'd been here twenty-five years, I'd had a wonderful set of experiences, and I was beginning to plan a very different kind of life. So there was a tremendous element of surprise in this for me.

RM: So it truly was not something you initiated?

SB: No. I was planning to move to California when the board approached me.

RM: And were they, to a person so far as you know, agreed that this was the way to go rather than to go outside? There wasn't competition for the position? I don't think that is the experience of many other women!

SB: I know very little about the board's process. Our board is very careful and deliberate. They had asked Frank Thomas to give them at least a year's notice at the time he decided he wanted to leave, and they were hoping he would stay much longer. So he gave them that notice, and from that moment I have no idea what deliberations they went through. All I know is that when they asked me to interview with them, I did that. We had a wonderful exchange, and I didn't have a great deal of time other than my long career here to prepare for the actual interview, which was a blessing because I could speak from my heart of my feeling about the place and my ideas about it. They offered me the job that day.

RM: That day?

SB: There was clearly a deliberative process that preceded that, but I am not a good interview subject for that!

RM: So you have had incredible support, from the board and from the staff, right? You did not come into a situation in which the staff was saying, "Gee, we thought they should go outside, or look for somebody else."

SB: Well, you'd have to ask the staff! Once I was selected, prior to this sabbatical, I went back to my regular job because Frank was still here, and we were still working together. I first interviewed every board member individually to understand what each person's visions and hopes for the institution were. I got a very good sense from that, and these were wonderful interviews. Then I sent an e-mail to every single person in the institution, all around the world. I said that I welcomed their suggestions and ideas, and I began convening small groups of people, both here and whenever I traveled to a field office.

There was an enormous flood of interesting e-mail and of face-to-face exchanges. I have a stack of hundreds of e-mail communications I got from people. I would then e-mail back and forth about their ideas, or I would write a letter. So I had a huge store of ideas that came from people I respect enormously, who know this institution as I do. It was with that in my pocket, finally, that I went out and talked to other people. I really ended up feeling I had a good sense of a variety of ideas I could choose from and move ahead with. It's been a remarkable process, and I don't envy people who take on these jobs without that kind of opportunity to consult so broadly within and outside of the institution.

A lot of the best ideas have come up from inside. I'll give you an example of one of my favorites. When I went to our office in Nigeria, we talked about the importance of hearing from everybody at all levels of the institution. A man who drives one of the foundation vehicles in Nigeria came forward with a suggestion which concerned his job of driving the foundation staff into a rural or urban area, where they go off to do their program work. He stays with the vehicle, which says "The Ford Foundation" in tiny letters on the side. People from the surrounding area often gather and ask, "What is the Ford Foundation?" So he said, "I would like to have you help me understand better what the foundation is so that I can speak effectively to these people, because all these people should know about the Ford Foundation and what it does. Maybe some of them would like to apply to the foundation."

Well I thought that was a wonderful lesson in thinking about the communication resources that you have in your institution, all the way through the institution. I would not have thought of that, had he not said it. In some of our offices, in fact, there's a concern about putting the name on the side of the vehicle at all, because of security issues and so forth, but in Nigeria in this office they find it a real plus. It produces useful conversation about what philanthropy is and about the civil sector that philanthropy is a part of.

MH: This June, Charlotte Bunch had her annual women's leadership institute at Rutgers, bringing women from all over the world to discuss human rights issues and share strategies. She of course is a beneficiary of the Ford Foundation, and I'm especially interested to hear you talking about the importance of strengthening communication with people in the field because I heard one of her participants discussing just that. This was a young woman who had been a member of the foundation staff in Africa—I don't recall which country—but she talked about her high hopes for the foundation and the future because there had been so much recent interest in hearing and learning from the staff in the field offices all around the world.

It is fascinating to me now to be reminded of this comment of hers and to realize that the initiative she mentioned came straight from the top.

SB: You know, foundations can only do good work if abundantly talented people who are out there come to them. You can't sit in these places and invent something, it's not going to work. It has to come out of the heart and soul and vision—and sometimes the fury—of people who see the world and want to make it different, people who see something wrong, see something that disappoints them, see something that confuses them. You have to respond to that fury or that optimism or whatever it is that brings them. So they've got to believe they can come to you. You've got to respond to them in a way that makes them feel supported.

RM: Is it your impression that that's a change during the period you've been at Ford? I must confess that practically the day before I walked into the Ford Foundation back in the early seventies, I didn't know what a foundation was, much less know how to relate to one for anything that I was doing. But I remember in those days the image was that foundations had agendas, that foundation officers went out and tried to find people to implement their agendas. The way you're describing it, agendas now arise from a lot of sensitive barometers and indicators of what's happening outside the foundation; and people come to the Ford Foundation bringing you *their* agendas, ideas, visions, and experiences. Then people here know how to build on what is brought to them.

SB: I think there is a change in thinking in the world that foundations mirror. The idea of the "grand design" is very powerful and very appealing; and there's clearly a foundation body of experience with grand designs. Many of the grand design experiences crumbled, though, because they were just that, designs created from the outside. It was difficult to get them rooted anywhere. So I think in many foundation domains you can see that such a change has occurred.

I also think that there is a myth of a "great man" theory in foundations and in other areas, because some of the great accomplishments of foundations, such as the Green Revolution, are seen today through a historically inverted telescope. What you're seeing looks like the design of a couple of single-minded people who sat down and made it happen. When you go back and look at where the ideas came from in the first place, it's a far messier picture. Yet because it's so far away in time, you don't see the mess; you see only the shimmering results and one or two people who got the credit when some idea worked.

MH: That's a good lead-in to our last set of questions, that focus on women and leadership. We are interested in your thoughts about the younger generation, and also about whether there is coming to be a more clear-eyed perception, as you're saying, about how change really occurs and how people effect change. We are coming to realize that a lot of what has been held up as the traditional way men have led never really reflected reality. You know—the great man setting out the vision, and the rest implementing it. These things can now be seen in retrospect as much messier, just as you say.

But is this one of the features that can be generalized about women's behavior in leadership roles? Are women, perhaps due to their shared experiences, more aware from the start that it's not likely to be a matter of one or two great individuals setting out the blueprints for change and then making that transformation happen—is that what you would say? In any case, do you think getting more women into leadership roles will make a positive difference? Do you think our daughters are going to be inspired the way a number in our own generation have, to pursue agendas for change? Will they be able to talk as you do about feeling blessed to be able to play a special role in all of this?

RM: You might also talk about how in the foundation world itself, as in politics and education, there has been enormous change. You're here at Ford, and there are other women who now head major foundations and also women in top executive positions in some of the smaller foundations. Do you, as a group, get together at all and talk as women leaders in American philanthropy?

SB: Different groups of foundation leaders do get together in various combinations, but there isn't one that I'm part of that is exclusively feminist or even female. We do talk a lot among ourselves, however, and there are now significant numbers of women, as you say, in these positions. I think one part of the benefit of having more women at the top is that the face of philanthropy will look more varied, as it ought to. It ought to reflect the country that it comes from. To the extent that there is racial and gender and other kinds of diversity in it, philanthropy will be seen as something that is a natural part of our landscape and not some elite, mysterious thing off in a corner.

As for the issue of how women behave in leadership, I am not one who believes that the biological differences between men and women are so powerful that they will make philanthropy or any other field truly different because women are leading there. I think some of the experiences that women have are different from men's, in their growing up and everything else. These can be powerful influences on their professional behavior. I think as a few more women move into leadership roles, it doesn't guarantee that you will have more focus on family or community issues traditionally associated with women. Not all women have those interests, after all. Putting a woman at the head of a foundation doesn't guarantee anything. But the more women you have who get into leadership positions, the more likely it is that the common experiences of women and the common interests of women are going to be represented in policy decisions. So I think it will have an effect in the long term.

RM: Have you seen any signs here?

SB: Having been at the foundation when women were a tiny minority of the professional staff to now, when from year to year they waver just above or below 50 percent, I have seen a different style emerge, a different organizational culture. We have changed a number of things, from our benefits to our notion of leadership style. So, yes, there are definitely changes here.

RM: What's the change in the notion of leadership style?

SB: I think a broader variety of leadership styles is accepted; it isn't always the directive person in control with a dominant idea that others are going to implement, as you said a minute ago. Again, mirroring change in the larger society, there is a more participatory, consensus-building style. There is broader interest in looking at the gender impacts of the work we do; it isn't the responsibility of one or two people who are sort of a truth squad. Because there are more women here, and because there are also more men who care about women's issues, people more often internalize gender as something they're responsible for thinking about. That's very different than it was before. It used to be always, "Oh, what does Susan think? Or Terry or Mariam?" I remember when Frank Thomas became president, someone talked this way in one of the officers' meetings and he stopped it immediately by saying, "This is not their responsibility, it's everyone's responsibility." That was a very important shift. I know that we have a long, long way to go still. But I'm amazed at the progress since the seventies.

MH: I agree, both about how far we've come and about how much remains to be done. One activity of the Institute for Women's Leadership we're involved in at Rutgers is to monitor women's participation in decision-making roles. Progress, as you say, has been real, even in leadership, but far too slow. For some time now, however, we've been observing what I think is a sea change in women's attitudes toward leadership.

I'm not talking just about eighteen-year-old college women but older women as well, especially professional women who want help in jump-starting their paths to leadership. Our entering students are far more receptive to imagining themselves as leaders than they used to be. There is lots of interest in the programs Ruth started at the Center for the American Woman and Politics for college-age women interested in politics and government; and Charlotte Bunch has annual global leadership institutes for grassroots practitioners as well as women working in governmental posts around the world. We're now putting together a leadership certificate program for undergraduates, but we're aware that educating larger cohorts of women to be effective leaders is only part of the task here. It's a big challenge.

SB: Yes. This year, we had a "Take Our Daughters to Work" day, as we've had for many years, and we had a wonderful group of young girls. I was introduced to them at some point in their day, with probably too much fanfare; and one of these little girls put up her hand and said, "I don't mean to be rude, but why are people making such a big fuss about the fact that you're a woman president of the Ford Foundation? Isn't that a perfectly natural thing?" I thought that her remark had both a good side and a sad side.

The good side was that this wonderful young girl feels the world is in front of her and it's there and she can get whatever she wants, just as I did. The sad side of it is that she doesn't yet see that there are a lot of people who don't think that is the case. We talked about that a bit. The difference I think in the task ahead of us from what we started twenty-five years ago is that we have managed to make a lot of changes by means of individuals adjusting their lives and challenging things. We have been driving the change process in that individual way. That has gone quite a distance and has even included changed laws and practice and many new ideas and new curricula. But if you step back and look at a lot of institutions, you have to admit that they haven't really changed that much. We still have a presumption about a pattern of work, for example, that is built on an obsolete model of households with male breadwinners and female homemakers. If this country is going to solve its social problems, we're going to have to reexamine that model. If we want to improve community life, men and women, who now both typically have jobs, are going to have to rebalance their work, family, and community responsibilities. This will require very profound social changes for people in this country, and I think we have not gone very far in addressing these very complicated questions.

RM: Yes, regarding these "complicated questions," I don't think we're in a much better place now, maybe in some senses slightly worse. I often think of this standing up in front of students in a classroom, young women with high expectations for the future. Some changes have helped, of course; but child-rearing responsibilities are not really any easier. In some ways, with all their personal and professional options, young women face greater challenges for coping with those decisions and plans, even though now one can say, "Well, I know lots of people who take their children to child care," in contrast to when we were younger. Of even greater concern, we don't seem to have very many good visions of what might be done to bring about positive change which is healthy for individuals, families, and the broader society.

SB: In one sense, women who are in poor communities, low-income women, are the clearest expression of that, the most extreme example, and a lot of the problems that they face are the things that the society has to think about for everyone. I think until we realize that, we're not going to get as far as we all hope we'll get. All of these promises that we hear in political campaigns are going to be just promises, just talk on *Larry King,* not real change. So I think we need to have a much more profound discussion about what kind of society we want to have and what the values are that we want most to protect and how individuals and communities and institutions have to be rethought over time.

MH: There's one level of leadership, then, that you've described that seems to envision the Ford Foundation helping to set those agendas or provide context for those kinds of discussions to take place in a wider arena than our individual households and communities.

SB: I wouldn't say set the agenda, but contribute importantly to the discussion and convene people to talk about it. Work-family programs in employment settings have often been thought of as something you do to help people adjust, something that is either neutral to the bottom line or negative to it. For the first time, we are finding results of studies Ford has supported in a couple of corporations showing that work-family programs are actually positive for the bottom line. You say to people, "Your work and your other life are intertwined. There is no way you can separate them the way we pretend you can, so we have to start thinking about how you're going to be able to do both more easily and joyfully. That's going to require some reinvention." The minute you say that, you invite people to begin talking about how the workplace can be better structured to do the work well while at the same time enabling workers to see to other responsibilities. Ideas for reform emerge that make for improved productivity as well as stronger families and community well-being. So it's not setting the agenda as much as helping move the agenda with new information, making the agenda visible to people, because it's really the people outside the foundation who set the agenda.

RM: What's the toughest part of the job? If you asked me about the years at the Center for the American Woman and Politics, I'd have to say that early on, like most of the women's programs around the country, getting resources and gaining credibility were the toughest parts for us. But at the foundation you don't have to say that, right? So what's the toughest part of the job?

SB: I'm having so much fun in this job right now, I'm not sure what the toughest part is. The toughest part of all program-related jobs in the foundation, I suppose, is that people see a pot of money, and so there is this endless flow of legitimate and wonderful demands made on you, everywhere you go. You sit down on an airplane, you go out to dinner . . .

MH: So it doesn't matter how big the pot is!

SB: No. People think of these jobs as ones in which you are always being Santa Claus and always saying yes. The opposite is true. You're continually saying no, and you say yes to only a fraction of projects. These are problems everybody should have, I know, but you feel you are often disappointing people who have wonderful, powerful ideas, and you can't do it all. I think since most people have never had the luxury of a job like this, they haven't thought about how it normally takes ten or twenty years to build an institution or to accomplish something. If you are serious, you're going to stick with a program a long time, and that means you're going to have to say no for a long time to a lot of other things.

The need for priority setting, then, balanced with reserving some support for the opportunistic response to ideas that come in and that you just never thought about. That's another conclusion I have drawn from working at Ford. If you look at any ten-year span of work that I've been involved with, half of the things I'm proudest of are things that we intentionally set out to do with grantees, and the other half are absolute surprises nobody thought would ever happen. So part of the challenge of this job is to be intentional to a degree, because you have to say, "I'm not going to do that; I'm going to do this, and with these grantees." But the other half is to keep enough time and money and energy for the fabulous wild cards that cross your path.

RM: Sounds like a good program for living.

SB: Yes, exactly!

MILDRED DRESSELHAUS

■

IN CONVERSATION WITH MARTHA A. COTTER
AND MARY S. HARTMAN

Mildred Dresselhaus, Institute Professor of Electrical Engineering at the Massachusetts Institute of Technology, was born in 1930 in a Brooklyn ghetto. The child of poor immigrants, she faced a strong class bias growing up in Depression New York and was discouraged from pursuing a college track in the public school system. Her early talent at playing the violin, however, enabled her to see middle-class New York, and she was determined to escape from poverty through education. After working three days a week teaching a retarded child to read and write, Dresselhaus applied to Hunter College High School and earned a perfect score on the mathematics entrance test. Her teachers encouraged her to pursue elementary education, then one of the few acceptable careers for gifted women. At Hunter College, a physics professor, Rosalyn Yalow (who received the Nobel Prize in medicine in 1977), recognized her talents and suggested that she

pursue a career in science. During graduate school, first at Cambridge, then at Radcliffe, and finally at the University of Chicago, Dresselhaus overcame significant discrimination. She later won a National Science Foundation postdoctoral fellowship for study at Cornell University.

Dresselhaus then accepted a position at MIT, where she worked in the Lincoln Laboratories for seven years before taking a teaching position in electrical engineering. The first tenured woman faculty member in the engineering school, she began her advocacy for women in the sciences at MIT by starting a forum for women students. Since then, she has worked to build a community among MIT's women faculty and students, in addition to assuming leadership positions both in the institute and nationally in her scientific field. Now president of the American Association for the Advancement of Science, Mildred Dresselhaus is a former president of the American Physical Society. Author of several books and many articles, she has been awarded thirteen honorary doctorates, and she received the National Medal of Science in 1990. The mother of four children, she lives in Cambridge with her husband and plays the violin daily.

MARTHA COTTER: You came from a situation of poverty and disadvantage and were offered little encouragement to pursue education. I know you were laughed at in a ghetto school when you set your sights on Hunter High [a very competitive high school in New York, then all-female]. How in the world did you acquire the self-confidence to persevere and achieve?

MILDRED DRESSELHAUS: That's a good question. I don't think that comes instantaneously. Self-confidence grows. You have some success, and that success leads to other success. Very few successful people have an inkling as young people that they will be successful in later life.

MARY HARTMAN: I agree, but then what was it that made you set your sights on passing that entrance examination for Hunter High School, the experience of success that put you on the path to so much more success?

MD: One of the overriding things for many who grow up in poverty is the simple desire to escape. I think it was sort of obvious to me that escape had to be through education. There is another side to my story that has to do with music school, which taught me a lot more than music by giving me an opportunity to meet people who were in easier socioeconomic circumstances. I was bound to ask myself, how do I go from where I am to where those kids are, and education was the means. It wasn't so much studying the violin, which I did and I'm still an avid player today. It was that cultural activities became an avenue to get to a new level. So what helped me is a vision of something different from what I saw around me. Maybe young people today get that from TV. TV does sort of make everybody equal, but at an intellectually low level, and with a high level of comfort. It is too much of a selfish approach to life. I think music school is much better!

MH: Were your parents encouraging you in your studies and your music school?

MD: Absolutely. I think that now a child who attempts to achieve academically is not a popular person, that there is peer pressure to be mediocre in academic studies.

MC: Let me back up a bit. You said you didn't have overall goals early on, save escaping poverty, and that you did not set out to be a leader. Was it then one goal at a time?

MD: Yes. Before I started high school, I had lots of menial jobs, jobs that everybody in our neighborhood would do for a lifetime. Working conditions were awful because people took advantage of little kids regarding both pay and working conditions. But this experience helped me in the end. People who have it too easy in early life have a disadvantage for later on, because they get to thinking that everything is going to be easy. Science is not that easy. You have to plug away to get at the laws of nature. They usually don't pop out at you, so you need diligence.

MC: Once you got to high school, was it easier?

MD: Well, it meant that I was mainstreamed all of a sudden. I was not swimming against the tide. There were a lot of talented people coming from very supportive homes. I did have a job when I was in high school, but so did many of the other students; probably 15–20 percent were helping to support their families and themselves. There was no particular discrimination against kids from the wrong side of the tracks except when it came to going to college and career planning. Then there was a difference.

MH: You mean to say that with that splendid high school record you weren't taken aside and encouraged to apply to various colleges?

MD: Oh, I did have a splendid record. But at that time, you know, and with no money, school advisers assumed I had to accept a simple college—not try for anything too fancy. Maybe it wasn't the right advice, but it all worked out fine.

At that time, they had scholarships in New York State for maybe twenty students in all. These scholarship paid something like half your tuition to attend Cornell. I won one of them, in addition to a regular state scholarship, so I was almost all the way to being a fully paid scholar at Cornell. But I couldn't see my way through for the part that wasn't provided, and people at the high school did not encourage me to try. They didn't think I could earn enough. So I didn't accept the scholarship. These days, a student in that situation would be supported somehow. Anyway, I went to Hunter College, and it turned out to be a fine place to go.

True, science education at Hunter was not very good, and there weren't many science majors. The high school had been very small and selective, and we had had excellent instruction since many teachers came from the college. But by the time I got to college, you could say I was overprepared. I took several majors at once, and it was still boring. Well, boring is not the right world, but it wasn't so much of a challenge for someone with my training.

When I started out in college, I would have loved to be a science major, but I honestly didn't know such a thing existed. I had been interested in science in high school, but I mainly did math then. In college I was strongly urged to go into education, since school teaching was one of the few professions for women. Another was secretarial work. I don't like to work for somebody, and *secretary* had bad connotations at the time. Maybe it still does.

MH: So you decided to be a schoolteacher?

MD: Yes, at first. I love teaching, and I set out to do teaching on the elementary level. Being a schoolteacher in New York was a highly respected, well-paid position then. At the same time, I was sort of fooling around a lot on my own with the science business. I had lots of time to do it because college courses were pretty easy and I was encouraged by the teachers. Hunter was a big school, like Rutgers, but also a little bit like Douglass College in that the students with some talents were given an unusual amount of encouragement.

Hunter cost five dollars a semester, which covered everything: tuition, lab fees, and books. We had a kind of all-college assembly at Hunter, where the president or the dean would talk, perhaps once a month. One message I recall very clearly, and which has in fact been a light of my career, was the following: "This free education is not free. We expect you to pay this back in service to society over your lifetime." I think that's a very good exchange for all concerned!

MH: I know that many distinguished graduates from Hunter are also very civic minded.

MD: Yes. Rosalyn Yalow comes to mind. She's from a about a decade ahead of me, and Gertrude Elion [another Nobel-winning scientist] is a decade beyond Rosalyn. We all have the same attitude and have discussed with one another how this message has influenced our lives.

MH: Bella Abzug was another famous Hunter graduate who said the same thing.

MD: Another message was also very strong. That has to do with the determination we developed at Hunter, the idea that somehow we would land on our feet and that we'd manage to figure it all out. What we didn't learn in the classroom, we'd learn by ourselves.

MH: How much did that have to do with being taken seriously as women there?

MD: Ironically, this was especially true in my epoch because of the GIs, who were there when I arrived in 1948. I will explain why. Hunter College became coed "temporarily" at that point, and it never went back. The GIs were about half the students in the science classes—although not half overall—but they were *not* the top students. The women were the top students. (The best students among the GIs had gone to other schools.) The men did have more experience—they were better than the women in the lab courses, for example, because many of them had operated a lot of equipment during the war years and some had been electronics technicians. But when it came to the theory classes, they were not anywhere as good as the women. Being at Hunter at that time, then, meant that one hardly got the idea that women couldn't do science, math, or anything they set out to do!

When I started college I thought the only thing a woman could do was to become a schoolteacher. But once in college, I had so many doors opened daily to me. True, I always looked for those doors, but in the end there were far more than I could open.

MC: One thing that interests me as a scientist is your assessment of the evolution of women's opportunities in science, especially physics and engineering. Shirley Tilghman, a molecular biologist at Princeton, says that young women today, at least in her field, seem to have lower expectations than women students ten years ago. They conclude, especially in this bad job market, that they won't be able to have both a career in science and a family. We tend to assume that these things have linearly gotten better for women in science over the years, but maybe not. How do you compare the generations?

MD: Mostly it is linear improvement, and while things may well be different in molecular biology, I'll talk about science areas with which I am more familiar. In the fifties when I was in college, expectations for women were low. Despite being encouraged in college, we found few careers out there. Once you got beyond schools like Hunter or the seven sisters, institutions just were not hiring women. In industry, opportunities were also quite limited, and there was a lot of discrimination. At the prestigious colleges, there were essentially no women faculty. Even in graduate school, women were not taken seriously.

When Rosalyn Yalow, nearly a decade before me, started in graduate school at Columbia, she was made a secretary since there were no research assistantships for women. She was not allowed to participate in class discussion and had to sit silently in the back of the room. They corrected her papers, but that was about it. When I was in graduate school, it wasn't yet equal but it was much closer. I spent a year at Harvard, and the women from *all* fields had to take their exams together in the same room because their presence in a coed examination setting was thought too distracting for the men. At Radcliffe College in my time, they had forty women, each one taking a different exam, and therefore students could not ask the professor for clarification of exam questions, whereas the men could. Also at Harvard they had fellowships that were only open to men. Women had to get their aid from Radcliffe, which had very little. The resources were different.

MH: What about professors? Were there professors who refused to teach women?

MD: Yes. When I was at the University of Chicago, I ran into that, but since I was a very independent student by then, it wasn't a traumatic experience. My professor, the only one supervising students in the area I was working in, solid-state physics, did not believe that women should be graduate students. He let me know that every time I met him, and he said that it was a waste of resources for the university to educate me since I was not going to do anything with my degree anyway. I was sort of tired of hearing this, and I applied for fellowship support outside of the university. Everything I applied for I won, and this professor was very upset with me because these were not fellowships limited to women, they were for everybody! He said how awful it was that I was taking these resources away from a man. Some others, of course, were not only friendly but very supportive. Enrico Fermi was a great, great supporter of women scientists.

MH: But those who thought training women was a waste got away with it?

MD: Absolutely, that was not considered a negative for a professor. At that time, it was an expected way for men to behave. Another thing I remember as a student was all the nude pinup girls on the walls. These were things you had to put up with in a lab to get your experiment working. It was not an environment in which women felt comfortable. But if you couldn't handle that, you knew you couldn't have a career in science.

MH: I'd like to fast-forward from the fifties to the sixties, with your appointment at MIT and your decision to look into the status of women students there.

MD: When I came to MIT, I came through the largesse of the Rockefeller family as a visiting professor, and then that worked into a permanent position. In 1968, I became the first tenured woman faculty member in the engineering school here at MIT, and that's not so long ago! We just did not have women faculty at MIT in positions of authority that could influence the future of the university. So, in addition to doing my science, I thought I should see what needed to be done that I could do better than other people, so to speak. We had a small number of women students—it was only about 4 percent when I arrived at MIT. At least *half* of them were on the verge of failure and leaving. At that time, our dean of women students, Emily Wick, who later went on to Holyoke as provost, welcomed my help.

I learned we had a bimodal distribution. A few women were very successful and would succeed no matter what. The other group, maybe the majority, got more and more beaten down. This was not because of lack of ability but just because they couldn't put up with it anymore. I tried to help. We had facilitation sessions that I ran for some time.

MH: What happened? Did you just encourage them to talk at first?

MD: Yes, mostly encouraged them to talk. You know, "What's on your mind? What's bothering you?" It was mostly isolation. So many had expectations of career and success dashed every semester. The guys would have a lot of fun beating the women students down. It was the thing to do around here. By bringing the women all together so they could all talk about it, they found out that so many of them were undergoing the same thing.

MH: "Oh, and I thought it was just me."

MD: Exactly, and that helped a whole lot. So many of them later on in life have come back to thank me and have said that I helped them finish their degree programs. And then they went on and were able to do the same for others. But when a new dean of students came in, he didn't think we needed any more activities for women, so he put an end to the dean of women's job. The students were terribly upset about this, so I supported them. Why not?

That was just at the beginning of the [Jerome B.] Wiesner administration, and he favored increasing women's numbers and support for women at all levels. The programs for women at MIT have never taken the form they have at Rutgers, where you have personnel with salaries and a special residence hall for math, science, and engineering students [at Douglass College]. The program here is mostly voluntary, but very successful. Now we're over 40 percent women at the undergraduate level in science and engineering. Also, the students have a much higher level of self-confidence, with expectations pretty much equal to the men.

So, while you have pockets with a decrease in expectations due to the job market, the market is tough for everybody. It's a little more tough for women because they hope for families and think that will disadvantage them in career placement, which is probably true. Molecular biology is a special case, though, because the apprenticeship there is so long, with postdoctoral work that often means people are well over thirty when they finally become independent investigators. In other fields, you start independent careers earlier. So I would say that in some sense, even though there are a lot of women in biology, the way it's all organized works quite negatively for women. There are likely to be some changes in that field though, partly because I don't think the men like it either.

MH: Tell us more about the different expectations of the new generation of women.

MD: They're confused because when they started their college educations, they had high expectations for their careers. Now when they graduate, many seem to be in a holding pattern. As long as you don't laugh at women for going into nontraditional fields, the situation is only bad, not terrible. There have not been many traditional careers out there in recent years, although this is changing now.

MH: Turning now to those women who *do* make it through—either to traditional tenure-track positions in science in the universities or in other careers using science—how do you assess what is happening to them in terms of power and recognition? Are their scientific contributions as readily recognized as men's? Are the doors opening more in other leadership roles, including administering departments or centers?

MD: Well, it's coming along. Take deans of engineering. Ten years ago there were very few; now there are quite a number. There are other indicators out there, too, but the problem is not yet solved. When you get to a certain level, men all of a sudden think, "Oh, the problem is taken care of." It *isn't*, but it is approaching solution.

MH: So you are basically optimistic that this upward, linear trend will include comparable leadership roles and influence for women?

MD: When I first came to MIT in the sixties, I thought it would take two generations for prejudice to disappear and for women to have equal opportunity. The increase in numbers, at least, has been much faster than I could have predicted. But there are so many problems that we haven't yet solved. I think we've done a lot in improving career opportunities, but we haven't solved the child-care problem very well. That's still a mess. We also haven't really solved K–12 education, so if you have young kids, you're probably worrying about them, and that's a distraction from your career. All kinds of things should go along with equal career opportunity that should make it possible for women to take more advantage of it.

MH: You end up with multiple and imperfect individual solutions. I was very impressed to learn that in one of your early positions, when your children were small, you announced to the lab head that you would arrive an hour later because of getting your children off to school. That took courage, especially as the other woman there reportedly had such trouble with the rigid expectations that she left.

MD: I left too, in the end. I wouldn't say it took so much courage to say I was arriving later, though. In terms of recognition worldwide, the two women researchers were doing almost the best work of anybody in that laboratory. I did not think they were about to fire either me or her.

MH: But wasn't it true that they kept after her so much that she left on account of it?

MD: Yes, but I would say it was misguided management more than anything. If you're trying to get the best results from an employee, you don't go around harassing the employee for things they can't fix—especially if they are giving a best-effort performance.

MH: Let me ask you some things about issues related to your lifetime in leadership, so to speak. You are, after all, an outstanding leader in research who early on achieved success and recognition. You have held many formal leadership positions in the profession. You were the first woman to chair your department here, you have headed many committees at MIT and on the national level, you are on government and industry boards, you're the president-elect of the American Association for the Advancement of Science, you're on the executive board of the National Research Council, you were the treasurer and first woman officer of the National Academy of Sciences . . .

MC: And the former president of the American Physical Society!

MH: How have you approached these and many other leadership roles? Have you felt that you couldn't really do what needed to be done unless you were in a position of leadership? Or have people more often singled you out and said, "Mildred, we want you to head up this or that because it is very important and we know you would do the best job"? How do you balance these demands others have on you and also your feeling that if you are in a particular place, you will be able to make a difference?

MD: You have asked a lot of questions all at once. Let me start with something that you didn't ask. All the leadership positions that I have had have one common denominator: none has required that I give up my science work. You have to remember that, because there are a lot of leadership positions that I could have aspired to or been asked to do. But I've always discouraged anybody from going further with such discussions because I like my students and I like my research. I don't want to give them up.

So first, there's a limit to what kind of leadership stuff I will do. That's an important thing to understand and perhaps has something to do with why there aren't more women leaders. Maybe many of us don't really want to do it all the time. I think the best job I could have is the one I have. I don't think being head of X, Y, or Z or of some government agency—being a senator or something!—are things I really want to do, or are things that are anywhere nearly as interesting as what I'm doing.

MC: So you do not take any primary satisfaction from holding leadership positions per se?

MD: Well, I would be just as happy doing none of them. I would say the ones that I've done, I've done because I think it's very important to break through this glass ceiling and give a message to women that they can do it too. So I've done a lot of the leadership things out of duty, not because they really were things I wanted to do. I don't know how many of the other people you're interviewing will say the same, but that's my story. Most of the things that I have led have been related to my work, rather than more general things. Once you do the latter, it's difficult to get back here!

So for running the American Physical Society, for example, or whatever, I use an equation, an algorithm, for such things; and I believe that's true of many of my women friends. We do it because there are still very few that are asked amongst women, so those who are asked simply have got to take on some of these things to make it easier for the next generation. That's a very important ingredient, which goes along with another responsibility—that you don't flub these things up, because you want to do a good enough job that people will have confidence that women can do any job that men can do.

MC: In your experience, do women and men lead differently?

MD: As I said, I wouldn't have had any interest if I hadn't felt this obligation to other women and also the need to do such jobs well because that goes along with the responsibility to other women. There's another thing that I'm not sure is a woman thing or a personality thing, and you can be the judge. I look around to see what needs to be done. It isn't that I do the same thing with every organization. If I think an organization is doing poorly because of administration, I pay attention to that, or if it's inhuman to people I pay attention to that, or if its science is lagging I pay attention to that. When I start out with these leadership-type things, I ask myself, "What are they doing well? What are they doing badly? Can we improve them?" I think any kind of job you take on you need to ask, "How can I make the company better, or how can I make the university better?"

More of the men who have taken over various leadership responsibilities, I think, look at these jobs as a way of beating their own hobbyhorse. Whether they're into environmental issues or whatever, they get into these positions and they just pursue those hobbyhorses. That's not a good way to help the organization achieve success; you're doing that for yourself, not for the organization.

MH: On a related issue, women leaders in different areas have often stated that their jobs were more difficult because they were women— either because they were being watched more closely and expectations were higher or that people on the inside, women and men, made it harder for them to do the job than if a man were in it. Did you ever experience this?

MD: Not very much. Let me give you some reasons why. Most of my jobs have been science related. I think such jobs are different because they can be quantified more clearly. I took over the Materials Center at MIT— that's this whole building, and then quite a lot of the rest of MIT. I did this almost twenty years ago, and I was director with a six-year term. When I took over, we were about to lose our federal funding, a bad situation! I took the job out of obligation, but after thinking about it, I said to myself, "Well, maybe I could do OK here; at least I have some ideas about what's wrong with the place."

So I took a number of steps, not all so popular. Some steps were against my best friends. When you're leading something, friendship has to be second place, unfortunately. After it was over, I had a lot of respect and support, since I'd turned our situation around within one year. We went from almost losing our whole funding to being sort of the best. I got the supplemental funds that were available for high performance every time, and I worked hard to do this. People were sorry to see me go. But I had said to myself I would stay for just six years. I became president of the American Physical Society at that time, so I couldn't do both jobs anyway. By then, I had got the needed money for the Materials Center, and I did quite a few things against the advice of the National Science Foundation sponsors. Still, the fact that we were so successful scientifically meant that everybody started using the same methods and approaches at other schools. That is why I say that leadership in science is much more quantitative.

Another thing. I had no other women in the organization; but my demonstrated success meant that the men wanted me to stay, so it was fine. When I was a department head, I had everybody in the department telling me about their personal problems. I felt as if I were a shrink. I think that being a woman *was* different, in this case. I don't think the men department heads get so much of that stuff. So I wouldn't say that the experiences were identical, but they were similar. Heading up the American Physical Society, that's pretty much a technical job. I just finished four years as treasurer of the National Academy of Sciences—that too is a very technical job. In such jobs, one gets evaluated by all the new projects that one has started. While I was treasurer, we did well financially, so that's good and another clear measure of performance. Members want you to succeed. After all, if you fail, they're failing too since they put you there. I really don't see the setups for failure that women leaders have reported. Maybe in middle management positions that happens, though. I think women should be very cautious about taking positions like that. Often they are tokens, and things may work badly in such cases.

MH: You make a strong case for the science-related nature of your leadership roles offering a clearer bottom line, a more obvious measure for success than other leadership positions.

MD: I'd add, though, that there's another thing you have to distinguish. My positions have been elective sometimes, but we don't really run for office. We're just as happy to lose. Most of the people, in all the jobs I've ever done, don't seek those jobs. It just sort of happens, and then you do them. It's different than running for senator where it's a political contact and you make deals with people. There are no deals in these elective jobs. We have some common objectives, which for the most part are obvious enough. You have a kind of goal to make physics improve the best you know how as head of the American Physical Society, or my job here at MIT is to make MIT improve or make science improve.

MH: So you're unlikely in an elective office, for example, to be selected to run as a sacrificial lamb by the equivalent of the party organization? That really doesn't happen at all in the science fields?

MD: It does happen to an extent. When I ran for the American Physical Society, I *was* kind of a sacrificial lamb. You brought up that term and it brought that home. The job was uncontested for many, many years.

Then, sometime shortly before I ran, the job became contested. There was one candidate that the board and the nominating committee thought would win and wanted to win. Then there was an also-ran candidate; that was me! Here I was running against a guy who was a Nobel laureate when I was a graduate student. He was really famous and I expected him to win, along with everybody else. Then I won. Surprise, surprise. The biggest surprise was mine. So in science we do have sacrificial lambs in some cases.

MH: With your success in turning organizations around, and your long record of achievement, you must get many requests to do this or that. What do people tell you when they try to persuade you to take a new position, and what do you tell them?

MD: It's very easy. The answer to that is that I only consider things where I feel I have a unique contribution to make. I'm asked to do far too many things—to run this and operate that. You know if you do a few things pretty well and have a track record, people will come back to you. I already have way too many things on my plate, and I turn down huge numbers of things. But I am doing this interview, for example, because I think it is very important for women to have the best information they can have. You have another generation of young women coming up, and they deserve the best encouragement we can give them, so we should find time. That for me has the highest priority, almost, of anything. So, in accepting A, B, C, or D, I always ask myself what can I do uniquely, where can I make the biggest impact—all within the boundary condition that I can keep my research at MIT still going. That sometimes means that I tell them I can't do it this year, but ask me again five years from now.

MH: But you are very clear about priorities, and I think this is critically important to tell young people. You need to say to talented young women, "If you want to move ahead and make an impact, then you're going to have lots of choices and you'll need to know how to pick and choose well."

MD: Far too many choices, though they are not always seen as such. When young people graduate and have a Ph.D. in something or other, they often have too narrow a perspective of what they can do with that education. That education can serve for a very large number of things. I just had a student over to my house the other night who accepted a job. He has a Ph.D. in physics and was a brilliant student. He would have been a great faculty member, but he has gone into business. He's doing computer stuff for a biology company. That's very far afield from anything that he learned directly from his Ph.D., but I know he is going to be a great success in what he's doing—he's very smart.

I think one of the things we should try to teach all our students is that everything that they might do in life is somehow connected with everything else; whatever they learn will be useful, not necessarily the specific knowledge, but the general approach, the methodology. I think, too, that despite a continuing tightness in the job market, the future is pretty bright for women in the sciences, especially if we keep working on all those other areas that still make it hard for women to take advantage of opportunities in science.

ANTONIA HERNANDEZ

■

IN CONVERSATION WITH MARY S. HARTMAN
AND LISA HETFIELD

Antonia Hernandez is president and general counsel of the Mexican American Legal Defense and Educational Fund (MALDEF), a national litigation and advocacy organization the uses the law, community education, and research to protect the civil rights of the nation's twenty-nine million Latinos. Since being named to the presidency of MALDEF in 1985, she has directed all litigation and advocacy programs, managing a five-million-dollar budget and a seventy-five–person staff. Headquartered in Los Angeles, MALDEF maintains regional offices in San Francisco, San Antonio, Chicago, and Washington, D.C.

Antonia Hernandez earned her B.A. at the University of California at Los Angeles in 1970 and her J.D. at the UCLA School of Law in 1974. She began her professional career as a staff attorney with the Los Angeles Center for Law and Justice, and in 1977 she became directing attorney for the Lincoln Heights office of the Legal Aid Foundation of Los Angeles. An expert in civil rights and immigration issues, she served as staff council for the U.S. Senate Committee on the Judiciary in 1979–80, drafting bills and briefing members on national issues.

The numerous boards and commissions on which Hernandez serves include the National Endowment for Democracy, the Los Angeles Annenberg Metropolitan Project, the Council on Foreign Relations, the Pacific Council for International Policy, and the Commission on White House Fellowships. She is extremely active in community affairs and serves as a member of the board of directors for the Automobile Club of Southern California, the Golden West Financial Corporation, the National Endowment for Democracy, the Kennedy School of Government at Harvard, the Women's Legal Defense Fund, and the Manpower Demonstration Research Corporation. Hernandez has received numerous honors and awards, including the UCLA Alumnus of the Year and the American Bar Association Woman Lawyer of Achievement Award.

Antonia Hernandez is married and has three children.

MARY HARTMAN: Antonia Hernandez, as president and chief counsel of the Mexican American Legal and Educational Defense Fund, you head what is widely recognized as the most important organization promoting and protecting the civil rights of Hispanic Americans. We're interested in talking with you about issues of leadership, about women and leadership, and about your own experience as a leader. We'd like to start at the beginning, so can you tell us something about your family background?

ANTONIA HERNANDEZ: First, I'm an immigrant. I was born in Mexico in the northern state of Coahuila. I come from a very interesting family, in the sense that there are several strong women; but I also have a very strong father. My father has always been passionately interested in politics, and my mother has been the spark as well as the hustler of the family! I'm the oldest of seven, and the first four were girls.

My father has an interesting philosophy. He always took the attitude that you work with what you have. As an example, when we migrated to this country, we were very poor; and I remember that on Fridays and Saturdays my mother would make tamales. Daddy and I would go sell them in the bars and garages. From the time I was a little girl, I was given responsibility. I knew I couldn't do certain things because of social inhibitions or prohibitions. But I can't say I ever had the sense that I could not do certain things just because I was a girl. I worked on the farms, and in the fields. When we migrated, my responsibility was to pack the box that had all of the utensils—the pots and pans that we carried with us. When the car broke, I had to help my father fix the car. So the message was, "You can do it."

The other thing was that in Mexico when my dad married my mom, he moved into her household. We had one of those extended families. Grandpa and Grandma always treated us children as special. Each of us was named after a saint! Growing up for the first eight years of my life on a farm, the usual sexual stereotypes just weren't there. I also had family members who were role models. On my mother's side, my great-aunt was a teacher and a school principal. I had cousins a couple of years older than I, and I even went to school early because I was always wanting to be like those older girl cousins. Partly out of economic necessity, my parents pushed us girls to do what we needed to do. In fact, in my family, it's the women who are the pushy ones. The guys are more laid back!

Among people that influenced my life, I would say my dad and mom come first—my mom because she sacrificed and worked so hard. Daddy was born in Texas and was from one of the families sent back to Mexico during the Depression in an exodus of Mexican Americans from the Southwest. But Mommy came here not knowing a word of English and had to adjust to a new environment. Just seeing her can-do attitude gave me a model. My dad always knew what was happening, especially in politics, both in the U.S. and Mexico.

MH: A common thread in our discussions with women we've interviewed is vivid memories of conversations about public issues around the dinner table when they were young. Was that your experience?

AH: Yes. For instance, Daddy would tell us every president of Mexico— who they were, and what they did. He would talk about Cardenas, who was the equivalent of Roosevelt in that era and a model of progressive leadership. When we came to this country, from day one my dad always voted. We saw that. He always read the newspaper in Spanish, and he brought used magazines at the Salvation Army store for us to look at pictures before we knew the language. He would listen to the radio and talk about politics with us. Although uneducated, he kept up with world events. He was always explaining things to us.

I am the most publicly active of the seven siblings, but most are involved in what my father defined as serving the public good. In his definition of the public good, it is true that then, anyway, there were some sexual-limitations. For a girl it meant to be a teacher. In fact, all my sisters are teachers. We didn't know we were poor because of what Daddy and Mommy gave us. We were close knit and had the love that is so important.

MH: What is the age gap from the oldest to the youngest child in your family?

AH: Twenty years. I'm forty-nine, and my youngest sister is twenty-nine. With each of us, Dad and Mom focused on the same two things. First, they wanted us to get an education, because they didn't want us to work "like donkeys," as they put it. (That's a cliché in Spanish.) "You can't work with your sweat," they said, "you've got to work with your brain." The second thing they always said was: "Be proud of who you are and what you do." The work ethic was very strong in my family. Work was held up as an important component of who a person is, and a big part of what makes you feel good about yourself.

MH: When you came to this country you were eight years old. Can you say something about your elementary and high school experience? Were you working then, too?

AH: Yes, I worked throughout my whole life. Along the way, in my education, I have benefited from the attention given to me, both positive and negative. Let me explain. When I came to this country, I knew how to read and write because I had gone to school three years already. I had started early. We moved into the housing projects in Los Angeles and I went to a predominantly Latino elementary school. I remember in 1956 that the kids didn't want to speak Spanish to me. To speak Spanish in America was not kosher! I remember this one teacher, Mrs. Moore, to this day—and very few teachers have made an impression in my life. I couldn't understand English, but she knew I could read and write Spanish. Math was no problem for me; it's a universal language. Mrs. Moore took the time to stay after school to teach me. I remember like it was yesterday that she would say to me: "You're not like them. I'm going to invest the time in you."

What she saw in me that was different, I don't know. It was positive for me, but negative for the others. They looked just like me; but I was the one she singled out. I remember that I skipped a grade and really got into the groove. I also remember my sixth-grade teacher, for the reason that he was the first Latino teacher I ever had. He was young, straight out of school. He spoke Spanish; and used to say, "Don't be ashamed of the fact that instead of taking a sandwich to school you're taking a burrito."

In high school there was another negative experience that turned out positive. You need to know first that I am very stubborn. I had a teacher who was the English instructor for college-bound students. Once I wrote an essay for him about going to college, about all my dreams and ambitions. Now he used to do happy faces and sad faces on our papers. When he wrote back, on the essay there was a sad face. He told me that I was just not college prep material. "Well," I said to myself, "I'll show you. I will shove it down your throat." Later when I made it, I had the chance to confront him with what he had done to me. It turned out that he was happy for me. I came to believe that he was a good and decent man. But I won't forget that in his assessment, I was not college prep material.

What else? To some, I was known as sort of a studious nerd in high school. I've always read with a passion; but I have always been multifaceted. I was very into sports, for example. I was a drill-team member. I was involved in a bunch of other activities, too. In fact, I have a couple friends who adopted the term *froufrou* for me, because I loved to party and dance. I didn't meet the stereotype, then or now, of a serious, in-your-face kind of feminist. The fun part of my life remains important to me.

So I graduated from high school, and I went to a junior college while I was working. There I had my first truly positive female-role-model professor—one of a handful of women other than my mother who made a real difference for me. She was Dr. Helen Bailey, chair of the history department at East Los Angeles Junior College; and she mentored a lot of the L.A. Latino leadership, elected and unelected. Dr. Bailey had traveled the world, and her special interest was in Latin America. She was brilliant and uninhibited, and like a lot of her other students, I took to her. She opened a world of possibilities for me. Because of her, my goal became, and still is, to get my Ph.D. in history and become the greatest Latina historian! I was going to rewrite the history of my people!

She said to me: "Why don't you go to UCLA?" I lived in Los Angeles most of my life; but I didn't know where UCLA was. I had never been outside the parameters of my neighborhood, and she pushed me to go. That's how, instead of going to a state college, I ended up at UCLA. Because of her belief in me, I became one of her closest friends. By the time she died, I was a lawyer and I did her will. I closed her estate. She also was an artist, and I have a watercolor of hers that I treasure.

MH: Could I back up a moment to the junior college decision? How did you make that?

AH: It was money. And closeness. I could walk to junior college. With my daddy, as I told you, some social things were traditional. A girl stays home—not just close, home!

LISA HETFIELD: When did you think about turning to law, and how did that happen?

AH: This gets back to my stubborn streak. I was always involved. When I got to East L.A. Junior College, right away I wanted to join the Chicano organization there. I found out where the meeting was, and I became the secretary of what was the first Latino-Hispanic Student Organization, right there at East L.A. Junior College. I helped recruit students to go to college. From there, I went to UCLA and started working with Project Upward Bound in 1969. At that time we were recruiting for UCLA from predominantly black and Latino schools. There were very turbulent demonstrations and boycotts.

I was already in the graduate school of education and getting my credential to teach. We don't have a lawyer in my family and I didn't know any lawyers at the time. But I remember one Saturday in February 1971, when I showed up for my job as a coordinator in the program, several of my favorite and most troubled kids did not show up because they were in jail. I remember that day saying, "I can't teach my kids if they're in jail. I'm going to go to law school to change the laws." That Monday, I walked across the UCLA campus to the law school; and they told me I had two weeks to sign up for prelaw exams if I wanted to go to law school the following fall. I did it.

Let me tell you a funny story. My father was waiting for me to graduate from college, as the oldest, so I could help financially with the other six kids down the line. I remember one Saturday I had to tell him about my decision to go on to law school. He said, in Spanish, "Why do you want to be a lawyer? They're all crooks." I remember telling him, "No, Papi, there's some who do good."

LH: How was the law school experience?

AH: I remember walking into one of those huge auditoriums in September of the first year. Practically all men—this was 1971, mind you. There were a couple of brown people, a couple of black people, and another woman who looked sort of Latina in this huge room. I was totally intimidated. I remember reading and reading and then I would go to class where the men, mostly, would just raise their hands and talk. I thought they were so smart. It took me three weeks to realize they didn't know what they were talking about; they were making fools of themselves. So I said, if they have no shame, and to be a good lawyer I have to make a fool of myself, then I have what it takes to be a lawyer.

That was my thing: I knew I was going to make it. I wanted to be a criminal lawyer. I wanted to change the law. I had this teacher in criminal law, and I studied hard in that class. I expected an A; I got a C minus. Everybody thought that was great, but I was disappointed. And you know, the

Latinos and other minority students wouldn't speak to their professors. My philosophy was, "Hey, I paid as much as they did. Everybody else is talking to them, why can't I?" So I got the courage to go and talk to the professor. I had this mindset that as a Latina and a woman, I hadn't done well because I couldn't write. That's what they tell you: minorities can't write.

So I went up and said to the professor, "I want to know why I did so badly. Honestly, is it because I can't write?" I remember to this day what he said to me: "No, Antonia, you can B.S. along with the best of them, that's not the problem. You just didn't know the law." It's the best thing he ever could have told me, because if he had told me I couldn't write, and reinforced the stereotype I had begun to believe in, I just might have quit in anger. When he said *that* to me, I thought, "Ah! I'm safe. I'm going to make it through law school. I've just got to read it over again, I've got to learn it over again, but it's no big deal. It can be done." I loved law school. I was in the Chicano student association. I was teaching night school to earn my way. I was teaching ESL at a high school, and I was involved up to my nose in activities. We did walkouts, and we took over the dean's office. We did just about everything!

LH: Was there a moment—maybe it was in law school, maybe it was earlier—when you first thought of yourself as a leader? Or did that not come until later?

AH: I don't see myself as a leader even now. I just see myself as someone trying to do the best she can.

MH: You will not be surprised to learn, then, that several of the other people we interviewed, whom the world sees as leaders, also don't think of themselves as leaders. For some it's because they have negative associations with the people who usually get called leaders. Pat Schroeder said she hated the "image" thing of the leader—you know, the guy cradling a telephone with his tie undone, tapping a pencil, looking awfully busy. Still, we are hardly the only ones who think of you as a leader. Why don't you see yourself that way?

AH: To me it's an awesome responsibility. I've always had to be a role model for my siblings and take responsibility. To me, it's onerous in many ways. Not only do you have to live within your own limitations, you have to live within the expectations of a lot of others. To say that I'm a Latina leader also means a lot. With that goes *more* responsibility. I know that if I succeed, it reflects on my community. And I know if I fail, it's not only Antonia that fails. So honestly, it's a burden.

LH: Tell us about your husband and children. When did they come into the picture?

AH: We truly have an extended family, and I couldn't do what I do without that family. We're very tight-knit. All my siblings except a sister, who lives a little further away, live within two miles of my parents' home. My parents celebrated their fiftieth anniversary this August, and we gave them a big party. It was brought to me clearly then that we all emulate what we see far more than what we hear. The strong values that our parents taught us really molded us—but it was *seeing* them live their lives every day that made the difference, watching them and not just hearing them talk.

I am married—over twenty years now—and we have three children. All my siblings except one are married, too; and there are no divorces in our family. Such things are always a possibility in a marriage; but Dad and Mom would be heartbroken. Things like that you just know. For example, my dad never believed in corporal punishment; but his lectures were worth a hundred lashings! I'd wish he'd punished me rather than say, "You disappointed me. I had this expectation of you. What went wrong that you did this irrational thing?" It's like, "Oh my god, I let down one of the most important people in my life." So there are always those constraints.

I'll tell you a funny story. For long, I had no interest in marrying, and until I was twenty-nine, I had no pressure from my parents. But finally my dad said, "Honey, it's time." He literally sat me down for a cup of coffee and said, "I don't know what you're looking for." I had been going with the same person for many years; and my dad said, "He's decent, he's caring, he loves you, we love him. You either make up your mind or you let him go. You can't play with people this way." I said, "Well, I guess it's time." My husband is Jewish. My brother married a Japanese girl. Another of my sisters married a Nicaraguan. Once my dad said to us, "You know, all I ever asked was to walk you down the aisle with a Pancho Villa. You have given me everything but a Pancho Villa!"

But my parents adore my husband, and my husband adores my parents. We live across the street from my parents. My husband has also played an interesting role in my career. You see, I'm not that ambitious, which is also counter to what many people think of me. When I graduated from law school, all I ever wanted to do was be a public interest lawyer in a small office in the community and help the people. I never planned my life. Far from having a five-year plan, I rarely knew what the next day would bring. I don't often say, "I want to do this and I'm going to have a plan to do it." That's not me.

When I met my husband, he was a lawyer in a rural legal services office where I went for the summer to clerk. After law school I got my first job, and I was quite happy with that job in a legal services office in East

L.A. My salary was $14,000, which was a lot of money in 1974. I got to take the cases I wanted. I had my little old lady clients with social security problems. I had constitutional issues. I had criminal issues. Then I got involved with the women's movement because I had one of the first sterilization cases. I was thrilled with that case, which I litigated against the county hospital for sterilizing women without informed consent.

I met all of these white women when I was working on that case. Now I'm going to say some things that you probably don't expect to hear. I had nothing in common with those women. These were white, well-educated, strident feminists. I'm a "froufrou" in the sense that I *love* being a woman. I've always loved being a woman. I couldn't understand the strident nature of the women's movement back in the early seventies. But I did get into that movement through reproductive rights. Here I am, a practicing Catholic. I still go to church every Sunday. And there I was doing a sterilization case, getting involved in the women's movement, getting involved in the issue of choice, and getting to know all of these women with whom I thought I had nothing in common. They were the leaders at that time, in the early seventies. But even then, when I was having all these new experiences, I was still in L.A., happy to be in L.A., doing my cases.

Then things really changed. Jimmy Carter ran for president. He won; and my girlfriend Gloria Molina, who is now county supervisor, went to work for Jimmy Carter at the White House personnel office. She wanted me to come to Washington. Now I'm very political, but not in politics per se. The most political thing I had ever done was vote, and to this day, that's all I do. Gloria wanted me to come to work for Jimmy Carter, and I told her, "No, I'm not interested." One day she called me again and said, "Now I've got the job you want. You're going to come." I said, "No I'm not." She said that Ted Kennedy had just taken over the chair of the Judiciary Committee, and he was looking for a Latino. I told my husband, and he said to me, "Antonia, people would die to be considered to be counsel to the Judiciary Committee." I didn't know what the counsel job was, and I could have cared less. I had just gotten married, we had just bought our house then, three blocks from my mother. Why would I want to leave?

So I said, "No." But you know what? If you say no in Washington, that makes you more attractive. I didn't know that then. So they sent a lawyer to interview me in L.A. Then they said they wanted me to come to Washington to meet Kennedy. I don't know what happened, but somehow I ended up meeting David Boise, who was then chief counsel. He was going to speak before the Ninth Circuit Court of Appeals conference in Palm Springs and asked me to meet him there. I said no. My husband told me I was crazy. So Michael [my husband] said to me, "You have to go to Saks." "Why?" I said. "It's so expensive." He said, "You have to get an interview suit." Now I'm a legal services lawyer, right? But I go to Saks, the first time ever. Then I drove my little Datsun to Palm Springs and I met David Boise at a coffee shop. We talked and we got along really well. It was a wonderful discussion. A week later I got a job offer. I said no.

David couldn't believe it, and neither could my husband. I went to my mother, and she said, "Honey, look, you're now a lawyer, you have a good job here, you just married Michael, you guys just bought a house. Your husband has a very good job. Why do you want to do this to your husband?" I go to my father, and he says, "Honey, have you talked it over with Michael?" I said, "Yes, he wants me to do it." He says, "If it's what you want to do and Michael agrees with it, you have my blessings." Meanwhile I'm saying, "Oh, my god. I don't want to do it. I hate cold weather. I didn't know what counsel to the Senate Judiciary was. I don't know anything." Michael says, "Think what you could do, the first Hispanic ever hired as counsel to the Senate Judiciary Committee." I'm saying, "I don't need that stuff. I'm happy here." Short story: he compelled me to take it.

I didn't know anything about the Senate. I didn't know anything about politics. I walked into this room in which Kennedy had assembled all this legal talent—all from Harvard, and from Yale. I'm the little Chicana and there's one black. All these pushy, assertive people saying, "I'm telecommunications," "I'm criminal," "I'm going to change the tort law," and so on. Kennedy had women at the beginning. One, now a federal judge, was there; and another, who is now an assistant to Madeleine Albright—all very assertive. I'm sitting there saying to myself, "Where's the bathroom?" But then I said to myself, "Okay, I'm going to do it. If they're going to do it, so am I."

But you know what? It was all so new, and I had opposition. This was one of the few times I had what I would call direct resistance from male Latinos. I remember thinking, "I'm this legal services lawyer from California. I don't look the part." Hair down to my knees, skinny—I looked like the public interest lawyer that I was. I remember the first day. We had flown in early Saturday morning on a red-eye after finishing work in Los Angeles the night before. It then started snowing. I was due on the job Monday, so I had to go once again on Sunday to Saks before the blizzard to buy closed-in shoes, a coat, and a suit. I literally didn't have winter clothes. My husband says, "Honey, go buy your clothes. You will be meeting the senator on Monday."

I had never met Senator Kennedy before I was hired. I was scared out of my wits. I didn't know anything about the senator. I knew about his brothers. I believed in the vision. I knew what they believed in, their politics. I didn't know the person. "So you're 'Antonier,' " he said. "Oh, my god," I thought, "I've got a new name." "And you must be quite a person because you were really wooed." "Yessir." ("What did I get myself into?") He said, "Okay Antonier, you're not only going to do immigration and civil rights issues, you're also going to be my Hispanic liaison."

The Texas male contingency of the Latino community didn't take too kindly to bringing in this person to Washington whom they didn't know— and a *woman*. I remember them saying to me at our first meeting, in different ways but with the same message: "The senator, with whom we have a really good relationship, did not consult us on your hiring. We want you to know who we are. We are organizations. We want you to know how you deal with us." I'm sitting there saying, "Okay, okay," and finally they said, "Well, what do you say?" I said, "You know, it's a good thing that you had nothing to do with my hiring, because since you had nothing to do with my hiring, I owe you nothing. I'm here and you're there, so you get it together as to who's going to deal with me." Where I got this, I have no idea. Afterwards, I said, "Oh my god, did I say this to these people?" I did, and then I added, "Now that we've got that straight, do you want to start all over?"

They gave me a hard time for about six months. They would try to go around me. I would come back to them and say, "Ah, ah, ah! Don't do that. For better or for worse, access to him is through me." I didn't know the rules, but I knew enough to know that if I was going to be successful in my job, I had to get control of the situation. It was painful, and on top of that, the white folks were very condescending. You know, "The little Hispanic needs to be tolerated." That was harder to deal with, because they were all kings and gorillas with their turf. You know, Kennedy has the best and the brightest. Everybody in the Senate has ego to their toes. That was tough. But I learned a great deal.

MH: That was a real training ground for what followed with MALDEF!

AH: Yes. In fact when the Democrats lost the Senate in 1980, Kennedy told all of us on the Judiciary Committee that he would help us find jobs, because he wanted to place all his people. He and the folks he put in charge didn't want me to go to MALDEF. They said they had bigger things in mind right there. The idea was, now that you've been here and got to know the whole community, worked with the press, learned to do a lot of things, and made connections with the African-American community, you are ready for bigger things. But as I said, the reason I went to law school in '71 is the same reason I'm still a lawyer today. I wanted to be a do-gooder, a public interest lawyer.

I learned how to use that position with the Judiciary Committee to help my community on immigration issues and civil rights issues. I used the position as much as I gave to it. At that time Vilma [Martinez, then president of MALDEF], called to say, "I want you to head my D.C. office for MALDEF." It was the day after the election! She had offered me the job before, and I said I had no interest. The day after the election she says to me, "Now you have an interest." I tried to say no. (She's was insistent.) Michael said, "It's up to you." I was also getting pressure for other options. I said, "I worked for MALDEF in '72 as an intern. It's the only organization where I can work with my community. These two years with Kennedy have been wonderful, but I went to law school to help Latinos." So I accepted Vilma's position and I headed the D.C. office of MALDEF for three years. That helped me solidify my contacts with the East Coast. Even though I live on the West Coast now, people think I'm an East Coaster. I have the contacts, I know the media. I got to know the women's organizations, I got to know the black organizations, I became a member of the D.C. bar. I got to know labor. I got to work with a whole different group of people. It helped me tremendously. I also started having children. Two of them were born in Washington.

Mike and I knew, however, that it was time to go back to our roots. As important as our work was, now that we had family, that was the most important thing. So we moved back to L.A. At that time Vilma had left and Joaquin Arula was head now of MALDEF. They didn't want me to leave, so they gave me a position in L.A. doing Title VII employment litigation. I did that for four months, and then for two years I assumed a lot of administrative responsibilities with the organization. Then I applied for my current position and was named the president and chief counsel.

MH: When you were an intern there in '72, the organization was just four years old. So you saw it from close to the beginning and you've played a key role in shaping the organization. How do you see its evolution and your own role? When you thought about moving into the position of president and general counsel, did you have plans in mind?

AH: No, in fact I didn't want to apply.

MH: I'm beginning to detect a pattern in your life!

AH: I get shoved into doing things I don't want to do. When Vilma left, people urged me to apply. That was in 1983, and I was already in Washington working with MALDEF. I said no. I had just settled into what I was doing, I loved being there, and I felt I was doing just fine. Then when I moved back to L.A., I was urged in 1985 to apply again. At the very last minute I did. I knew the challenges of running. I didn't go in with a vision, but I did go in with specific objectives. I'm a community grassroots person. MALDEF works the mega side, the macro picture of major policy. For me, the challenge was, "How do I stay in touch with my community, how do I truly reflect their problems and aspirations?" What I had to offer was my involvement, my connections in Washington, and my ability to work the process. I knew how to fund-raise. I also liked program development and the substance of the law. When you go into administration, you become a paper shuffler. I understood that, but I didn't want a lot of the administrative responsibilities. As you know, I also encountered problems because they tried to fire me a year and a half later. It was a huge problem and it was covered nationally.

Still, I knew what I wanted to do, and I was excited by the opportunity to head MALDEF. 1998 is our thirtieth anniversary. For twenty-three of its thirty years, MALDEF has been governed by a woman. Outside of the women's organizations, you just did not find women heads of such groups. I was dealing with Jack Greenberg, Julius Chambers, Ben Hooks—I was the only woman. In 1985, when I was elected, I was chosen by the overwhelming majority of my board, with the exception of four men. I didn't fit their image of a leader, and they didn't want me to take over MALDEF. Well, I got elected, and unfortunately they got elected to the leadership of the board. For a year and a half it was hell. These four took control of the executive committee, and then they tried to make a coup by firing me and then hiring their friend Tony Anaya, because he looked like a leader! He was an ex-governor of New Mexico, a man of course, and part of the old boys' system. I not only was a woman, I was nobody's patsy. I had my own ideas of what the institution of MALDEF should be, and I had the connections with the foundations, with the money people on the East Coast. Needless to say, they didn't like that. There was a big fight.

MH: Did the other members of the board who had voted for you initially come to your support at that point, or did you feel that you were having to fight alone?

AH: The thing is—and I think this is a woman's trait—we don't like to reach out for help. We don't want to admit that we're having problems. So for that year and a half I really tried to deal with the leadership by myself. The general membership and my board thought that everything was peachy keen. It was not until the firing became public in 1987, and they had a press conference to announce my firing, that it all came out. Then the board came together and overturned the decision of the executive committee, and I stayed on.

I was never fired because the executive committee never had the authority to fire me. But we had to sue to enforce the MALDEF bylaws. We went to court in Texas. That was the other thing these guys didn't know about me. If they had come to me and said, "Antonia, step aside for the good of the community," I would have said, "Up yours, I don't need this, you can have it." But they challenged me publicly. I told them, "You know what? I take on the best. You're insignificant to me. If you take me on publicly, you have a fight." In the end, these four left the board. I never read any books about consolidating power, but I'm a disciple of Machiavelli! I put my own people on the board. It was a very public fight.

That was a very defining moment. Having my parents see on television and in the newspapers the daughter who has done just about everything being publicly disgraced. It was like, "Oh my god, I have failed my parents. I have brought shame to my parents. I can't do this." My husband said, "Antonia, you've got to fight. You have no choice. If you fight and you lose, I will respect you for it. You cannot walk away without a fight because you are right." I said, "Well, I don't have a choice. I have to fight." It was very difficult. It called on me to do things that as a woman, I don't like to do. But it also taught me that I'm capable of doing what needs to be done to get the job done.

MH: This was in 1987?

AH: Yes, and like I said, it brought out the best in me and it brought out the worst in me. It is probably good to know your extremes!

MH: It may have sharpened your focus on what you wanted to do in that next decade, too.

AH: It did. I became more confirmed in my definition of MALDEF as much more involved with community, much more grassroots, and much more activist. It also made me more aware than I had been of the problems with being a woman in leadership. I'm a risk taker by nature. There's very few things that I will not try. I like to have risk takers around me, too. I hire the best and brightest and then I let them run. Most of the time they do great, although on occasion we have had major blunders. Still, it's not for lack of trying and not for lack of doing. I think that's one of the things that was a legacy of this experience. I hire very talented, very committed people, but people who are independent. If you want change agents, they don't stop being change agents just because they work for you. They're troublemakers all the time.

LH: Did you, from that experience, have a different attitude towards power? You said you knew then how to consolidate power, but did you then become more powerful in your own sense of yourself?

AH: Not in my sense of myself. Although I then was perceived as very powerful, and to this day as someone you don't mess with, it is the perception that becomes reality. I have not since had to go to the extremes I did then, but people know. I seldom get angry, and I seldom pick a fight. But they know they don't mess with me! If you want to approach me, you can get just about anything with honey and with rationality and with "let's talk about it." I'm not one that wants the limelight. Since a lot of folks do, I'm quite happy giving them the limelight. In fact, that's my approach to getting along in the men's world.

I once had a question by a white man. It was so funny because it was really a white woman who wanted to ask the question in an audience because I heard her saying, "Ask Miss Hernandez how she deals with machismo in her community." I said, "The same way I deal with sexism in *your* community. It's no different. You have a different name for it, but it's the same thing." There is a predominantly male leadership in the world that I deal with. I have objectives. I want things done. To me it's not that I have to be in the lead to get the things done. It's how do I bring people along to get the thing done. If I have an idea, and I know that if it comes from my mouth it's not going to get very far, but if it comes from him it will work—well, I work it so it comes from him. And then I come along supporting his idea, and I'm quite happy. I don't need to be out there.

MH: Do you think that's more a women's leadership characteristic— that is, the view that the object is to get stuff done, not to be recognized for getting stuff done?

AH: Yes and no. I think in the older generation, we have learned to find ways of getting what we want. The younger women, no. They have a different experience, a different environment, and different expectations of themselves and society. Sometimes I get upset with some younger women who want me to mentor them. I admire their lack of patience, but I say, "Wait a minute. I wish you were a little more patient." I admire their cockiness, but at the same time it seems that there's something missing; perhaps it is a sense of balance, a sense of give-and-take, a sense of how the real world is. But then the question is: "Is my world the real world, or is their world the real world and am I outdated?" It's my mode of operation, appropriate for my generation and the one before me, but perhaps not for this one. I don't know. What I know is that the generational differences are there.

LH: Tell us what is special about the MALDEF leadership programs.

AH: I think that there are very few born leaders. So we at MALDEF said, "Okay, what are the leadership skills that you need to be a good employee, a good student, a good professional, a good businessperson, a good head of a civil rights organization? What are the skills?" Budget, finance, how to influence power, how to deal with the media—those are some. So we put together a curriculum. Then we said, "Not only are we going to train you, we're going to place you on boards and commissions." Since we are a very small organization, and since we can't be at every table, our philosophy is that we've got to be sure that there's someone at every table. We work a lot on issues of how to be accountable, how to be ethical. We deal with the challenges of leadership positions, the difficult decisions you have to make, the balancing act. We do all this with an activist perspective, because we want to create agents of change.

MH: I think that the program that you developed on "parent empowerment" is exciting as a way to encourage leadership not only in the wider world but within the home.

AH: You know, when I came into the leadership of MALDEF, there was a Chicana rights program, and I didn't like it. It was a separate program for the women that made no sense to me. I had to make sure that it was not just the females that care about women's issues, that males care about them and think about them. Men as well as women need to think differently about women's issues and to incorporate women's perspectives.

LH: What are your thoughts on education for leadership, and what advice would you give to ambitious young women?

AH: You know, one of the things that I have found in looking back— not at why I've been successful, but why I've enjoyed my life—is that I have always felt comfortable being who I am. A woman, a Latina, just me. No better, no worse. I've always known that I was going to be a mother and wife. I never saw it as being incompatible with wanting to be a lawyer or an activist, or working with my community. I could not be happy and content if I were not a mother and a wife. But I could also not be content if I was not exercising my gray matter and being involved in the community. I wanted both. For me, the message to women is: "Whatever generation you're in, whatever you want to do, there's a balance to life. Find out what things really make you happy, and then find your own balance."

I also tell women that I've been in the business of change for a long time, that change is slow and incremental and you have to have the patience for it. I have never thought that I was going to change the world in a year or two. When I die, if I can say that this little sand on the beach was able to make a couple of waves of change, that's fine. Having a realistic perspective of what you can and cannot do is important.

I also feel that sometimes as women, we've had to deny a certain part of us to have success somewhere else. There is no such thing as a super-woman. In my own case, I daily walk a fine line. I'm daily on the edge of barely doing this and barely doing that and staying on top of things. It's not all the glamour it is made out to be. It helps if you don't take yourself too seriously and learn to laugh at yourself.

A lot of young women don't want to hear that. They want a formula. They come to me and say, "I have my five-year plan; I have my ten-year plan." And I say, "I've never had a plan in my life." All of a sudden I'm not the person they thought I was. "I want to be here in five years," they say; "where do you want to be in five years?" I say, "I don't know, but I know five years from now I want to be alive, I want to be happy, and I bet you that by keeping my options open, I'm going to explore possibilities that I never would have dreamed about if I only focused on getting somewhere."

LH: Do you have your own definition of leadership?

AH: To tell you the truth, I don't even know what the formula was for me, let alone others. But I do think part of leadership is knowing when people around you want you to lead them. To me, that's leadership. I've got to be in tune! The staff that I have are not there because of salaries, they're not there because of fringe benefits, they're there because they have a passion for the work. My job as the head of the organization is to find those people that have the passion, that have the commitment, that have the work ethic, and then give them a work environment in which to move the institution forward. That's my job. I don't make leaders. I identify people and give them opportunity. A lot of the young folks come and say, "I want to be a leader." And I say, "God, that's chutzpah." Then I say to them, "I'm going to test you. I'm going to test you at your work, because you're not the only one. I'm going to give you the opportunity to be a leader. The only limitations you're going to have are the limitations you put on yourself." That's been the approach.

One of the things that has helped me is I'm very intuitive. I can read a room and I can read people very quickly. Then I try to find my place in that room and with those people. Then I set to work to advance my agenda, and my agenda's very simple. It's how do I help the Latino community? How do I serve as a bridge?

MH: At this stage in your leadership and your presidency, are there any specific things that you would identify as part of that agenda, the next steps for MALDEF? Or is it all part of this listening to the passion, interests, and focus of the people that you work with?

AH: Yes, but I don't want to mislead you, just because I listen. I listen to figure out how I can be in synch with them, but I also know where I want to take them. I know that what I bring of value is that I am a risk taker, and I'm willing to push and shove. I just had a conversation with the current chair of my board—a retired corporate CEO, Republican, and white. He was worried, because he thought that after twelve years at MALDEF, I might be thinking of leaving. I told him, "I think about leaving every single day!" He was one of those who overturned the decision when they tried to fire me, and I was touched when he said: "You know, Antonia, what I like about you, and the reason I accepted the role of chair, is that you push us. That's unusual. You bring us along and you push us. We have trust that you can deliver, that we know what we're doing, but we're always following you. You're not following us." I think to some degree that's true.

For the Latino community, in addition to the traditional emphasis on political involvement, I have always believed that to advance, we must have economic involvement as well. Entrepreneurship is very important. I've always been a businesswoman, and I believe in liquidity in my community. I've loved business. Whether my dad and I were selling my mother's tamales or she was crocheting doilies and I was out selling them, we've always been hustling. I've always been a businesswoman, and now the business I am in charge of is the business of change. Our product at MALDEF is change.

In addition to economics, I think that the media represent a very important area. We have been beaten up royally in the last ten years. I want to develop a media project to change the perceptions society has of Latinos. MALDEF does litigation, advocacy, and community education, and our work is cut out for us there. Very soon, especially in Texas and California, we're going to be moving from the minority to the majority. But it won't do any good if we're not educated, if we're not part of the mainstream. As we become the majority, we can't just ask what's good for Latinos; we have to ask what's good for everybody. We not only need to solve problems for ourselves, we need to solve problems for everybody. So how do I help to get my community to go from the mental state of a minority to the mental state of a majority? It takes a whole different way of thinking of issues.

How do we interact with other communities of color? As African Americans become more threatened, how do we collaborate, how do we connect? How do we do something different and not just say: "It's my turn, move over"? How do we learn to share power when no one else has learned to share power? How do I tell my community that to be successful, we have to be collaborative? How do I convince them we have to share and that we can't emulate the very system that has excluded us in the past?

MH: Is it possible to do better in our schools and our colleges, as well as in our homes, at teaching some of these things about power and collaboration? Universities have always claimed, for example: "We send leaders out into the world." But we know what color and what gender most of those leaders, even now, are likely to be. How can we change that, and how can we change, as you say, the way people think about sharing power?

AH: I think simply talking about it is one way. I'm not too appreciated when I start talking about these issues, even within my community. "Wait a minute, Antonia," they say. "We just got to where we are, and nobody shared with us. Why do we want to share?" So I think first we have to articulate all this. I have to have the chutzpah to go to my black brothers and sisters and say, "You know what? I'm coming to the table, but I'm coming as an equal. That means you're going to have to give. If you force me to fight for it, I'm going to fight to win at all costs. But if we collaborate, it's going to be win-win. None of this stepdaughter, or stepchild business. You're going to have to start thinking differently." Now, that's also not very popular.

The same thing with women. I'm a Latina, I'm a woman. Does the white women's movement represent me? No! Does that mean I don't have things in common with them? No! Does it mean that they cannot be open to the experience? No! We've got to move to the reality of where we are instead of what I call delusions that "We're all so collaborative and inclusive." B.S. Because the leadership talks to one another once every six months does not mean there's communication. We have to say, "We have commonalities and we have differences. Let's talk about the differences, but let's concentrate on the commonalities." People look at what you do, not what you say. So it's not what I say, it's how I run MALDEF. It's not what I profess, it's what organizations I am involved in, what conferences I participate in, what stands I make. That's what people notice, and that's how they're going to be able to say, in the end, "Ah, this is who she is."

Finding that equal relationship is what matters, then. I think it's happening, even though we have a long way to go. I think the younger generation is not so strapped with historical failures, although I worry that they don't have the wisdom of certain experience. The issues, after all, are not just about blacks, Latinos, and women. They are generational, too. With new technology and global economic power, our kids are functioning in an entirely different world. We have to acknowledge that.

LH: Are you optimistic?

AH: Yeah. I am a Pollyanna, absolutely. I think we've already made great strides. If you look at history, the progress that women have made, the progress that civil rights advocates have made in the past fifty years—compared to the past five hundred or so—is phenomenal. We don't see it because we're right in the middle of it.

Change is going to be so much more rapid from here on, too. How do we make our women, who have often been more traditional, adaptable? That is going to be a real challenge because you need to be adaptable, you need to be flexible. At the same time, though, you need to know your bottom-line principles. How do you provide "constants" in an ever-changing world? To me, that is the biggest challenge of my life. How do I provide the values for my children that my parents did while at the same time helping them adapt to rapid change? When I die, it's not finally what I did as president of MALDEF that will matter most. It's what I did to shape these three human beings I brought into the world. Did I give them the values to be good human beings? Did I give them values to guide their lives well? I think that is an open question.

MH: And a profound one. Thank you so much.

BELL HOOKS

∎

IN CONVERSATION WITH DEBORAH GRAY WHITE, CHARLOTTE BUNCH, AND HARRIET DAVIDSON

A Distinguished Professor of English at City University in New York, bell hooks is one of the foremost theorists of race and gender in the world. Born Gloria Watkins in Kentucky in 1952, hooks received her B.A. in English literature at Stanford University. After earning her M.A. at the University of Wisconsin–Madison, also in English, hooks received her doctorate in American literature at the University of California at Santa Cruz, with a dissertation on Toni Morrison. She is the author of numerous books, among them, Sisters of the Yam: Black Women and Self-Recovery, Yearning: Race, Gender, and Cultural Politics, Feminist Theory: From Margin to Center, *and* Ain't I a Woman: Black Women and Feminism. *Before accepting her professorship at City University, hooks taught as an assistant professor of African and Afro-American studies and English at Yale University and as an associate professor of English and women's studies at Oberlin College.*

In her scholarship as well as in her life, hooks has advocated an understanding of the experiences and the boundaries that define identity and allow for self-actualization. Indeed, many of hooks's academic stands, as well as her distinctive views on leadership, derive from her own remarkable experience and background. Growing up a gifted child in a working-class family, hooks felt the presence of those around her in their support of her intellect; yet she also felt the oppressive nature of apparently self-evident gender boundaries in her patriarchal family structure. As she contemplated leadership, she found that many of the weaknesses of the black and women's liberation movements are rooted in this model of patriarchal leadership. Therefore, much as she has urged a rethinking of gender and race in her teaching and writing, hooks urges a redefinition of leadership as well. A liberatory movement, in hooks's term, must rethink leadership to allow people to lead in the most effective manner. In this sense, a leader can write as well as rally. Most important, hooks writes, a true leader must be able to connect with people, a connection she herself has often been able to forge through literature that dares to use an intensely personal voice to create bridges of experience with readers of both sexes and all groups.

DEBORAH GRAY WHITE: What effect did your family and childhood have on your understanding of male and female roles and your development as an outspoken voice for feminism?

BELL HOOKS: Much of my early feminist thinking came from being raised in a gender divide. I did not have to be educated to know that the black family had these incredible gender divisions. Coming from the rural South, I didn't know anything about some notion that the normal black family was single-parented, because most black families in the world I lived in were multilayered and men were present. Even if fathers didn't live with you, they were present, because our town was so little. So the whole idea of the absent father figure was new to me when I went to Stanford as a seventeen-year-old and was bombarded with this stuff about the matriarchal household. I wondered, "What about the households I knew growing up, where what the men said was absolute law?" Our mother could tell us we could go to the store, but if Daddy saw you putting on your coat and said, "Where are you going?" and you said, "Momma said I could go to the store," if he said, "No you can't," and then you said, "Well, why not?"

he could say, "Because I say so." Now my mother never had the power to overrule a decision that *he* made. Never.

DGW: So you decided that you did not want to be like your mother?

BH: No, it was that I grew up seeing male power as something for which no reason or argument had to be given. It was simply the power vested in the father by virtue of his maleness that I resisted.

DGW: Where were you in the family?

BH: I was the middle child of seven. I think it was important that there were six girls and one boy. My brother was in this female-dominated household in terms of quantity; but males still ruled. My brother had a single room, and he had power and privileges that we girls didn't have. I gave a talk a while ago that my brother attended, and it was one of those magical feminist moments. Here we were in an auditorium of about four hundred feminists, mostly lesbian and transgender and transsexual, and my brother was sitting there with his family. They had come from church. I'm reading something I wrote that says, "My brother didn't have six sisters. He had six slaves." All eyes turn to him. They all know he's there, because he's one of the few men and he looks exactly like me. He sits there and I see him weeping as I read a passage about the division in our household, where he was completely cut off from us because the gender divides were so clearly established. I think that played a big part in shaping my early thinking about gender and patriarchy.

DGW: So where was race?

BH: It's interesting to think about how I grew up in severe racial apartheid. I went to all-black schools, I lived in all-black neighborhoods, and whiteness was very much a signifier of danger. I think it is precisely because there was such apartheid that race did not seem a central determining factor in the household. White people and the power they held over us were outside. They were away. My world as a young, black female in the South was so shaped by domestic politics—not just the politics of my parents but the fact that my mother lived a short distance from her mother—that my father felt that he was constantly competing with my mother's family and her brothers for control over this universe. I heard my father say that he was not going to be dominated like my mother's father was by my grandmother. So there was such tension around gender and domination that these things felt more real than race. Race was public and at a distance. Gender was constantly present.

CHARLOTTE BUNCH: When you were growing up, were you an outspoken child?

BH: That's exactly how I took the name bell hooks, which was the name of my mother's mother's mother. What I remember is that I cursed a lot as a kid. I still do. I was six or seven when somebody first said, "You must be bell hooks," referring to my great-grandmother, who apparently cursed like a sailor. I heard so much about this woman of fierce speech that I had only known when I was a small child. When I started to write, I was living with a black male intellectual academic, and we used to make these books for each other. I gave myself the name "bell hooks" because I was involved with feminism and we were all into "no ego, no name." I was influenced by people like Charlotte Bunch and others who were saying that it is ideas that matter, not our personal identities. This man then made my first book for me as a birthday present, the first bell hooks book ever, called *I Nearly Wept*. It was a book of my political poems. I must have been nineteen or twenty. That was the beginning of that writing persona, my identity as bell hooks.

CB: Did you have support for being outspoken from your mother or from others?

ʙʜ: I had a lot of support from Bebe, my mother's mother, because she was outspoken—the one who was perceived as dominating her husband. I feel that a lot of who I am is also about the region of this country that I came from. Kentucky is its own unique location. In the world where I grew up, seeing black men go into the coal mines of Appalachia, I would hear stories from my grandmother about my people coming from the back woods. One characteristic these people were supposed to have was a kind of feudal notion of honor—people who kept their word but who would kill you over something in a moment. I feel that that culture was given to me by my grandmother, while my mother resisted it, since she wanted to be modern and not to be associated with the backwoods.

CB: Do you feel you have a split personality? Are you different when you're bell hooks than when you're Gloria Watkins?

ʙʜ: Not at all. I was smart enough to realize I had a conflict with my desire to write and speak out and my training to be a Southern belle. I was soft of speech, the lightest girl in my family, and the one with, quote, "good" hair. The dreams for me were of a good marriage, a marriage that would take me out of the working class and lift me up higher. More than some of my sisters, I was pressured into a certain kind of behavior. My mother resented my looks, perhaps because she had not been the lightest in her family but had been one of the darker, though she's not that dark. My grandmother looked white and lived in a white neighborhood, which was unusual in this apartheid world; but she had this land that she had bought from some white people that she had worked for. My mother had a mixture of resentments and treated me rather badly, so it wasn't until I was an adult woman that I realized my darker sisters envied me in any way. I was whipped so much and so emotionally tortured that it never occurred to me that I was being groomed for the right marriage. My mother was thinking of a Kentucky racehorse and putting her money on me, the one who in the end disappointed her and never married.

I had the oddest experience of talking to my ninth-grade teacher the other day, to whom I have not spoken since graduating from high school. She said she remembered me as this person who said things in ways that no one had ever said them before. I was in constant conflict with my parents and with people at school, and she remembered that I would sit in my high school classes and weep with rage and frustration because of the racial apartheid. We were at these recently integrated high schools, and the white teachers were often cruel, although she was one of the white teachers who was progressive.

CB: How were you able to take a public voice, and what does that assumption of a public voice mean to you as a woman, and particularly as a black woman?

BH: This goes back to the primary institutions of black life in a segregated world, the school and the church. Church and school positioned me to have a powerful voice in that we had all this attention on talent contests and presentations. I also was very much into reading and reciting poetry, which I did from the age of ten or so, at school, for the entertainment of my peers. We would have normal pep rallies like other schools, but before them we would display our talents. I might read the poetry of Wordsworth in the high school gymnasium. I think people forget the old black schools, because even though it was the sixties, the mentality of the segregated South was often twenty years behind. It was all about making us cultured people, and one of the ways was reading poetry. In addition, I was chosen at my church to read the Scripture every Sunday for one of the morning offerings, and I got tremendous feedback when these old women would shout and tell my mother, "When that child reads, oh!" Now there was validation!

I feel so sad sometimes when black intellectuals talk about the struggle to maintain contact with the black community, because part of what I think makes my work different is that I haven't had that difficulty. I can go back to my home church and the deacon will stand up and say, "She's written another of these feministic books, and I think the whole church should rise at the end of the service and shake her hand, because she belongs to us." I'm going home on Saturday to do a book signing, and my mother said, "The whole church is planning to come, and the new minister just can't wait to meet you." They know the church was the heart of my coming into myself as a public voice.

I still think that there's tremendous historical and cultural work to be done on the place of black women in the church, because when black women could not have voice and presence anywhere else—and despite the patriarchal nature of the church—we received tremendous affirmation there. Women from my community who supported me in my efforts to "be somebody" were women I met in the church. I wouldn't have met them anywhere else because we did not socialize cross-class. That's another arena black people have yet to write and talk about, that moneyed black people from church were interested in gifted kids no matter what group they were from. There was this whole sense of racial uplift. Our church was moneyed, so when we went to college, it gave us all money.

DGW: As a black intellectual, do you think of yourself as a leader? You're saying that these people from Kentucky, ordinary folk, are going to buy and read your book?

BH: I know that the folk read my books because they—do you know what they do that is awesome? They send me envelopes with money. That is so unique, I think, to a certain kind of black spirituality. People say, "I tithe, I read your book, and it has nurtured me. In the spirit of tithing, I am sending you this twenty-five dollars." And they say, "I know that you don't need the money, but I want you to take this twenty-five dollars and buy something special just for you." So my career as an intellectual is very different because of being a Southerner. I have had this constituency rooted in a folk world.

I decided that there was so much discussion of my work recently that I had to come out and talk more about where I came from and to say that I've had infinitely more affirmation for being a thinker, for being smart, in that segregated world that I grew up in than I ever got in academe, period. Now Cornel [West] will say that it was when he went to Harvard that he really had a sense of what it is to be an intellectual. It was just the opposite for me. My notion of being an intellectual was formed in the racially segregated world I grew up in, by black teachers who said to me, "You are gifted. You were put on this earth to do something with knowledge." That sense of entitlement was given to me there in that working-class world. My parents, who didn't have any money for frivolities, still made sure that I had certain books. I think that has a lot to do with why the ties I have with my community were never broken. It wasn't just me, either. The town that I'm from has an unusual number of black Rhodes scholars. The writer Ted Poston came from Hopkinsville, and a lot of other black thinkers and intellectuals.

DGW: There have been numerous articles about the "new black intellectual," and I'm sure you know that you are put in a class with Houston Baker and Cornel West and others. One of the comments that has been made is that this is a group of leaders that needs to be listened to, that they are inaugurating an era comparable to that of Du Bois. How do you see yourself in relationship with this group? After what you have just described, are you resentful of general criticisms that these leaders are removed from their communities?

BH: I think many people don't realize the gendered nature of fame, and that part of why I don't see myself like these men is that I know I don't have support structures. I know I don't have anyone else making a phone call for me unless I pay them myself. That's not to be grumpy; but my status isn't the same as theirs, much as it may sound that way.

I don't make the money they make. And to the extent that those support structures are important for getting work done, I don't have those. I answer my own phone. If you get some correspondence from me, I typed it up or wrote it. My life has been overwhelmed. I sometimes say to people I have the stardom without any of the things that normally go with it. I have a good salary, an above-scale salary as a distinguished professor; but people forget that I've only had this job for two years. Before that, my salary was in the thirties for many years. I say that in defense of Cornel West too. People forget that for a thousand years, Cornel did talks for nothing and ran all over the country.

Part of the bad thing about the media focus on us as though we just landed on this earth is that it starts with where we are now, rather than where we began. In the heyday of my comradeship with Cornel, we were two normal, overworked, and underpaid academics whose idea of a good time was driving on Friday nights to a little black club called the Elks Club to dance where nobody knew us as academics. We had this anonymity and could be with our people without there being any of the overt class divisions that would have been there had people known that we were these professors from Yale. That shaped a lot of our thinking and writing, rather than the experience of being known and celebrated.

I have come to believe strongly nonetheless that rewards are very important; rewards affirm people, they give people a sense of entitlement, they help you to continue to do what you do. Like so many women, I worked a long time without reward. It's interesting to me that the point in my life when I'm finally being rewarded, I am also being attacked for being rewarded. That reminds us of the servant/served paradigms around both race and gender. Black people have served so often in this country without reward that even other black people come to think that there's something kind of up-pity about you if you wish to be rewarded. There's a difference around gen-der because there has been no precedent of highly rewarded black women academics and/or intellectuals. Who would have thought that a feminist thinker, a thinker on the left, would be able to do work that would receive any kind of mainstream reward?

DGW: Do you see yourself as a nationalist?

BH: I feel I am totally *not* a nationalist. Every discourse on nation in the world requires control over women's bodies, and until there's some kind of conception of nationhood that is not rooted in the patriarchal mindset, I repudiate nationalism of all kinds. I don't repudiate identification with one's community, but I don't think nationalism has to be the way that one does that. One of the things I said in *Killing Rage* was that it is hard for me even to use flag imagery. I chose the image of the flag by a black woman artist, Emma Amos, for the cover of the book, although I realized that on some level I didn't even want to touch the discourse of nationhood. Yet I feel that if we don't touch both nationalism in terms of a more universal American identity and nationalism in terms of black identity that we leave that discourse to the conservatives and to the Right. So I've been trying to enter that discourse in some way, but most of the time I have chosen in-stead the discourses of racial uplift and self-determination. Black self-determination, along with feminist thinking, have been the two primary forces or standpoints that have energized my work. They were there from the beginning and will remain there for the rest of my life and beyond.

DGW: How do you deal with the nexus of race and gender which is so central to your work, when demands coming from the feminist world some-times ignore issues of race, or when demands from the black world ignore gender?

BH: Some of the most visionary thinking within feminism has come from women of color and black women in particular, precisely because of our stake in creating some kind of theoretical discourse that brings these things together in a noncompeting way. We have to be constantly educat-ing people around that. One thing that brought that home to me was the Million Man March, when I tried to say that I fundamentally opposed that march because of the militarism, imperialism, and patriarchalism in state-ments made by Farrakhan.

People have not understood what I meant, and I've had black people stand up in audiences of hundreds and say, "You're not supporting black men." I say, "I love black men and I have been in solidarity with black men since the beginning of my public work, but when black men offer patriarchy as the only force that can heal black life, I urge all black people to resist that." What is sad to me is how our work is not done, how our work clearly has to be ongoing, because what has happened is that there are generations of young black men and women who have no idea what patriarchy is and no idea what I am talking about when I say I will not support patriarchy as an answer.

I said publicly on the radio and TV, "Black men can march by themselves for days with my approval. I would love for black men to be marching for black self-determination and opposing sexism and misogyny. I'd stay home and even be glad to cook, which I hardly ever do anymore! I'd stand in the soup kitchen of the movement if those were the values that black men were marching for." But people have difficulty hearing that.

DGW: When you talk about "killing rage," aren't you afraid that since so much of that rage is misogynist, that you are undermining our message?

BH: I guess not, when the book's full title is *Killing Rage, Ending Racism*, because I think that black people situate that immediately. Perhaps it's a sad statement, but black males don't even elevate the anger they feel towards us women, in misogynistic moments, to rage. It's presented often as a very dispassionate anger. I don't think that for a minute, when black men see *Killing Rage*, that they associate it with anything that has to do with gender. "Rage" is immediately a race-loaded word; we have a rage about racism. Black women have a rage about racism that we don't have about gender.

When the O.J. [Simpson] verdict happened and, in my class, black students cheered, black *female* students, I said to them, "If I'd come in here and said that Susan Smith [a white woman charged with drowning her two sons] was found not guilty, would people have cheered?" They were angry, first, that I would even make a gender analogy with race. I then said, "Well, what about male violence against women?" They said, "We feel that a woman should be strong enough to leave. It's not that we don't take violence seriously, but we feel that the woman should be able to leave." Then I said, "How come you guys aren't ever saying O.J. should have been strong enough to leave? Why shouldn't he have been strong enough to leave his violence, his white addiction, and his drug addiction? I don't hear any of you saying that *he* should have been strong enough." I try to explain how their very different expectation for females is itself an expression of sexism.

CB: When black men are feeling in a rage against racism, they feel justified in raising and expressing it in a misogynist way?

BH: Black men I talk to feel that black women are in cahoots, honey. In the movie *Jefferson in Paris*, the black man says to his sister, "We want to be free," and the sister acts as though she has no conception of freedom. He tells her she is stupid, blinded by her worship of white male power; and you get no sense that he thinks she's liberated or has anything that he desires. What you get is the sense that she is an enemy to his freedom. So the rage he expresses at her, that takes the form of misogyny and sexism, is not seen as that at all; it's seen as the rage of one who wants to be free but who is being held back. I feel the message I get most often from Hollywood, from black men, is that black women are betrayers; we are willing to keep the black man down because we are in cahoots. If we were actually resented because we were perceived as more liberated, as some have argued, then we would be recognized as people capable of leading. But I think it is clear that part of the message of the Million Man March was that black women cannot be leaders in the liberation of black people. I'm saying that rage is not perceived as connected to discourses on gender, and to me that failure of perception is critical. They see rage as being always and only about race. They don't see that it gets expressed *via* a discourse about gender.

DGW: How do we change that? After all, as black women, we are taking the brunt of all this rage that comes out of the black male community.

BH: I read in the paper the other day that black men are victimized by racism and that that feeds their violence against black women. I said, "Hold up. What about the fact that black women are victimized by racism, and yet we're not killing and raping and doing all of those things?" In the popular discourse, black men are enraged by how wounded they are by racism, and they go home and express that rage in domestic violence. What about the black woman who's beaten down by racism and goes home and doesn't rape and beat and mutilate her children and her man? Then people go through little twists and turns to say, "But that's not the same." They end up returning to patriarchy and their sense that black men are entitled to a space of freedom within sexist thinking that women aren't entitled to. So female rage at racism will never be equal to male rage at racism because women have less right to freedom. This is why I feel black feminists do not have any energy to waste attacking one another because we have so much work to do to try to disseminate feminist thinking in a way that can be understood cross-class by masses of black people.

I get more correspondence from black men than any other group, and a lot of times they're just begging for books that will help them understand what we mean by sexists and patriarchy. One of the major failures of the feminist movement in general is that we didn't produce a body of work for men and boys that retheorizes masculinity in ways that are liberatory.

So much work on masculinity is done by white men who privilege their own lifestyles and identities as the model, so black men don't relate. Black males will say to me, "Is there a book like *Sisters of the Yam* for us?" I was stunned because that book was not something I imagined black male readers poring over. The books for black men that deal with gender are coming out of Afrocentric thinking and are, finally, anti-feminist.

DWG: One root difficulty here is that the whole paradigm for leadership, black and white, is based on a patriarchal and autocratic model. So as black men want to become leaders, their concept is to be more like the white men who have been leaders.

BH: Yes, that was true of white women, too. It is part of what has fucked up feminism.

CB: I think that's a useful point, to look at how these issues affect white feminists as well, because I think the autocratic model of leadership has messed up everybody. Clearly, it has made it hard for feminists to lead in different ways. What would you say about the kind of leadership that is needed now in the public world? When I hear comments bemoaning the death of the public intellectual, for example, I think these critics are often incapable of acknowledging either black women and men or white women as intellectuals.

BH: Or as capable of having a universal appeal. For every black man who tells me he's reading *Sisters of the Yam*, there's a white woman who says the same thing. Now I've read self-help books directed at white people all my life and been helped by them, but one of the arguments I had to make for publishing *Sisters of the Yam* was that I felt others than just black women would read it! When we try to publish books that are race specific, we're told that they will not have universal appeal, whereas white people write books every day that are race specific but believed to have universal appeal.

I think part of our difficulty with leadership is that we conceptualize it unidimensionally. We conceptualize it solely in terms of overt public activism, and I think that we must begin to think of leadership as multilayered and as diverse. There *is* no unitary leader who is out in the streets. Leadership is a collaborative project. For example, people often ask me to speak at rallies, but I don't have a "rally" kind of voice. It is high-pitched; and the farther I have to reach, the higher it gets. It's not a stirring voice in that kind of space, and I say, "I'm not the person to do this." To me that's not a repudiation of public leadership; it's saying part of a good strategy is conceptualizing leadership around the task to be done. We have tended to think leadership comes first and that the work that needs to be done comes later, rather than first imagining the work that needs to be done and the individuals best suited to do it. If we did that, we would have better models of leadership.

I've never used the term *public intellectual* until recently because I don't see myself as a public anything. Part of writing twelve books so far is that I'm home by myself more than even I think is healthy, and I want to change that. Part of why I stress the difference between being an academic and an intellectual is that I do think that the nature of contemplation is private; it is not collaborative and it cannot be shared. Many people don't know—because my books are very accessible—that I read a lot, at least a book a day. Having decided on a need for inclusive work, for knowledge of many different spheres, I realized this was hard to come by in other ways, since formal teaching tends to be highly specialized. In my own life, this breadth has come from having the luxury of time, because reading is about privacy and time. I say, "Okay, I don't know a great deal about Tibetan Buddhism." I then go and get every book I can find, and I read, say, a hundred books in a month on Tibetan Buddhism. I have the space.

I don't buy any kind of bullshit that women can do it all. I think it's central to the amount that I've written that I do not have children. It's central that when I left my long-term partnership, I began to write much more because I had lots of unmediated, uninterrupted time. When we talk about interdisciplinary work, very few people mention that for that work to happen, you have to be able to read and study a great deal, and that takes time. Some people have mistaken my naming these things as flaunting a certain positionality, whereas I see it as saying, "Let's stop being unrealistic with young women about what it really takes to do certain things." The fact is, I wanted to have children and I waited, because I also wanted to write books. Having been raised in a house where there were small children when I was a child, I had a clear sense of what parenting takes. It's no wonder that I didn't try to have a baby until I was thirty-nine, and then I wasn't successful. I'm clear about the realities of time, and I'm clear about the realities of money. I waited to have a baby until I thought I could have a nanny. Part of the dilemma women have had, and black women particularly, is that we are made to feel that we don't need these things.

As for power, that is something I knew I had when my family and community recognized me as a thinker and a writer. When I got to college and people started not recognizing me as that, rendering me invisible, I felt as though I became the person who had to give myself that recognition, who had to stand in front of the mirror like I now tell my graduate students to do, and say, "I am an intellectual. I can write this book. I have something to offer." I think people are naive in thinking that women within patriarchy or black females within white supremacy and patriarchy will just have some inner will that leads them to work against the odds. That is bullshit. Then I became fortunate enough to have a black male academic/intellectual partner who affirmed me in his own ways. I am here to testify that that boyfriend went out in rain, sleet, and snow to get whatever book I needed. I am writing about my development because I want people to understand that there are black men who are not opposed to feminist thinking, who are trying to work through the same contradictions. I feel very positive about the fifteen-year partnership I had with Nate because in it I did blossom as a thinker and writer, despite the fact that that relationship finally became repressive of those very things he had nurtured in me. I think we see this particularly in professor-student mentor situations, where there's an imbalance of power. He was a tenured professor, and I was trying to write my dissertation.

HARRIET DAVIDSON: I wonder if you could talk about the kind of transformational leadership that can come out of writing, out of art, out of things that aren't traditional channels of power.

BH: Going back to the idea that I am not a particularly public person, I have no interest in public leadership for myself. I was telling my best girlfriend this morning that I was sick of hearing my own voice and that it was partly because my spiritual practice involves lots of silence that makes the public speaking difficult. I do it with such skill and ease that people imagine that I'm really into it and like it, but for me, it is a form of activism because it is something I do against what I take to be my nature. I feel that I could serve feminism and black self-determination better by writing at home for the next twenty years and that other people who are happier there should be on those stages or out in the streets. Things change too. You can want to be publicly talking for five years, and then there may be five years that you want to be doing something else.

Part of our problem with the unitary vision of leadership is that we don't imagine shifts in skill, activity, or possibility. We think you should be on a road and keep going on that road, rather than that there might be something you give at one moment in time and at another you withhold and do something else. As a Christian most of my life, I drew a lot upon the notion of Jesus as a leader and the idea that at one moment he is speaking but at another moment he is going into the desert. Cornel and I had a long debate for a couple of years about our role, because Cornel had a much more public vision of leadership than I did. I was very interested in a balanced life—not working ourselves to death. Cornel identifies himself more with Christianity today, and he made what I felt was a patriarchal argument that we are called to sacrifice. I argued that God is a God of love and that we're not called to sacrifice our lives on the altar of activism, that we are instead called to bring a greater wisdom to bear on the notion of leadership, and the ways we go about leading.

A Buddhist teacher that I have used most in my work is writing a lot more lately about the danger of one-dimensional leadership and activism and how crucial it is for us to measure and weigh and balance and come up with new understandings, new senses of leadership. I think if anything has been detrimental to movements for black self-determination and feminism, it has been that we work our leaders to death—to a kind of intellectual and emotional death. I think people don't want to acknowledge how much the quality of your work is affected if you're in a different city every day and then don't sleep well at night. I think that reconsidering all of these things about one-dimensional leadership and the harm we are doing to our leaders will help bring us to transformative notions of leadership. I said this in *Sisters of the Yam*, when I started looking around and realized there were all these black women writers sick with cancer or other illnesses— all between the ages of thirty-five and fifty or so. It couldn't be merely accidental; there are too many of us suffering. I thought there must be something about the level of stress brought to bear upon us, the fact that most of us do not have support structures in our lives that enable us.

Just the other day I said to some guy in North Carolina, "Hotels are really structured for men." I suggested that historically, they were invented for businessmen, and a lot of the comfort of a hotel is about people geared up to serve men. When women enter that space, the support is not there in the same way. If there is not a chain lock on my door, I don't feel safe and I don't sleep well. I have been in hotel rooms where people try to get into my room because they were given the key accidentally, and the result of things like that is special stress for females. Even today, when I come out of my house and a white limousine driver looks at me and he's picking up a black female not dressed in professional clothing, nine times out of ten he will not open the door for me.

DGW: He thinks he's got the wrong place.

BH: Even when he finds out he's got the right person, I don't conform to the idea of who he was called to serve. I think all these things are about the levels of stress when you try to go out and be a leader. While black women lead effectively, I think often the emotional costs to us are grave. For example, I've been saying I want a partner, and people have been saying, "You're kidding, you like writing those books." I feel that the fact I have had to insist on the need for intimacy and partnership in my life is to counter a cultural myth that somehow the rest of the world needs partnership and intimacy, but black women as individuals need to be able to go on and conquer the world by ourselves.

We were reading *Song of Solomon* in my class, and talking about Pilate, who has no support structure—how she is a kind of model of black female leadership. Morrison is fond of female-dominated, utopian households, but you still have the sense that the female leader never has anybody to fall back on. She can never take a day off because there is nobody powerful, charismatic, smart, shrewd, or wonderful enough to take her place. We were talking about how these female leaders are constructed as monsters, as otherworldly; and I said, "Well, are they goddesses or are they monsters?" The students finally said, "They're monsters, because only monsters can sustain themselves at this level."

I was thinking particularly about Bertha Harris's work about lesbians as monstrous, because they're constructed as alone. "Can you have sex and power as a black female?" we asked ourselves. "Is black heterosexuality doomed?" Within black women's fiction, you do not see a model combining ecstatic black sexuality and power for women. The powerful surviving women are often the women alone. I feel this is a demand people put on women. I think of Audre Lorde, June Jordan, Pat Parker who died of cancer. A disproportionate number of us have had life-threatening illness, and I think it is tied to these demands on our black women leaders.

HD: As a follow-up on the question about transformative leadership that comes out of writing and art, I am struck by the language of witness and testimony that you use. How do you see that? As a way to educate, a way to transform, a way to lead?

BH: Absolutely. I think that anybody who's looking at my work would see that in my first two books I say very little that is personal. What I found in trying to reach audiences cross-class was that if people felt that your academic language was unfamiliar to them, or even your style of being, they wouldn't listen. That's when I began to think not only about the power of storytelling but about the power of personal testimony. I found that if people could identify with you through the act of personal testimony or confession in some way, they were more open to grappling with different jargon, different paradigms. So you see a shift in a lot of my work. Particularly in a piece of writing where I think I may be presenting an audience with something unfamiliar, I will rely much more on anecdotal confessions and storytelling as a way of illustrating. The genius of feminist theory was its call on all of us not to be afraid, to utilize the confessional within a larger framework of the theoretical—not to abandon the theoretical for the confessional, or to privilege the confessional as an end in itself. I don't think anybody could find a piece of my writing in which the sharing of something about my life is done gratuitously or for no purpose. It's usually to emphasize or illustrate a point, to clarify something, never for its own sake.

HD: Do you think the power of that storytelling can be generalized as a model for the way women lead?

ʙʜ: I think first of all we have to look at how it's one of the few aspects of what might be traditionally defined as feminine or female traits that patriarchal leaders have appropriated to rule the world. If you look at those locations of power where men, and white men in particular, have had tremendous control, storytelling is one of the few strategies of engagement that they deploy. This is true of male leaders globally, and also of alternative male leaders like Malcolm X—in speeches and in voice. These are often men who in their private selves and lives were very reserved but who understood the power of testimony and witness and sharing. They might not ordinarily have shared anything in their daily lives. We can hardly find a speech by Malcolm X in which he does not first draw on some kind of personal anecdote to illustrate the depths and profundity of a thought.

When we talk about black tradition, it is the power and privilege of the patriarchal black male preacher; and personal testimony is at the heart of how he will get his message across. If he's not sharing a story from his life, he is sharing a story illustrated by someone else's life; but it is still the primacy of that intimate quality of sharing that is fundamental to the capacity to connect and lead. I think real leadership, like real community, is about connection. There is no leader anywhere on the planet who does not organize in part around the capacity to connect people to one another— to connect them as speaker and audience, but also to connect them to many others beyond themselves.

CB: A remaining area we would like to explore with you is what you would like to pass on to younger women about leadership and how you would encourage them to take leadership initiatives for themselves in different ways.

ʙʜ: I would go back to say that another genius of the feminist movement was its bringing to the fore the notion that we are better able to lead if we have also chosen the path of mental and emotional well-being for ourselves. The therapeutic model of feminism, more than any other political and social radical movement in this culture, is what I would uphold as positive. It enables young women to begin to imagine the possibilities for a leadership in which one's goals and tasks are not undermined by a lot of dysfunctional behavior, often in one's family of origin. That there is a model that says, "I can be a better leader to the degree that I am healthy, emotionally well, and self-actualized" sets a baseline for a very different notion of leadership than the patriarchal model that used to make us feel that leadership qualities were inherent, that it didn't matter if you were doing screwed-up things in your private life as long as you were a charismatic leader.

Feminist thinkers, myself included, have said that our movements have been undermined by people who may have great leadership abilities but whose very skills are compromised by unresolved personal dilemmas. In my own analysis of radical social movements in the U.S., I concluded that those movements have often been so damaged by the dysfunctions of leaders that we need to begin anew with different educational approaches. We need to help create a rising generation of young women and men committed to feminism who want to build on a foundation of selfhood that is healthy and strong. This would mean that a different sort of person would come into leadership, one who is truly capable of representing communal interest, not someone who is driven by ego-centered needs for stardom, authority, and power. We have had too much of this negative model of leadership in the black liberation and feminist struggles. I'm excited by the fact that we have better pedagogies now to promote self-realization and that we can hope to dissuade young people from the destructive notion that they can split mind and body and do damaging things in all other areas of their lives and still be fantastic leaders.

CB: Could you say something in conclusion here about the differences between self-actualization and selfishness in a leadership context, as I think there remains a lot of confusion on this point?

BH: Absolutely. Selfishness to me is about a kind of narcissistic obsession with one's identity, whereas self-actualization suggests that the self is something we have to create. We have to do that consciously and willfully; we are not inherently who we are, and our destinies do not simply unfold in a magic carpet kind of way. In fact, we must be ever mindful and thoughtful about where we want to go and who we want to be and what we want to do. To me, that is very different from a narcissistic model of selfhood that says you just get to sit around and indulge whatever thought or feeling or impulse you have.

To think in terms of self-realization, self-actualization, is first to think in terms of a notion of the social structure of identity, which is already counter to a narcissistic model that says, "You really won't have to do any work because you are already who you are by the time you're six years old, so everything you do is just a living out of that." The problem with the terms is that many people are disturbed because they use that individual word *self*. But the fact is that there is a quality of inner growth that is not collaborative, that is not communal, that really is the self having to come to terms with our being in isolation.

I think part of why spirituality has remained so important to me is the understanding that part of being a healthy subject is being able to be with oneself, to be alone, to know who you are in the moments of aloneness. It is a model that says that the self is forever changing, is never fixed, that you do in fact have control over your actions, your thoughts, your experiences—even as you are simultaneously a creature of destiny and fate and circumstance. I think that that kind of self-actualization is crucial, and a necessary first step for anyone who wishes a life of worth, as well as for anyone who undertakes to lead.

LOIS JULIBER

■

IN CONVERSATION WITH MARY S. HARTMAN
AND ADRIENNE COLELLA

*Lois Juliber is currently executive vice president and chief of oper-
ations, developed markets, at the Colgate-Palmolive Company. Born
in Brooklyn in 1949, she earned her B.A. at Wellesley College, where
she first became interested in a career in business. Juliber went on
to Harvard Business School, where she earned her M.B.A. before
taking her first corporate position with General Foods in 1973.
During fifteen years at General Foods, she worked in product management and general management with such recognized brands as
Kool-Aid, Post Cereals, Stove Top, Shake 'N' Bake, Good Seasons,
and Minute Rice. It was also at General Foods that she acquired the
hands-on management approaches that have marked her effectiveness as a business leader. In 1988, Juliber joined Colgate-Palmolive
as president of the Far East/Canada division of the company. Her
experiences and travels in many Asian countries gave her exposure*

to different cultures and helped her in leading a company commit-
ted to promoting diversity. In 1992, Juliber became the company's
chief technological officer, where she brought a business perspec-
tive to research and development, manufacturing, and systems,
bringing these departments closer to the company's long-term busi-
ness strategy.

Lois Juliber attributes much of her success to what she calls a
"gender-blind" upbringing, in which her open-minded parents sup-
ported her as both an ambitious scholar and a competitive athlete.
Indeed, Juliber first understood her leadership potential in childhood.
Yet it was also her experience in many different aspects of interna-
tional business that led to her success in her promotion in 1993 to
the presidency of Colgate–North America, where she brought sig-
nificant growth to a previously stagnant division of Colgate-
Palmolive, as well as to her subsequent promotion to executive vice
president of the entire company. Finally, along with her competitive
talent and strong ambition, Juliber cites adaptability to new business
philosophies in changing times and an ability to manage a well-
trained team as the keys not only to her own flourishing divisions but
to effective business leadership anywhere.

MARY HARTMAN: You just said that when you started work twenty-three
years ago, it was much harder for young women coming out of school and
wanting to enter business than it is now.

LOIS JULIBER: It's very different now. There is a great scene in *The
Heidi Chronicles,* written about my generation, where two sisters are discussing careers, and its clear that the younger sister by ten years just
doesn't understand the changes that have occurred, doesn't appreciate the
barriers that were broken down in such a short period. Young women now
are so lucky.

MH: They are. Sometimes you want to shake them when they seem
to take hard-won opportunities for granted. But other times you think, "Why
do I want to parade them through all that dreary past?" *Your* story, though,
is anything but dreary. Who was there for you along the way who inspired
you to achieve, to choose business, and then to rise so far?

LJ: Okay. I was born in Brooklyn, and I lived there until I was about
nine or ten years old. My family then moved to Long Island, where they
still reside, as does my one sibling. I am the baby, the younger of two daughters, which defies all the stereotypes about leaders.

When I was young I was big and strong. I was basically this height and size by the time I was ten or eleven, and I was always a good athlete. Sports and competition have been an incredible thread as you go through my whole life. When I was three or four years old I was competing in a sack race, and even by that age I was already used to winning. I lost the race and threw a tantrum on the spot. I'll never forget my father sitting me down, trying to make me understand that there are times when you can't win, and when you run into those times, you've got to be gracious and congratulate the winners, even though it may be very painful inside. Supporting others who do better is an important characteristic of leadership in terms of helping others, making people feel good about what they have accomplished.

The second important leadership event in my life was when I was about fourteen years old, at summer camp. I became a so-called color war captain. What did I know about that? But it was during that week that I came to understand my ability to motivate and to lead. There were about a hundred and twenty girls, and I realized that I could motivate people to do more than they ever thought they could do. This is an extremely vivid memory.

What else? When I was in junior high, out of the blue one day I was called in to the English teacher's office—a very intimidating man—and he said, "We'd like you to be editor of the junior high newspaper." Now, I wasn't the best English student and I wasn't terrific at writing. But there was a recognition on his part of something I came to understand later. You don't have to be technically the best at something to lead it. Through my career into very senior leadership positions, I have kept the conviction that you don't have to be able to do everybody else's job very well. What you have to do is put it all together effectively and smartly. This leadership (or perhaps management) characteristic ends up derailing a lot of people: perfectionism versus seeing the whole picture.

I have more sports experiences, needless to say! My whole early leadership experiences are very sports driven. You may be better served to find a counterbalance to me, because my story is so extreme.

MH: You're right in suspecting that other stories have been different. More of our stories have been: "I never really saw myself in a position like this when I was growing up; it was gradual." What I'm hearing from you is that you recognized yourself as a leader at a pretty early age.

LJ: Pretty young. When I speak to groups, one of the things I stress in career choice is the need to be brutally honest with yourself about yourself. I say you need to determine what you like to do, what you don't like to do, what you're good at, what you're not good at. I tell the story that early on, I knew I couldn't follow others and that I had to lead. By the time I was a teenager, not only did I realize I was a leader from this one experience of leading a hundred and twenty people for a week, but also from regularly being selected to run things and being elected to things.

ADRIENNE COLELLA: What were your career aspirations during high school and junior high?

LJ: The first thing I wanted to be when I grew up was a gym teacher, which was predictable! Then in the late sixties I got fascinated with computers. I thought I wanted to be a systems analyst and in fact took the first computer class Wellesley College ever offered. But it was when I started to take economics courses that I found a discipline that put together sociology, history, mathematics, psychology, and business. From that point on, I knew I wanted to be in business. I was twentyish at that point. I did fool around with other areas. In college, I started out thinking I was going to do history. I helped create an American studies program at Wellesley, but by my sophomore year I wasn't interested anymore. So I searched until I found something that gave me an end result, which was business, and the academic studies that would get me there. It wasn't as if I was not focused and directed by the time I was twenty-one. I was.

MH: Let's go back a little bit to look at influential figures. We have a clear sense that you were exposed to some things that really took off with you: the summer camp experience, the athletics. How about the role of your parents generally? We've already seen a very supportive father.

LJ: My parents had tremendous influence and impact, though I don't think they knew what they were doing at the time. I have an incredibly supportive family.

MH: What about sibling rivalry? Did that have anything to do with your competitive spirit?

LJ: No, the opposite. My sister is very different. She is not athletic, she is not competitive; but she is a leader also, who got there a different way. My parents claim they made all their mistakes on my older sister, and she would probably agree! They were totally supportive of me.

They encouraged me to experiment, do dance, do whatever. As I got older, and this is maybe ten or eleven, the message was: "You can achieve anything you want, as long as you set your sights on it." They didn't reinforce me with big gifts. I got big hugs! And I had a gender-blind kind of upbringing. I *do* use that term consciously. My sister and I hypothesize that since I was the baby and the last, and my father was a great athlete, he decided to make me into a bit of a tomboy. Yet he was just as interested in my going to parties and having a boyfriend, so it really wasn't the stereotype of "This is going to be my surrogate son." But really my father did enjoy the fact that he had two little girls. An only child himself, he was thrilled with his daughters.

My sister's story is also interesting. I didn't play with dolls when I was growing up. Whenever I got dolls, my sister, who was [deleted] years older—but you're not allowed to print that because we made an agreement that I would never tell her age—my sister would take them. She was very prissy and frilly and I was as tomboyish as they came. I did well in school; she never buckled down. We were completely different kids. She married very young, at nineteen or twenty. I married at thirty. She had children almost immediately. I don't have children.

MH: Are you married now?

LJ: I am married. She, when her oldest boys went to college, went back and enrolled in law school at age forty-one. She is a lawyer now, a law professor who does a lot of pro bono stuff. She has been president of all sorts of associations, but none of this when she was young. So we are kind of doing similar things today, but we started at different points in our lives.

MH: How did you decide to go to Wellesley?

LJ: In those days, the Harvards, Yales, and Princetons were not open to women. I wanted to go to the best school, so we looked at all the prestigious coed schools and women's schools. One rainy May day in 1966, my parents and I drove onto the Wellesley campus and my father said, "This is where I want my daughter to go to school." I said, "I agree." That's where I went, and I had a tremendous education. In gratitude, I do a lot for Wellesley today.

MH: It's where you discovered your sense of vocation?

LJ: Yes. The other thing that I got from Wellesley was a tremendous comfort level with being with women, working with women. In high school, I had some very close girlfriends, but not the same kind of appreciation for women—not the same camaraderie and support that I developed in my four years at Wellesley.

AC: That affirmation helped in the next steps we'll ask about: business school, your early career, and the path that you took.

LJ: It helped tremendously. Yet in shaping my career, the one person who has been most influential is a man. He is the one who gave me my first job out of business school at General Foods, and he did not match any corporate stereotype whatsoever. This is 1973, and I go in to meet this person. He is short, kind of with-it in the way he dresses. I get into a conversation with him, and I learn he is a single father, which was unheard-of then. I also learn that he's just come back from a six-month sabbatical at the Cordon Bleu [cooking school]. What this said to me was, in *this* company, you don't have to fit the norm. You can be different, and you can be yourself. This man, who is still a very close friend, has always been his own person. It was really because of what I saw in this individual that I chose to go to work for him at General Foods; and for the first five years of my business career, I worked in his organization.

"Mentors" didn't exist in those days, but I knew that he was watching out for me, that he was subtly managing my career, giving me the best experiences. At times he took incredible risks, giving me jobs that by the normal standards I shouldn't have had. I am forever grateful to him. It was only a few times in that five years that he ever said anything about my career to me. We would talk about the business and related issues, but only on very rare occasions did he ever say anything about my management style, how I approached an issue—what I would call the less quantitative, results-oriented side of the business.

There have been other people who have taken risks on me. Certainly when I came to Colgate nine years ago to run our businesses in Asia and Canada, our chairman and our COO took a tremendous risk because here was someone who was going to be new to Colgate and had never worked outside the United States.

AC: So you were brought in to Colgate to go over and manage Asia?

LJ: Yes. Absolutely fantastic experience, probably one of the two most unbelievable experiences of my professional if not my personal life. The CEO and COO and I talked a lot about my managing the Asian operation, because I would be a woman in Asia, which could be difficult. But we said it was worth a shot and we would take the risk together.

Within three months—the assignment lasted from 1988 to 1991—it was so clear that it was a match made in heaven and that we had bet smartly. Acceptance of women for the most part had historical precedent—in the Philippines and India, they had had female political leaders even though there had never been a highly visible woman in business. In China, if you go back to the age-old shopkeeper mentality, it was always the wife or the mother who was not out front selling, but sitting in the back, where she managed the money. Japan and Korea we never conquered. Luckily, Colgate's businesses there were very small.

MH: Let's go back to China. I was intrigued by the shopkeeper mentality you mentioned, but isn't there a lot more to what made that situation work better for you than Japan?

LJ: This is what I found, and this was very important throughout Asia. Usually they accept you initially because of your position, the title. But I found the way to penetrate business in Asia was to get the people to trust you. Once they trust you, they will do unbelievable things for you. Within about two to three months, I was the same way! I would come back to New York and fight for them and stand up for them. I became a very strong advocate for Asia. Now, the downside of that is if you say, "Go," and they have some reasons not to go, sometimes they won't tell you outright, so you have to learn how to tease out what their real issues are, get them to tell you what's wrong with the idea. What I had to learn over time was that from their body language, you could sense when they said, "Yes," whether it was a *real* yes or a qualified yes.

MH: Did you have people with you for assistance in these matters or did you have training in culture or language?

LJ: No, all I did was read a book—a simple series of books, really—on the "Do's and Don't's" for every country in Asia. The human resource person I worked with, who was from the Philippines, gave me these books, which turned out to be critical. From day one, you saved yourself from making the standard Western faux pas. In certain countries you can touch people; in other countries, you can't. In certain countries you can point; in other countries, you can't. I don't speak any of the languages; but in that part of the world, business is conducted primarily in English, though I know some salutations. I did a fair amount of other reading, too. My college roommate reminded me that even going back to our freshman year of college, I was fascinated with Asia. I wrote many papers on Asia. So there'd been a long-standing interest, but I had no formal training whatsoever.

AC: What would you counsel young women about overseas assignments, especially when they may not be accepted in other cultures or countries?

LJ: Well, first of all, a young woman, as I said before, needs to figure out who she is. Until then, there is constant friction or inner turmoil. I then think that regardless of whether she wants to do business overseas or here, she needs to ensure that she gets experiences that are pretty broad. A tendency we see in all of our young people, not just women, is that they become very vertically oriented: "I want this job, then I want the next higher job, and the next." I don't think that's the future reality. I think the future reality is more breadth, more horizontal and less vertical.

I also think that over time, while industry will still value the individual with some kind of technical expertise, the ones who will be singled out will be those who have seen more and done more. So I think it's very important to get wide experience. I also think that it is very important to find a few people who really believe in you. Whether you call them mentors or not, its important to use them and have access to them.

MH: Talk a little about those fifteen years at General Foods. You mentioned this man who was a mentor before his time, facilitating your access to varied and challenging assignments. A recent Catalyst report says women still aren't getting enough of those assignments, that too many women are written off, early on, as candidates for this grooming. How did you develop the breadth that enabled you not only to move into the position here, and go to Asia, but to run with it?

LJ: It was very different then. General Foods was a very structured, hierarchical, consumer products goods company. Basically my career was managed for me at General Foods. I had a series of moves that gave me depth in one area, then broadened me in terms of applying what I knew to other businesses. They gave me the experience of running a staff function, which involved developing a certain amount of humility and understanding gained from moving out of the limelight into the support area. Ultimately I moved into general management positions, smaller and then bigger. When I came to Colgate, Asia was very much a broad-breadth experience. You had to deal with the whole business, not just marketing—which is where I started my career—but everything that a company has to do.

AC: Why were you chosen? Surely General Foods didn't plan everybody's careers and provide these kinds of experiences for everybody. Why you?

LJ: I really don't know, and I never asked. Probably one day I will ask this man why I was chosen. But certainly when I started I had a level of curiosity, perspective, analytical skills, energy, ability to present myself and my ideas. I also had an ability to get stuff done. There was perhaps an inner strength or characteristic that they saw, though I have no idea. You perform well, you deliver results, and it gets recognized.

MH: You talked about their willingness to take risks. I think they saw someone who was willing to take risks herself.

LJ: But my General Foods experience was risk free. I describe it as leaving the womb when I left there, because it was so secure. The risks I took were on the business, but the personal risk was very limited. Actually for me to leave there and come to Colgate was a huge risk. I could have stayed there forever; and the truth is, one of the things I find young women averse to doing is taking the real career risks.

MH: Can you talk about something that you did that you're especially proud of when you were at General Foods? Then we want to hear more about what's on your agenda here, and what you're proud of doing here.

LJ: My claim to fame at General Foods had to do with being part of a team that took a business—Kool-Aid, of all things—from being a product nobody cared about, that wasn't growing, to a huge business today. I started out as the worker bee on the team (assistant product manager) and then all of a sudden one day I was in charge of the team (category manager). This was in the 1970s. I think the other thing that I did that was very important to me was the first general management position I had, which was running all of the dry grocery products. These included businesses that weren't growing, that were sleepy, and I had to figure out how to grow them and how to energize the people. Those are two General Foods examples.

Colgate's been a tremendous experience for me. My Asia experience was unbelievably fulfilling. I was there when we signed our contract to enter China for the first time, and we also experienced tremendous growth and increases in profitability in Asia. We put certain parts of Asia on the map for Colgate, which was great. My next job after that was chief technological officer of this company, where I was responsible for things I knew nothing about—research and development, manufacturing, and systems. My last math and science courses were in my freshman year at Wellesley. My contribution in technology, in about two and a half years, was bringing a business perspective to a technological organization and linking our technology closer to our business needs. In the process of doing that, we made the decision to move to a completely new systems infrastructure so that, around the world, every Colgate company, and there are seventy or eighty subsidiaries, would be operating off the same systems platform. We did a long-term strategic plan then, which still drives our technology investment today.

The last two and a half years I've been running our North American business, which was a business that was not growing, and we are now growing very profitably. We are exceeding our own expectations and my management's expectations.

MH: What did you do that made the difference, do you think?

LJ: First thing we did was getting the right people doing the right jobs. People really do make all the difference in the world, and one of the things a leader has to do is select who can play on the team and who may be brilliant but can't play on the team. Secondly, we looked at the business, realized that we had a few issues. We needed growth and developed a lot of compelling new products. The business responded almost instantaneously, and it has been an incredibly rewarding and fulfilling experience for all of us. The key, though, was putting the right people in key positions. You can have brilliant strategies, but you have got to bet on the people first. Along the way, you have to take some tough people decisions and business decisions.

AC: Back to how you personally manage. Is there a difference in the way successful female and male managers behave?

LJ: I know what answer you want, and I'm not going to give it to you.

MH: I would say we're committed overall to more women moving into leadership positions, but we want or expect no single answer here.

LJ: It's funny. I see all different types of male leaders and female leaders, and in terms of the female group, I cannot give you a stereotypical answer or categorize this. We have a bunch of very successful female general managers in our North American business and they are as different from each other as they are from me. The same is true if you look at a comparable group of male leaders.

AC: So a wide range of styles and behaviors works for both sexes?

LJ: I will tell you—and my sample isn't large enough—that even my "girlfriends" who do what I do, whether they run Seagrams or Publishers Clearinghouse or whatever, are as different as can be. Some may be more people-sensitive than others, some may be more aggressive, some may be more strategic—we run the full gamut.

AC: That's actually encouraging.

LJ: I'm sure you've read this. The last major study I saw on this was from the Center for Creative Leadership, and it said that the characteristics that make for successful leadership are pretty similar across genders.

AC: But people are still pushing the idea that there are big differences in styles. Some new studies are reporting that women are better managers in the current global climate, where there is greater need for the more inclusive negotiating styles women allegedly have.

LJ: The perspective about women managers as more nurturing and more sensitive and more, quote, "motherly," I have not generally seen in practice. I will tell you, though, that to be leading an organization of over thirty-five hundred people, you do have to have humanity, you do have to have sensitivity, you do have to deal with a lot of very delicate issues. Then, too, there has been a real shift that I have seen in the past ten or fifteen years or so with the globalization of business and the diversity of workforces. Managers who used to be able to get away with being totally insensitive will not be able to do that in the future.

MH: So there may be something to this idea of drawing on what has been more of a female tradition or style?

LJ: Yes, the stereotypical female characteristics, whether real or not. I do think that these characteristics will become something that all good leaders will have to display more of in the future.

Leadership is having vision, having energy (which is something we haven't talked about), having a game plan, choosing the right people, giving the organization a lot of room but being there, having that sixth sense to know when they're in trouble and being there to pick them up, slap them on the back, and send them off on their way again.

MH: Let's talk about that energy and the whole business of time management, since it plays into how you keep your energy level up, and what you do, and what a typical day looks like.

LJ: I think being a leader of a sizable anything requires tremendous energy, tenacity, and stamina. It is just not a nine-to-five job. No matter what people say, it is twenty-four hours a day, seven days a week, and you are totally engaged. It doesn't matter whether it's me running a company or a college president. You are on call constantly, you can never get away. It comes with the turf. The thing about energy and stamina and loss of privacy, by the way, are areas that are grossly overlooked. You can't keep out of the press, out of the media. They want gossip, they want tidbits, they want insight—and it's very tough. The truth is, you have to figure out a way to have a life. That becomes a real challenge.

MH: Let's spend a little time on that. A recent *Catalyst* study of women in corporate leadership ["Women in Corporate Leadership: Progress and Prospects," 1996, *Catalyst.*] says that although nearly three-quarters of the women managers surveyed were married, a significant number were separated or divorced. Also, only about two-thirds of the women have children, whereas over 90 percent of comparable male executives have children. I think those numbers are fairly significant. How do women managers arrange to have a life? How do *you* manage to do it?

LJ: My own experience—and this is not a generalization, this is me— is that I had to make some choices. They were about successful career, successful marriage, potential of children. In my case, my career is pretty successful and I have a solid marriage. We made the choice not to have children, which was a very tough decision; but it was very difficult for me, or for my husband and me, to have everything at the same time. When I move out in time, ten to twenty years, I am seeing women who are no longer making the same choices I had to make. Now, is it because twenty years ago it was so much more demanding, you were held under such scrutiny that you didn't dare take a day off? I don't know. But I do think today the work environment is more supportive for women. In this organization, and

I am sure in others, we have more and more women who are raising families. You'll never know about the quality of their marital life, but you see more women who are choosing to have a family, and I think it's terrific. I think that when Catalyst repeats that survey in ten years, you may see a different profile.

MH: Talk to us about your experiences of people reporting to you, people who are peers, and people to whom you report—men and women.

LJ: I've never worked for a woman. I've only worked for men, and that's basically been a pretty positive experience for me. I've found for the most part they've been extremely supportive and almost pride themselves that they have me working for them, that I'm happy, and that I will sing their praises. So it's a funny kind of pride, but I've found that the men I've worked for in my career thought it was terrific. Today my direct reports include two women out of seven, and it's wonderful. Just as I know I have a different relationship with everyone who works for me, I also have a different relationship with the women who work for me. This is not the first time that I've had women work directly for me, but it is very nice. Sometimes, though, I think I hold the women up to different standards, because knowing the kinds of challenges that lie ahead, I realize that they need to be as good if not better than the overall peer group. But having said that, I think that it turns out to be a real win-win, because they in fact have their first experience with a female role model.

AC: Do you make it a point to mentor other women in the organization?

LJ: I watch out for the women and minorities in the organization. My own experience is that it is unhealthy for me to mentor women who work in my organization. It is bad for the organization, and I worry that it can backfire on the women. Over the years I have mentored other women in the corporation, who were not in my direct organization. That works pretty successfully. But I do think that people don't understand the seriousness of mentoring. It can be destructive as well as constructive, and it needs to be well thought through.

MH: We learned not long ago that Texaco executives engaged in highly disturbing conversations condoning the exclusion of African Americans from advancement in the company. It takes little imagination to think of similar conversations about women.

LJ: If a woman and/or a person of color is in the room, such conversations almost never occur. The thing that none of us ever knows is what happens when we're not there.

Colgate's a very interesting company. We have a chairman who is adamant about diversity, treating people with respect, and treating women and minorities as well as disabled and international people as total equals. The chairman sets the pace when it comes to these behaviors, and ours is quite outspoken about it.

MH: When I was going around talking to corporate leaders at the time of my college's capital campaign, I was explaining to one CEO who seemed interested in working with us that I would like to work with their senior woman presenting our leadership initiatives to a wider corporate audience. This CEO turned to his head of corporate giving with a puzzled look, and it became clear that neither could identify who their senior woman was. It was a real moment, though neither appeared embarrassed.

LJ: I view the CEO as responsible for that. I will tell you my Colgate story. Our chairman, obviously very progressive, took a look at his organization nine years ago and said, "We have a lot of women in the middle of the pipeline, but we don't have anybody close to the top. I think it's very important that we have a senior executive role model who is female in this company." He went out and they started a search for a senior-level woman. As he puts it, we identified someone (me) who not only could play the role as the senior woman but also could run a big piece of our business. They then followed with a similar search for a senior minority for the top of the company's ranks. They went out and found an unbelievable woman who is currently the deputy general counsel for Colgate. This CEO really saw the need; he required role models and people who could succeed in this organization. It is an incredible tribute to his leadership, in having the guts to say, "We've got good women but they're not going to grow fast enough, so let's go out and bring the talent in." The payback for the company is in business perspective and also that very visible senior women and senior minorities enable you to attract more and better people. But to make it work you need the undying support of the top of the organization.

MH: I want you to make some predictions. We talked at the very beginning of the interview about how women today have it a lot better. Yet the corporate area, unlike some others with the exception of high political office, perhaps, remains a real challenge. I recall the figures from a survey in 1990 showing that just 2.3 percent of Fortune 500 companies have female corporate CEOs or VPs—and they're mostly VPs. Of that small group, a miniscule 3 percent are minorities. If you were gazing into a crystal ball in 2025, what would it look like? That's part one. Part two is, do you think there is anything all of us can do now to make a difference and to increase the pace of women's entry into top-management positions?

LJ: Many believe that we are not making progress fast enough, but I maintain that there is a pipeline that had to be filled. We had to admit women to business schools, and then we had to let them have the right experiences coming up through organizations. I think we are just starting to see a big change. My class at Harvard had only twenty-eight women.

AC: When did you graduate?

LJ: 1973. Five years later, there were one hundred twenty women. The explosion happened after me. I think that to attain the real senior leadership positions, you've got to have a lot of experiences. You need the breadth, and if you don't get it, the probability of succeeding is low. I think that if somebody were to track the numbers in terms of when women graduated from business schools, they would predict an incredible ballooning of women in more senior positions soon. These are capable, competent women, and my sense is that by the year 2025, rather than the two CEOs of Fortune 500 companies today, you will see a lot more. These are women who have the right experiences coming through the systems.

Yes, there will still be barriers and obstacles and subtle discrimination, but I think it will be less than it is today. And today it is less than it was twenty years ago. So I am actually optimistic.

MH: As you're looking at this group coming in, and the group just behind them, are you seeing things that you wish were there in their education or training that are not there? Are you seeing qualities of personality that you wish either were there or not there?

LJ: It's hard to generalize, but I think that the older women have much more of the pioneering sense: "I will do whatever it takes." Younger women, maybe because they never really had to fight, take a lot for granted. There is a sense of entitlement about certain kinds of support. But then again, the world has changed in twenty years. While there are some differences, I think the competent women who exhibit strong leadership throughout their careers will eventually ascend. The one area I and others worry about is that we have seen that younger women are less willing to take real career risks. They are more likely to say, "Give me the game plan and I'll execute it." What we've got to do is increase the level of security or confidence that if they do something a little bit different, they can eventually get where they want to go. We need to increase their risk orientation.

AC: Why do you think women are less likely to take career risks?

LJ: I don't know. Maybe it's because they don't truly trust the system. Twenty years ago, it was all one big risk. You never knew what the rules were, and I think a number of us got comfortable with looking at and doing things differently. In those days, after all, starting out as a woman in business, you were already doing something pretty odd. The question I used to always get was, "What's a nice girl like you doing here?" Today, of course, women in business are much more accepted.

MH: It takes a lot of energy just to answer that question over and over, too. Let's circle back to you right now and what challenges you see out there in the next few years. I'm not asking whether you plan to stay here but rather what would you like to see yourself do, here or elsewhere, that you haven't done. Also, do you have any regrets associated with the career moves that you've made, anything you would do differently?

LJ: I am amazed at my own career. I never ever expected to be president of a big company. When I started out, my first assignment was on Kool-Aid, and my long-term career goal was to be the product manager of Kool-Aid. This is what I thought would be reaching the heights and the limits. You know, it's just a question of perspective. Once in a while I do pinch myself. Is this real? When I was being interviewed coming out of graduate school, people would ask, "What do you want to be?" Twenty years ago I said, "Oh, I want to be president of a company." I did not believe I could, but it was the right thing to say to get in the door. So now I'm president of a company—an operating company.

If there is a regret, it is that I stayed at my first employer too long. I didn't have the guts to leave because it was so comfortable. Yet there was a world out there that was changing. The company I worked for, General Foods, was acquired by Philip Morris in the mid-eighties, and it took me a while to get up the courage to leave. It was a painful, painful decision. I talked to Colgate for over nine months. I had been thinking about leaving, but I just couldn't do it. Finally, having done it, you realize that there is a greater world out there and tremendous opportunities, so the biggest regret is I didn't get on with this sooner.

As for the now, I love what I do. I love working with the kinds of people I work with. There's nothing more thrilling than to see someone grow in front of your eyes, and with some of the people I work with, I can see a transformation that I know I participated in. There's also the thrill of winning in the marketplace. So I really love running a company, and I also love the people side. What is important to me, and I've always felt this in all my jobs, is to leave behind a business that is healthy and growing, an organization that is strong and able to manage with you or without you at the helm.

MH: Is it possible to translate in any formal way the qualities that you've been expressing to us, to communicate these things to younger people sooner in ways that actually work? Is there any kind of leadership education that makes sense to you? Or is it better just to have a series of incredibly good, smart, inspirational people like you come and talk to students periodically?

LJ: Role models are important, and I think that the sharing of the experiences is very important. What I do, very selectively, is just that. It takes a lot of time, and it's quite intimate. You end up exposing a lot of yourself. The giver of this needs to feel comfortable with such self-exposure.

In my business career there is one training program that had a dramatic impact on me. I went to it when I was out of graduate school eight years, a program in leadership. I was a middle manager, and it was the first time I was ever exposed to 360-degree feedback, which can be both constructive and destructive. It was the first time that I was able to see myself as others saw me, and that was one of the most transforming experiences of my professional life.

AC: Do you use 360-degree feedback now?

LJ: Yes. But this was 1981. Maybe I had that experience one or two years too late, but it not only changed me as a leader—it *made* me a leader. A true leader, a motivating leader. It really changed me professionally and personally.

As for what we should be doing from an educational standpoint, there are different points in life when people are especially ready for training and development of leadership skills. If we could find those experiences or exercises that have a transforming potential, experiences that can make people think in fresh ways about themselves and about inspiring others to focus on worthwhile goals, that would be incredibly valuable. But short of that, exposure to leaders who are willing to talk pretty candidly about their experiences is, I think, a very valuable thing.

MH: Is there anything that we didn't ask you that you want to talk about?

LJ: One of the things that you never asked about were the leadership experiences that weren't necessarily positive. It's very interesting, because the reason that this leadership program I went to was so important was that I was your classic type A kind of manager when I first started out. I had tremendous capacity, I was pretty thorough in my work, and anything I was asked to do I could do better than most other people. One of the things that I had to learn was to step back, to give others room, to let them shine, to stay in the background and be proud. For someone who had always been the bright young girl, what an incredible experience that was. We can call it just growing up or becoming mature, but it is more. To succeed in the future—for me to succeed today—is to be comfortable with just letting the organization go. Being a leader is often stepping back and giving others room, not demanding perfection but figuring out how to allow others to get the job done. This was a very important negative experience for me, learning one of the major things that I had to change if I was to advance.

AC: Did you realize this yourself or were you told this?

LJ: Well, I kind of knew it, but I dismissed it. I was told it by supervisors, but I dismissed it because they didn't know the real situation. It's only when I started to hear it from the people who actually worked for me that I realized that perception is reality. You can make all kinds of excuses but you really have to start to deal with it.

Also, it is important to realize that styles and behaviors that may have worked at one point in a career need to be constantly examined. Leaders all need to recognize change in the environment and to make appropriate changes in their behavior.

AC: Your story, and your good advice, are real gifts to a new generation of women with aspirations to break through that glass ceiling.

KAREN NUSSBAUM

■

IN CONVERSATION WITH DOROTHY SUE COBBLE
AND ALICE KESSLER-HARRIS

*Recently named director of the new Working Women's Department
of the AFL-CIO, Karen Nussbaum served in the first Clinton administration as director of the Women's Bureau, the only federal
agency specifically engaged in the concerns of working women. She
was born in 1950 and grew up in an activist liberal family in Chicago.
The social upheaval of the mid-1960s marked her coming of age, and
after attending the University of Chicago for one year, she left to become more involved in political activity, especially the anti–Vietnam
War movement. At eighteen, she moved to Massachusetts, where she
took a clerical position at Harvard University. It was there that she
began to see the plight of women office workers, who were margin-
alized by the feminist movement as well as by organized labor. Re-
sponding to these workers' needs, she began organizing on a small
scale at Harvard and soon realized that workers at other institutions*

and businesses were also organizing fledgling groups. In the spirit of student activism of the late 1960s, Nussbaum engaged with her colleagues to create a larger movement, bringing the successes of the organized peace and civil rights movements to the workplace.

The immediate result of Nussbaum's efforts was the formation, in 1973, of "9 to 5," a support network for women office workers and, later, a sister organization and union, Local 925, for the representation and defense of clerical workers. Nussbaum attributes the early successes of "9 to 5" not only to its spontaneity but to its unique form of leadership. For Nussbaum, leadership resides in advocacy, grassroots organization, and managing through a comprehensive participatory program rather than by fiat. Central to this philosophy is the understanding of the cultural milieu in which organization takes place, an understanding Nussbaum took into the federal government with work at the Women's Bureau from 1993 to 1996 and, now, into her position as the head of the first women's unit within the AFL-CIO. On her agenda, with mandates from a poll of working women conducted by her department, are issues of equal pay and child care as well as encouraging increased voter participation by working women.

DOROTHY SUE COBBLE: We don't have any preconceived views about what feminist leadership is; but if you think there is such a thing, how would you describe it?

KAREN NUSSBAUM: I don't have a theory of feminist leadership. I think much more in terms of practical application: a combination of what I think will work and a commitment to working with women. When we started "9 to 5," we never used the term *feminist*. It has never been important to me to establish the sanctity of the term or of theory around it. I can talk to you about how I decided to do the work that I do and the way in which I do it.

DSC: Fine. Begin by telling us about how your background influenced your work.

KN: I come from a liberal, Jewish family in Chicago where reading distressing novels about social injustice earned high marks. There was a lot of discussion about those things in my family. My mother was a Reform Democrat committeewoman in our largely Republican community. My father was more an intellectual than an activist; he only went to a year of college but was well read and now is a theater director and actor. He became very involved in the avant-garde Hull House Theater, and I would go watch his plays as a teenager. He'd be doing Ionesco or Pirandello, and I would sit there, stony faced, while everyone else was laughing, as you were supposed to do at theater of the absurd. You're supposed, after all, to laugh at the absurdity of the situation. I had no way to make sense of all that, but I knew something was very wrong out there.

My parents provided a rich cultural milieu and were concerned with social issues, although they were not particularly activist until the sixties. My father was a small businessman, and neither of my parents had been involved in anything more left wing than Reform Democratic politics. There had never been any union activity. But this supportive environment, combined with the turmoil of the times, led to next steps. In the sixties, my parents and we three children participated in a peace vigil in front of our town library on Saturdays. At one point, my mother invited Staughton Lynd to speak at our community recreation center. He had just been indicted for traveling to Vietnam without a visa, so the John Birch Society sent my mother postcards with crosshairs on them. The community center refused to let her hold the meeting, but somehow they managed to hold it. We marched for civil rights, too, and as children we thought we were living the kind of moral life of integrity our parents taught.

ALICE KESSLER-HARRIS: Talk a little about coming of age in the late sixties and what it was like for you.

KN: I was eighteen in 1968, and what might normally have been individual angst was part of a much bigger activist context. I went to college because I thought it would be a great way to get involved in politics. You have to understand that in 1968, academic advancement was not the most interesting thing happening. It was far more interesting to be involved in the real world, and I got involved in the anti-war movement and the student movement on my campus at the University of Chicago. I left school after only a year, but that year gave me a base for the kind of life I found most satisfying: being totally engaged in trying to fix things that need fixing.

This was just the beginning of the women's movement, but that wasn't my way into a political life. I wanted to work with women in their own lives—not as part of a women's movement organization, but with women as workers.

DSC: So what did you do next?

KN: It's not as if I sat down and planned it all through. I left Chicago and went to Boston with the idea of getting more involved, somehow. I got a job, and because I was young and a woman, the kind of job I got was as a clerical worker. I became a clerk-typist at Harvard

University. Like so many women, I felt that nobody knew who I was. I couldn't think of why my boyfriends, for example, thought they should be my boyfriends, since they didn't actually care to notice anything very significant about me. No particular incident started me off. It was what I saw going on around me.

The most powerful motivator in the early days of organizing working women was the issue of respect. We didn't produce grand analysis or statistical evidence, but women responded to the basic message of respect. At Harvard, when we put out a notice for a meeting for women workers, fifty people came. One woman thought it was far more important to be considered for promotion than to get a salary increase. They talked endlessly about the issue of who got the coffee. I know it sounds ridiculous, but women did not want to feel they were office wives. They were real workers with real jobs, and making coffee symbolized the lower-class status of women as workers.

AKH: Were you working with anyone on this or were you on your own?

KN: A woman in my office, who was not involved in anything, came in one day with *Sisterhood Is Powerful*, a book I never actually read. I began to realize that the ideas of women's liberation had seeped down almost everywhere, and though the women in the office would have rejected being part of a women's organization, or identifying with the media's image of women's liberation, they were questioning what was happening to them. I had already identified problems in the larger society that I thought it was worth engaging with as part of a group. So my best friend, who was also working at Harvard, and I started an organization. We knew about organizing because we had come from the peace movement, so we knew there was a form available to us to try to pursue some solutions.

There were only ten or twelve people in this group, which we called the Harvard Office Workers Group. It met Wednesdays at noon. We had no program; we didn't really know how to move things ahead. One of the defining moments for us was when we organized a protest to Nixon's wage freeze, which limited our pay raises to 5 percent. (Now, the notion of a wage freeze at a 5 percent increase seems unbelievable.) We distributed a petition around the campus and got hundreds of office staff to sign up. Then we requested a meeting with the head of personnel. We practiced for a month, assigning a different role to each of the twelve people in our organization. We met formally with the head of personnel, in his office, around a big table and we all acquitted ourselves beautifully. He said, "I'll get back to you." He never did, or maybe he sent a letter thanking us. We had thought the combination of being articulate and having a petition would be enough. It wasn't. We said to ourselves, "We took it this far; what do we need to do now?"

At the same time, we started nosing around other universities and other workplaces and began to find that there were isolated little bubbles of insurgency everywhere. The experience of most people was similar to our own: they would do something remarkable and then feel defeated. For example, the eight secretaries in another department at Harvard prepared a memo that read, "Re: Alterations in the Job of Secretary." In it they wrote up their concerns, which ranged from not being requested to go make a Xerox copy while sitting at their desks on lunch hour, to thousand-dollar raises, to being promoted to research assistants. Management met with them and gave them all raises, but they didn't get anything else. They threw up their hands, ready to quit, while I was thinking, "Wow! This is fantastic! Look what you did." A friend who was working at Prudential did something similar in her workplace, and I met women at MIT with thirty-two issues on their petition. But nobody knew anybody else was doing any of this.

DSC: So this led to your founding "9 to 5"?

KN: Actually my friend Ellen Cassedy and I founded it together. It seemed to us at that point that we needed to help people understand they were part of a larger movement and a longer struggle, so that whatever victories they enjoyed, however small, added up to something bigger. We decided to build a citywide organization. We wanted to tap into people's sense of wanting change and give them more support. Throughout all of this, we just followed our noses. The two of us quit our jobs, got our first grant, and lived on fifty dollars a week. In 1972, I was not concerned about my future, and neither was my friend. I had no career goals. I had no idea what I was going to be. I tried to do what I thought was important, to help solve problems I found exciting and that affected me. That was an option in those days in a way that is less true now. We had virtually no exposure to the labor movement, and we weren't part of a women's organization.

So we put together an organizing committee (although we didn't call it that then) of about ten or twelve women from all the workplaces that we had learned about. All of us contributed money so that Ellen Cassedy could go to the Midwest Academy in its inaugural summer and get organizer training. We applied community-organizing tactics to the workplace. We built an organization that we would like to be in. We talked about things in a way that we would find interesting. That's how we came up with the name "9 to 5" and with the slogan "Raises, not roses."

AKH: Were you still meeting at noon on Wednesdays?

KN: No, by then the Harvard group was done. We had moved on, combining our sense of injustice with the tools of organizing as a group. But we had no preconceived idea of what kind of organization we wanted or any of the language that goes with that. When I sat down to talk to someone and saw her flinch if I used the word *organize,* I didn't use the word again. It was common sense. We did spend a lot of time on the name for our group. We also spent a long time trying to figure out how we would refer to the group of women we were appealing to. Should it be "clerical workers," should it be "secretaries," should it be "women workers"? We ended up with "women office workers." You know, most women—at least in those days—didn't respond to the notion that they were workers. They thought of themselves as secretaries or office workers. We wanted a definition that women felt comfortable with, not so narrow that someone else with a different job title felt left out, or so broad that it was hard to identify with.

We recruited people in lunch meetings. Many days we'd have two or three of them. That's also how we recruited additional staff. We recruited Judith McCullough, who was working as a secretary at Travelers Insurance, that way. She now works at the Service Employees International Union. We also recruited Janet Seltzer, who became a community activist in the school system. We worked as a team, which is what I've always liked. I enjoy working with very collaborative people.

The organized women's movement wasn't doing what we were doing. It was not active in the workplace. It was taking on issues of individual empowerment, or social issues like abortion. It was addressing the issues of professional women at the top, or women not getting to the top, but there was no working-class focus. Of course, people didn't use the term *working class* then; they don't use it now. But for average American working women, there was no organized women's movement that seemed appealing. We thought at the time that what we were doing was expanding the women's movement and that the only way to do that was in terms that made sense to the people we were recruiting.

DSC: How did you go about it?

KN: I drew on my own experiences, which were the kinds of things any working woman could tell you about from that time. They are perhaps inflated anecdotes by now, but they still speak to what was moving people then. One day I was sitting in my office at noon while my boss was out to lunch. A student came in, looked me dead in the eye, and said, "Isn't anybody here?" That probably wouldn't bother me today, but at the time it seemed emblematic of the problems. One of my jobs was assembling monthly notebooks for a committee to review. I was in the midst of this with papers spread all around me while I tried to put them together when a male professor walked by and said, "Why aren't you smiling?" I thought, "Well, what's it to you? I'm doing my job; leave me alone."

Those things burned us, long before we found out that clerical workers earn less than any kind of factory worker. It wasn't until after we had started "9 to 5" that we began doing research. We had demanded a meeting with the chamber of commerce, which insisted on a written document describing the problems. We found out there was only a handful of things women could be—nurse, secretary, teacher, or waitress. We also found that there were more clerical office workers than any other kind of worker. We said, "Boy, we should have more power than that!" This became the first of many "9 to 5" reports.

We didn't have many members, so we had to find ways to leverage public opinion. Humor was often an effective way. We used to do these great skits, which were lots of fun for the members. We had committees for different employee groups, including a publishing committee; and we did a wonderful skit about Big Yellow Publishing, with all these funny names for the bosses. Everyone loved it. We would actually do these things in front of the companies and invite the media.

In one case, a woman called to say she had been fired. Her boss, a lawyer, had called her in during her lunch hour to get him a sandwich, which she dutifully did. Then she went back to eat her lunch, when she got an angry buzz. "You got me corned beef on white, and I wanted it on rye." She said, "I'm sorry but it's raining out and I'm on my own lunch hour." He said, "If you don't get me corned beef on rye, you're fired." She refused. She called our office, and two days later we were out there with forty "9 to 5" members with placards that said, "Boss says, 'Rye bread or no bread!'" The media came, and it was big news. She never got her job back, but she was one satisfied secretary.

AKH: Talk about your move to the union movement and how that developed.

KN: "Nine to 5" operated on two principles. First, develop the natural leadership. Find the natural leaders and help them emerge. You can find leadership in anybody. We wanted leaders from the constituency. Second, show victory. You have to give examples of success. We often joked that we would claim anything as a victory. At a party for me when I left Boston for Cleveland, they wrote a phony press release that said something like, " '9 to 5' predicts sun will rise in morning. Prediction upheld!" It was so important for people who had for so long swallowed their grievances and had no way of understanding them except as personal failings, to see that there was something they could do that might succeed. Doing that encouraged people to think that taking the risk was worthwhile. You needed to have an organization so that victories weren't so fragile, so that you could build on those victories.

We came to the idea of unionizing women gradually. For my part, I experienced two epiphanies. One was at a peace demonstration in 1972, one of the really big ones in Washington. After the main march, a little group demonstrated in front of the Justice Department. They were chanting, "What are unions for? General strike to end the war." I thought to myself, "Mmmm, unions as organizations for social change. What an idea." First time I had ever heard it. It planted a seed for me.

AKH: It's funny, those of us who study union history think social change was central!

KN: I know, but that's the kind of thought you had in the sixties, because most unions then supported the war. That was the public perception.

The second epiphany came from a wildcat strike at Corcoran's, a restaurant in Harvard Square. Eight waitresses were abused one time too many by their boss. It was similar to that group of women in the bank in Minnesota, the Wilmar 8, who went from nothing—no money, no power, no understanding—to a long strike. These women at Corcoran's went on strike, and I was on picket duty one night a week. I would walk around in a circle in front of Corcoran's for two hours, and over that long, cold winter I began to appreciate the power of the idea of women's equality applied to the workplace. I saw how this possibility changed these women, how it could move them to heroic action and be a powerful motivator. That is what made us understand that we might really be able to help blend the women's movement and the traditional labor concerns in a meaningful way. That was really the precursor of making "9 to 5" a citywide organization.

There was a third influence, a labor educator name Frank Lyons. We didn't know a lot, so the staff used to go to his class for union representatives one night a week at the University of Massachusetts. He took us under his wing, and after we'd had "9 to 5" going for a year or so, he asked us what we were going to do about a union. We said, "Uh, we don't know. If someone wants to unionize we'll refer them to a union." And he said, "That's stupid. You're going to do all the organizing and then give the members away?" So we said, "Oh, okay, we'll keep them. I guess we'll start our own union." We didn't know what we were talking about or what we were doing, but having the question posed to us at this pivotal moment moved us along. We wrote a proposal about what we wanted to do, which included full funding and a charter—autonomy and money—even though we had no members to offer. We weren't affiliated with a local or anything. We went to ten different unions with the proposal that they should fund us to organize clerical workers, even though we had no members to offer, or dues, or anything.

One of the group went to the local Teamsters. She was told, "Well, you can't organize women workers because they think with their cunts, not their brains." Not everyone was as bad, but everyone said no. Some people offered to hire us as individual organizers; other people told us to come back when we had some members. Then we met up with the Service Employees International Union [SEIU], and there was a great general organizer named John Geagen who got it. He offered us money—practically nothing, but money—*and* a charter, *and* a chance to organize workers. So we started our own union.

DSC: That must have been quite an experience.

KN: When we organized our first workplace, a tiny little publishing house called Educators Publishing Service, the boss sent us a letter soon after we had organized, but before we'd negotiated a contract, announcing that he intended to give raises. We didn't know that he was obligated to do that. In fact, not only was he obligated to do it but we could have said no. We didn't know any of this, so we said, "Wow! This union stuff is great!" We had a terrible time with the contract. I'd never negotiated a contract. We finally came to an impasse, and we formed a picket line in front of the company on a Saturday when they were showing the new books. We had a conga line. We banged pans and spoons and maracas and chanted, "EPS is un*fair!*" We had signs that said, "EPS: Every Person a Slave." On Monday, I got a subpoena, and I called the union lawyer. We'd been in violation of the law. It was all just totally seat of the pants.

AKH: In retrospect, do you think you lost anything by unionizing?

KN: We maintained the two organizations as sister organizations. We believed very much that you needed an open association that could attract the widest number of people. So "9 to 5" was a public organization for individuals all over the country, an entry point. Local 925 was for people who wanted to have the power of a union. In Local 925, we had an organization that had the character and concerns of the working women's movement but the power of a trade union. I think our members didn't experience what the leaders—myself and a couple of others—experienced in battling the trade union bureaucracy. But we also thought of ourselves as being a force to help transform the trade union movement. I think it was useful to maintain the separate organization, because it gave us an independence within the union movement; "9 to 5" was all mouth and no body. It had no organization dragging it down. We weren't negotiating contracts; we didn't have long-standing relationships with employers that we had to worry about. We were agile, we were fast. We could identify an issue, write a report, and change the debate.

All that was the real strength of "9 to 5," and it was something very hard for the unions to do. "Nine to 5" had a limited decision-making process. We didn't have to worry about a large board of local leaders of their own organizations, with a number from a traditional, more conservative framework. We didn't have to bring anybody along. We had a certain independence. The Coalition of Labor Union Women opened up the whole labor movement. Together we helped make it more modern.

We achieved that, partly with John Sweeney's support. He wasn't the president who brought us in, but he allowed us to become a national union within SEIU. Before that, we'd only been a local in Boston. He supported us all along the way. One of the first big corporate campaigns that SEIU did under Sweeney's leadership was to go after Equitable Life Insurance Society. This was an ill-fated campaign, started because we found a group of ninety clericals in Syracuse who were really hot to trot and wanted to organize. We organized them in a snap and then discovered that there were ten thousand other Equitable employees out there, so that we weren't going to have an easy time getting a contract. It required a huge corporate campaign, and Sweeney totally backed us. Equitable was the first of a long series of aggressive campaigns. He's now known for that kind of organizing.

AKH: Can you talk about what is different or special about organizing women?

KN: I've always felt that you organize women in different ways than you organize men. But you organize blacks differently than you organize whites, and you also organize language minorities differently. That's always been true, and those differences are important. Any good organizer meets people where they are, and people aren't all at the same place. Effective union organizers in the South meet in black churches, or women office workers meet at lunch. You must understand the culture in which you're operating. You start with something people feel comfortable doing, and if it's bringing something to the bake sale and they have to show up because they have to deliver it, well, that's the way you get them to the meeting. You have to be painstakingly conscious of these things. You can't just call a meeting and hope that people are going to come. It is extremely intensive work to organize people who aren't used to being organized. But you've just got to do it.

At the time we started "9 to 5," many unions were just passing out hand-bills in front of buildings and not having anybody respond. We developed new tactics for our organizing, because prior tactics were not working. Other organizers were coming to the same conclusions. Now these tactics are more widely diffused throughout the labor movement. They are much more labor intensive in recruiting and leadership development and being engaged—not just in the workplace but in the community as well. Labor organizations now have a more open leadership, which is often a charac-teristic of women-led organizations. They have more levels of developed leadership, not one leader for life and a membership with no strata in be-tween. You could say one is a male model and one is a female model, but there are plenty of exceptions. Lots of organizations led by women aren't like this, and plenty led by men are more more developed in this way. I think of it as good organizing, as having seeds in the women's movement but not *just* the women's movement—just as the women's movement was itself part of other social movements.

DSC: How do you assess the developments in labor organizing since founding "9 to 5"?

KN: In the late seventies and early eighties, I had a theory that union organizing takes place in waves and that it's spurred by social movements. Just look at the socialist movement and how it helped spur union organ-izing here in the thirties, or look at the impact of the civil rights movement on the public sector and hospital organizing in the sixties. Now I thought the next big organizing wave was going to occur because of the impact of the women's movement on traditionally female jobs. That's why "9 to 5" was needed if you wanted to do business in the new emerging trade union movement. It was a great theory, but unfortunately what happened in the 1970s and 1980s was an extremely severe attack on unions and the be-ginning of the most sustained decline in wages and living standards for American workers since the Depression.

Just as our union, Local 925, was getting its charter, the fastest grow-ing industry was union busting. We didn't know what hit us. We expected we were going to have a big, stable organization and that we would see a withering away of "9 to 5," the association, as we took our rightful role in the labor movement. We got smashed over and over. These businesses had not traditionally been unionized, and they were damned if they were going to be the first ones in the new wave. We never had an easy election.

Between '73 and '75, I was an organizer for "9 to 5"; and when we started our union in Boston in '75, I went over to the union and became an organizer. I did that for a couple years, and then we realized that we needed to go back and broaden the base again. Unionizing office workers was like using a dentist's drill on a brick wall. We decided to make "9 to 5" a national organization, and I became a national organizer working to help people think of their efforts in a bigger context. A few years after that, we decided to make the union national. I headed both organizations then, until I moved to the Women's Bureau.

AKH: How do you deal with leadership in a bureaucratic government framework?

KN: When the Women's Bureau job came along, I wasn't looking for a job. I was happy within my own organizations. SEIU [the Service Employees International Union] put my name in. I'd never thought of the Women's Bureau, but my name got circulated and eventually I went to meet Bob Reich, the secretary of labor. I had a reputation as a strong advocate, and that's what Bob wanted at the Department of Labor. There wasn't a conflict for me in the position, then, since my history of advocacy was regarded as a plus.

At the bureau, I spoke to women nobody else hears. I had an almost unfettered opportunity to talk to working women and not catch much flack for it. It was like "9 to 5": we spoke in a language that was accessible; and one of our main goals was to engage working women—surfacing what their concerns are and demanding change. But there were so many more resources there. It is just a bigger, more complex playing field. I'm completely delighted with what I was able to do.

At "9 to 5," every time we wanted to start a new campaign, we'd pass out surveys and write up a report. You get the attention of the press, and then you get even more people involved. We also decided to do a survey at the Women's Bureau; but since we were the government, we got sixteen hundred organizations to help us distribute the survey, and forty daily newspapers to print it. Millions of surveys went out, and over a quarter of a million women returned them. It asked, "What do you like about your job, what don't you like, and what needs to be changed?" I liked being able to engage that many people and to deliver the message that this is a rightful goal of government, that government is best when it asks people questions and listens to them and then develops public policy based on their responses. It wasn't just about polling. We didn't just do a scientific random sample; it was also a popular effort; and then we had a mandate. We focused on the issues working women told us they cared about.

DSC: It seems that with "9 to 5," you could actually go back with survey information and build an organization. At the Women's Bureau you tried to use such information to convince companies to change by offering publicity and incentives, but you were not actually building an organization.

KN: That's not the role of government. But it is what working women are looking for. When I went around the country and met with working women, I'd have a group of twenty women from different jobs, or maybe all women from one hospital, or twenty-five poultry workers, or whatever. I'd sit there for an hour and a half and talk with them about their jobs. I always had the feeling, at the end of those meetings, that these people didn't need to be talking to the Women's Bureau director; they needed to be talking to an organizer. They all knew what their problems were, but they didn't have the first idea about what the solutions might be. In their world, the sphere of possible change is so small, and there's no one getting out there helping women understand what they might do to try to solve their problems. They might say, "Well, maybe I could ask my sister to watch my kid." The sphere of possible change is perceived as so small. We'd talk about their options, and I tried to put them in touch with supportive organizations in their area. But I often thought a grassroots organization should be there, going around the country and talking to people.

DSC: Is there a different way of organizing women? Do they need this first step of empowerment that men don't?

KN: I think there's been a tremendous change in the way women view themselves as workers. When we first started "9 to 5" over twenty years ago, the most common experience was that women blamed themselves for whatever failings they had on the job. Perhaps it was because they hadn't gotten a higher diploma, or the boss wasn't in the right mood when they asked for a raise. The word *discrimination* was not popularly accepted, and you could not talk about organizing. By the time I was at the Women's Bureau, when you talked to a typical woman worker, she felt that she was a permanent member of the workforce. She supported her family. She was fed up with the way she was treated on the job, and she didn't think it was right.

The other thing is that over the last ten to twenty years, wages for men, particularly white men, have dropped sharply, but wages for women are going up somewhat. There's a theory that says that it's those people who have some hope that are in the best position for demanding change. It's not the people who are on the road down that dare to say, "I'm going to risk everything now." You've got this combination of women who have changed their self-image in a significant way, who are experiencing slight improvement in their position as workers, and who also exhibit a practical, day-to-day approach to "How am I going to get my family through the next month?" That creates an interesting combination which would lead you to think, "If we want change, let's work with women to make it."

Working women are also pivotal in changing the political world. Women in traditional jobs, high school–educated, basically low-income women are the "best" voting block. (Actually, the best voting block within *that* group is African-American women!) What I mean by that is that such women are the most likely to vote on the basis of concerns for their families and for others—in favor of education, health care, and old-age security. These women are the swing voters. They're the voters who defeated Bush in '92. They're the voters who stayed home in '94, and because of that, the Republican Revolution took place. If women had voted in the same numbers that they had in '92, then you wouldn't have had the changeover in Congress. Since the identification of the gender gap in 1984, the women's movement has been calling attention to it. I think it is plain old sexism that political leaders have felt more comfortable courting men.

DSC: What did your experience of working with the corporate world show?

KN: What I did was help to show women that if they stood up, they could achieve something. The campaign that we did, "Working Women Count," asked women what they cared about and showed that there's a supportive framework for making demands. We challenged companies by saying, "Whatever you've done so far, you've got to do more. And that's all we're counting; were counting what you do from today on. What are you going to do that makes work better for women and their families now?"

Originally we hoped to get government action on pay equity, paid leave, or expanded family leave. But with the 1994 elections, it was clear that no supportive legislation would be considered. It was never even going to have a hearing. I met with groups of workers and employers to ask for recommendations they'd like us to propose to the president. The human resources and personnel people told us, "We really need the threat of something hanging over us or else it's hard to get the company to do anything." Someone said, "We could really use the threat of new legislation. We don't really want new legislation, but the threat of new legislation would be helpful."

One woman, who was the head of personnel for a big construction company, said, "Well, when there's a really important program for me in the company, I go to the boss and say, 'You know, the labor investigators are going to be here next month.' " "Then," she said, "I go to confession!" She knows the Office of Federal Contract Compliance is not coming for a long time, but she needs the threat. As I listened to her, I thought, "Oh, brother, even that isn't going to work anymore." It was clear we needed an alternative, popular form of momentum. The threat of government action wasn't credible enough anymore. We had to do the best we could to create a culture that said, "You're expected to meet this standard. This is what working people need. We are setting these standards of improvement out there for you." Admittedly, it is a weak tool, but more successful and more powerful than I used to think. It can only work in a long-lasting way, however, if grassroots organizations step in, use the momentum, and then try to build on it. That's what I hope happens.

AKH: We've talked about how leadership develops among women and how you organize women. But how do you move from there to getting power for women in an organization?

KN: How do women become empowered? How do they exercise power within an organization? My approach has always been to work with people where they are and help them take the next step. I've often thought being a good organizer is like being a good lover. In the absence of a huge, spontaneous movement, you have to be very sensitive to the person that you're working with. In the very early days of "9 to 5" there was an article in *Business Week* that said something about us being patient. I felt at the time, "Well, good, but I hope not too patient." You can't wait forever, but you also have to understand that it takes five lunch meetings before someone will make the first commitment.

The nicest thing anybody ever said about me was at the time I left "9 to 5" to take the Women's Bureau job. One of the union members said that I never asked people to do more than they could but that I always knew that they could do much more than they thought they could. I thought, "Oh, how perfect." That is what you want to communicate, a kind of confidence that moves people but doesn't make them feel you're demanding the impossible. That's my approach to empowerment. Before you know it, that person is leading the picket line or speaking before the press, and she's a changed person.

You can express power in many ways. When we first started, negotiating contracts was a totally male thing. There were no women doing that, or hardly any, in 1975; and on top of it, we didn't know very much! Then we realized that actually the power was not in the person but in the organization. As long as the organization was behind you, it didn't matter what you wore, or how you spoke, or what your personal image was. It was whether you had a base that meant anything. As we negotiated several contracts, I began to understand that there was an advantage in the other side's not knowing what to expect from us. They thought we wouldn't do a good job or be smart enough; that was an advantage!

DSC: The women's movement historically has had a somewhat ambivalent relationship to power. Has it been difficult for you, being a spokesperson and having power?

KN: I haven't felt conflicted by it. I think I'm good at what I do, and I'm glad for that. It's a pleasure to have the opportunity to do what you're good at. I also believe that my successes aren't *my* successes. No one's successes are entirely their own. You work with a group and you share successes and failures. That's always the way I've felt about whatever group I was working with. I'm not in this to advance my career. What has been important is not where I go next but whether I am helping to build something that I'm proud of. I think it is helpful to have a spokesperson, or two or three spokespeople. These are issues of strategy, not personality. For example, at "9 to 5" we said, "Okay, if we're going to get this message across, we need to have someone the media can identify," and I got assigned. I got good at it. I like it, but I can do without it, too.

AKH: Didn't that produce jealousies, as in some other women's organizations where people used to insist that media assignments be rotated so as not to develop "stars"?

KN: We made sure that in addition to myself speaking as the director of the organization, for the most part it was different members who were speaking. If we did a press conference or an action someplace, members were the press spokespeople. I have seen organizations where only one person speaks, and I don't think it works very well. But I also don't think it works well to rotate it. We were interested in building a permanent organization with ongoing power, and we thought that one piece of that was being identifiable to the press. We always thought of our press strategy as leverage.

One of the things I'm good at is strategy, and so I think I've held the leadership positions in my organizations honestly. Of course there have been times when I thought that I wasn't a good enough leader or manager; but I've generally believed that successes and failures both belonged to whatever leadership team I was part of. I never thought I should be doing something else—maybe I never had the imagination to think of what that would be, but I certainly had those occasional panic attacks like, "Is this working? Are we going to collapse? Where do we go from here?"

In the late eighties, in fact, I got away from it all. I was sitting there watching the election returns and seeing George Bush elected in 1988 and thinking, "I have got to get out of this country." You know, the eighties were really terrible. We had been pretty static in our growth at the union. There were problems inside the union, and so I left for a while. I took my three kids and went to Brazil for four months. It was like cleaning out my carburetor. All I did was try to speak Portuguese and get to the grocery every day because the refrigerator didn't work. I just tried to live my life. What I found hard there was so different from what was hard at home. I set myself a project of studying Brazilian social movements during their political democratization. I went out and just interviewed the people I was interested in talking to. I wanted something totally different.

Then, when I came back, I felt different. I felt I had a better sense of what was important and what wasn't important. What was unimportant was internal political infighting. What was important was building a program. You lead with your program, and if your program is strong, people will come to you. It sounds simple, but I had lost that along the way because I had been snowed under with political infighting. It worked. We put much more emphasis on leadership development within our own organization, and we focused on building the kind of organization we could be really proud of. Then, if it worked, it worked; and if it didn't, we would have failed honestly. We put lots of effort into leadership development; we put even more effort into organizing. We stopped trying to get power through internal means and instead built our power from our base.

That's the way I operated inside the Department of Labor, too. You lead with your program. Internal machinations were not interesting to me. I have always believed that wasn't the way to get support for your work anyway, and it didn't matter whether anybody thought I as an individual was smart, because all that meant was I was a smart person in somebody else's meeting. What mattered was whether we could get support and resources— political, financial, or otherwise—for a program. I think we've been successful.

AKH: So you think that within the Labor Department you were able to get what you needed to run the Women's Bureau?

KN: When I first got there, I met all the staff in small groups and got briefed by them on what kind of work they do. They told me about the hundreds of publications that they put out and how they were focused on women and business, and other things. At one point I said, "Well, I thought we might put out things about job rights—let people know what their job rights are and encourage them to pursue them." One of the women said, "You mean, advocate?" I said, "Well, yes, that's kind of what I had in mind." She applauded. They had had twelve years of Republicans, and many of the former directors really had no relationship to women's employment issues at all. We started a campaign called "Don't Work in the Dark, Know Your Rights." Nobody had done that there in a long time. I went around the country meeting with every different kind of worker I could find. I brought that experience back into the bureau and made decisions about where I spoke based on how many working women I would reach. That was unusual for the bureau. The huge survey we did was also unusual for the government. The criterion was, "Am I reaching working women and am I helping them improve their jobs?" That wasn't typical. Like "9 to 5," we weren't an enforcement agency, but we had some authority that we could build on and reinforce. We developed such an interesting program that both the Department of Labor and the White House wanted to take advantage of it. We did five White House events, which is probably not that common.

DSC: It seems one of the connecting threads for you is that you really want to change women's notions of what is possible, not create change from the top down or transform things through legislation.

KN: Right. The question is: How do people solve their problems? not: What is the problem? That's what I'm interested in working on, and I am most interested in working on it with women—not *only* women but mostly women!

As an individual, I have enjoyed being the head of an organization. It's a lot easier than not being the head, because you get away with more stuff than if you weren't! I could never be a consultant. I need to be part of an organization.

AKH: We have talked about empowerment, but now talk a little about power within the organization. There's a skeptical piece of me that wants to say, "It sounds wonderful as long as you're in charge and you can pursue these programs, but how did you build for the Women's Bureau a status that could continue after you left?"

KN: Practically speaking, you cannot do that in the government, since the way the government is set up is that political leadership changes every four years, and that leadership determines what is going to be important and what isn't. In government as head of the Women's Bureau, I could and did do things that helped reinforce the bureau as an institution. But if a new administration should come in that is not interested in the average working woman, they will just stop everything. That is their prerogative. Government is not like an organization. The government is the government.

AKH: You've left the government and are now at the AFL-CIO as director of the new Working Women's Department. Why did you decide to make the change and how do you like the new job?

KN: I went into the government to "serve" (as we say in government) working women from a new vantage point, to learn how the government works and to take a fresh look at how to reach working women. But my heart has always been in organizing, rather than in serving—that is, in building organizations in which people help themselves, rather than crafting policy or delivering service. I expected to stay at the Women's Bureau for one four-year term and then go back to the labor movement in some capacity.

The lure of the labor movement became irresistible when John Sweeney, president of SEIU, my old union, joined with other union leaders to issue a challenge to unions to take up an activist agenda, put organizing at the top of its priorities, and remake ourselves as a movement for all American workers. Sweeney ran for president of the AFL-CIO in the first contested election of the labor federation. I remember riding to work on the Metro one day and reading a headline that said something like "Sweeney Declares Labor Irrelevant." "Fantastic!"—I nearly said out loud. Finally union leaders were admitting just how bad things were and how much change was needed. Sweeney, Richard Trumka (who became the youngest elected top leader of the AFL-CIO), and Linda Chavez Thompson (the first person of color) won the election. Even though I loved my Women's Bureau job, where I had been working for three years, I was thrilled to be asked to create—for the first time in the hundred-year history of the American labor federation—a Working Women's Department at the AFL-CIO.

DSC: What can you tell us about that position so far?

KN: I thought I knew a lot about working women, but I was surprised to find out two things. First, nearly 40 percent of union members are women, which means around 5.5 million women who are members of AFL-CIO unions, making us the largest working women's organization in the country by a factor of about 100. Few would have thought of us that way, though, because we didn't act like it. Our opportunity, our future, would depend on doing that. We needed to change what we did, how we talked, and who spoke for us to reach out to working women.

The second fact I learned was that in the last twelve years, more women had organized into unions than men. Most people are aware of the gender gap in politics, but there is also a gender gap in organizing. Women are more likely to say they would join a union tomorrow if they had a chance, and more are likely to support collective action. So, in addition to matters of simple justice and women's equality, by focusing on reaching out to women we are building on an important and largely unrecognized strength.

I've applied the lessons I've learned over the years to my new job at the AFL-CIO—that an activist program is the best way to gain the involvement of working women and the support of leadership. In less than two years we've moved towards becoming a voice for working women as well as a powerful and credible working women's organization. We did a national survey called "Ask a Working Woman"; traveled to dozens of cities, meeting with working women and community and union leaders; and held a breathtaking conference of nearly two thousand women, bringing together union women and women who aren't represented. The survey gave us a mandate to focus on equal pay and child care as policy issues, to become a major force in elections through our "Working Women Vote" program, and to build on our organizing strength in unions. It's an exciting time to be in the labor movement; lots is at stake. There's a huge battle ahead of us, but the potential for working women becoming an organized force to be reckoned with has never been greater.

DSC: Can you tell us about when you felt proudest in your leadership, and why?

KN: There was more than one proud moment, for sure! I was proud to share the stage with President Clinton, the First Lady, and Secretary Reich at a White House reception for one thousand women celebrating the 75th Anniversary of the Women's Bureau. I was proud to have leaders like President Sweeney, Governor Ann Richards, and Congresswoman Maxine Waters come to our Working Women's Conference and see that something special was happening here—that a new chapter of the women's movement is being written. I'm proud when my children reflect the values my husband and I try—awkwardly—to instill.

Two other moments come to mind. One was back in the seventies, when I was very active in the peace movement. We had called a demonstration for April 30, 1975, which as it turned out was about two days after the war ended. We went ahead and held the rally in the Arlington Street Church in Boston, which has these fabulous acoustics. The place was jammed. It rained the entire march, so everyone was soaking wet. There were probably a thousand people there—people who had truly been the heart of the peace movement. Somehow, I got chosen to be the emcee, and I got to introduce all the speakers and say something about what each meant to the whole effort. I felt so proud. We didn't have delusions of grandeur. The American peace movement had played a small but important role in achieving peace. We were *with* history, not butting our heads against a counter-trend, as in the labor movement. To be able to appreciate that was exhilarating.

That's one kind of proud moment. It's been more than twenty years since then—many of them years when we haven't been *with* history, at least not on that kind of scale. But there have been other kinds of proud moments.

I mentioned the time one of our members said I never asked her to do any-thing more than she could do but that I always knew she could do more than she thought she was capable of. Then there is the letter I got from one of the staff, when I was at the Women's Bureau, who said that she'd been in Indiana, and a woman who'd been at a conference where I had spoken came up to her and said, "I heard Karen two years ago. She encouraged me to file a suit and I just won the settlement. I think it's because she said, 'You've got to take a risk and you've got to be prepared for adversity.' " I felt, "Wow, that's what the whole thing is about."

JACQUELINE PITANGUY

■

IN CONVERSATION WITH CHARLOTTE BUNCH
AND BARBARA A. SHAILOR

A Brazilian social scientist and feminist activist, Jacqueline Pitanguy was the president of Brazil's National Council for Women's Rights (CNDM) from 1986 to 1989 and is the founder of CEPIA (Citizenship: Studies, Information, Action), a nonprofit independent research organization concerned with public policy, human rights, gender violence, and reproductive health. Born in Rio de Janeiro in 1945, she was introduced to international education early on, attending high school in both Brazil and New York State. She spent her university years at the Pontifical Catholic University of Rio de Janeiro and the Université Catholique de Louvain in Belgium before graduating from the Institute of Sociology and Politics at the Catholic University of Chile in 1970. Pitanguy completed her graduate study in the department of political science at the University of São Paolo in 1985; since then, she has held academic positions in several institutions in Brazil and Chile,

teaching sociology and political theory. Pitanguy has also conducted extensive research in her fields, including work on prison conditions, health and sexuality, women's political engagement, and conditions for low-income women in Brazil and Chile, and has consulted with UNICEF, the Latin American Faculty of Social Sciences, the United Nations Population Fund, and the World Bank, among other international agencies.

As president of the CNDM, the first Brazilian governmental organ for women's advocacy, Pitanguy led the fight against the traditional "defense of honor," which had successfully exonerated thousands of Brazilian men who had murdered their wives. In addition, she worked to establish special police stations all over the country to handle crimes against women, including rape and domestic violence. In 1991–92, Pitanguy held the Laurie New Jersey Chair in Women's Studies at Douglass College, Rutgers University, and now continues her directorship of CEPIA. Among her many other honors, in 1989, Pitanguy received the Medal of Ordem do Rio Branco, the highest decoration from the Ministry of Foreign Affairs, and the Ordem do Merito de Brasilia, Brazil's highest command. She is currently on the governing board of UNESCO's Institute for Education, on the board of the Inter-American Dialogue, and is a member of the International Human Rights Council.

Barbara Shailor: I am interested to know when you first thought of yourself as a leader, or did you consciously see yourself that way?

Jacqueline Pitanguy: I still have a certain difficulty with the term *leader*, because I would prefer to see myself as someone who is multidimensional. Rather than seeing myself as a leader, I think of myself as someone who can be a leader in some areas and yet be full of doubts and very vulnerable in others. Thinking about leadership as a dimension that dominates my life is not something that I have done. I do, however, see myself as someone who takes initiatives. I have taken initiatives throughout my life, even when I was in school.

BS: Can you cite some example in your early life where you saw yourself taking the initiative?

JP: Yes, at the secondary school where I studied. I was educated in a very traditional French nuns' school, and I took some initiative in challenging the nuns to respect the students more, because they were always ready to assume we had done something wrong. All the time we were having to prove we were not doing something wrong, and I took the initiative in organizing the students to protest. The nuns told us that either we accepted their rules or we would have to leave. We decided to leave, which was something unique for the school.

CHARLOTTE BUNCH: How old were you when this happened?

JP: I was fourteen, and in that adolescent moment! It is so hard to be an adolescent: to discover what life is like but also to be full of uncertainties because of all that is happening, including all the changes in your body that you're not very comfortable with yet. Then to have all these nuns pointing a finger at us for what seemed like most of the time. A big part of our lives took place in school, after all. I remember I was picked up at six-thirty in the morning and brought back at six-thirty at night. It seemed that the nuns were always after us, especially in relation to sexuality. Always there was something related to sin.

The nuns had a meeting with the parents and said that they couldn't deal with our class because our class was too united. It was quite something that we managed to organize ourselves together and say, "We don't want to stay in this school because this school does not respect us." So there is an example of initiative. It was not only me, of course, it was a group of us; but I was part of the group and among the first to urge that we should all be together in deciding to leave that school. We did leave, in the middle of the year.

CB: That's a pretty powerful example. I think that taking the initiative is one of the most important characteristics of leadership. This example shows the leadership isn't one "man on a white horse" directing everything, but rather several of you making something happen by helping people to see what they want and articulating it effectively. After that happened, did you feel some sense of the power that went with the statement you and your classmates made?

JP: I don't think I was fully conscious of it. We were facing a difficult situation in the school and we got out of it. We certainly felt powerful at the time, but we were also adolescents dealing with all the uncertainties of adolescence. When I think back, I suppose it was one of the more important initiatives of my life; but at the time, I didn't think much about it, except that I was able to change schools and be exposed to another environment where what mattered was the students' intellectual ability and not so much what they were doing or thinking of doing in their private life, or religious life. Something that has remained, though, is that the group of us who were together in that situation are still close today, so many years afterward. We still meet, and we still feel a kind of pride.

BS: At age fourteen, it was a very courageous thing to take on the "system," especially in the kind of school you describe. How did you have the courage?

JP: I think it was that at the moment, it was so very difficult for us to survive in that environment. There had been a change in the director of the school, and the atmosphere was suffocating. I think we felt that anything would be better than staying there. We took a risk. Our parents might have made a deal with the school, and we might have had to stay in that atmosphere. But that was a risk we were ready to take.

In general, I think one of the most important things to remember when you take initiatives in life is to confront the possibility of failure. You have to be ready to fail, but you also have to put all your cards on winning. You just tell yourself that if you don't win, it's all right. You'll survive. I think if people see themselves only as winners, then they will only go for sure things, for victory with the big *V*. That makes them very fragile. Society places too much value on winning, and that is not good for leadership, because someone who takes the initiative has to understand that failure, or not winning everything you want, is part of life.

CB: Did your own parents support you?

JP: Yes they did. My father, a physician, was very supportive, and my mother was also a person who was deeply moved by a sense of justice. Neither were rigid Catholics; and they told me that while the nuns were saying that the problem with us students was our solidarity, they themselves actually cherished and valued solidarity. So they said go ahead and leave. I think it was a revolution for the parents, also, although I wasn't very conscious of that at the time. This is another point: you cannot be too self-conscious. If you take yourself too seriously, you get paralyzed protecting your image.

CB: Would you say your family was generally supportive of you as a woman doing things in the world and that this helped you in becoming a public person?

JP: I lost my father when I was fifteen, soon after that school incident. I feel very often, even today because he was such an interesting man, that I would have liked him to know me as an adult. I am sure we would have shared many things. My mother was always supportive, in what is a peculiar way in that she never thought anything I did was extraordinary. She just thought, "Why not?" I remember once when I was heading the National Council [for Women's Rights in Brazil], I had a very difficult meeting coming up with the president of the Republic. I called her and said, "Mother, I'm scared. I'm going to talk with the president." So she said,

"The president is a normal man. He has insomnia, he has problems of digestion and nausea. He's just a normal man, and he is aging. He has the functions of the president to perform, and you have other functions of your position; but it is just two human beings, here. Go ahead and talk to him and don't make a fuss over it. You're very well prepared."

This was fantastic for me. She would also be like a mother and say, "If you can't talk to the president, who can?" And then I would feel, "Well, why not?" So she was very supportive. She was much older, and she came from a generation where women did not work outside the home. She studied, liked literature, and was very refined—much more so than I am! She had read all the classics and talked with familiarity about everything, but she never earned money—never in her life. I think that makes a big difference in our generation, in our way of seeing life and of placing ourselves in life. But internally, she was free.

BS: Tell us about your development as a leader after adolescence.

JP: Well, I had two youthful experiences of going away from my home, my country, that were important. When I was sixteen I came to the United States as an American Field Service exchange student, and I lived with an American family in northern New York. For the first time in my life, I experienced being by myself. I had to speak English for a year, and never a word of Portuguese. The family was very undemonstrative, and I had come from a very warm family where we would often touch each other. This family would maybe give one another a kiss on birthdays—but very quickly, like that!

On the other hand, there was something about the mother that has kept us together to this day. She was very self-contained in terms of her gestures, but she was generous in her soul. She really loved me, and I loved her. This was important for me to understand, that in the absence of familiar environmental signals, you can relate to a person and you can understand that a person likes you and that you like that person. Today she is eighty-nine, and we've built a strong relationship. I think that I gained a lot of understanding through her about being able to connect with people from very different cultures.

It was very different for me then in the U.S. in 1963, since I was really made to feel foreign. It was interesting to be someone from Brazil, since people would come and see if you had two legs and two arms and so forth, so being exposed as a foreigner and at the same time trying to apprehend what is common, what is human, with everybody, was fascinating. In high school I made a lot of friends.

Then the second experience of leaving home, after I went back to

Brazil, was when I went to Europe. This was the big moment of changing worlds, in the late sixties. Being young and by myself in Europe, I was trying to discover the world through certain authors.

BS: Who were you reading?

JP: I was a good Latin American, so I read and reread Marx, and for a time I thought I had my compass, just as more religious people had their compass in the Bible, or the Koran. From Europe I went to live in Chile, and I was there when Salvadore Allende was elected president of the country. I was able to see a peaceful transition from a Democratic Christian regime to a socialist government and to feel the hope that was part of a shift to a more egalitarian society. So I am also part of that Latin American generation that has had a diaspora, going from here to there and being persecuted by military regimes. Many of my friends have disappeared.

CB: Did you meet your husband when you were in Chile?

JP: No, he was from Chile; but I met him in Europe and moved with him to Chile. When I was there, it was a time of great change in that society. I was immersed in the whole process to such a degree that my own personal being was somehow not there. I always joke with my friends that I didn't have a mirror in those days! Now it's true that I *did* have a small mirror in the bathroom, but I didn't have a big mirror because my looks were not really important then, since I perceived and defined myself basically as someone engaged in the structural changes going on in the society. This is something that perhaps Latin Americans understand better. You feel you are immersed in a historical process. It is a fantastic feeling, but it is also very alienating.

CB: Can you give us more of a sense here of your personal biography at this time?

JP: I was recently married and I was at the university studying sociology. Allende was elected in 1970, and one of the most important emotional experiences of my life was the night of the election, going to the Alemeda to the Presidential Palace and celebrating what we thought was going to be a peaceful transition to socialism. In Brazil in 1964, we had had a military coup d'etat, so the situation in Brazil remained very bad. (I'm part of a Brazilian generation that had twenty-one years of military rule, so democracy is something that we cherish a lot.) When Allende came to power, people were escaping from Brazil to Chile because in Brazil we were under a military dictatorship and Chile was still the land of freedom and liberty. All that changed by 1973, when the Pinochet military coup took place in Chile. By then I was back in Brazil, so you can see that for me and for many of my generation there was general upheaval throughout this period. Some of my friends migrated to Argentina where it was still kind of open, since the military horror had not yet taken over the country. But there was a real diaspora of my generation of political activists.

CB: Could you talk about the period when you had your children and how your feminism evolved?

JP: I became pregnant in Chile in 1971 and decided I wanted to have my first child with my mother in Brazil and be close to my family. The situation was already very difficult in Chile by the time I left. I was very thin, and I was already eight months pregnant. I said to my mother when I arrived, "I'm going to look for a job." She said, "No one will hire you. I never heard of such a thing." So I went to the Department of Sociology at the Catholic University of Rio de Janeiro and told them I had research experience and needed work, admitting that I was about eight months pregnant. The director was someone I liked very much, and she said, "Okay, you work here a month and prepare a project. If it's a good project and if we are able to raise the funds, after you have the baby you can come here and work on it."

Well, I wrote the project, we raised the funds, and I started working after Andrea, my daughter, was born. My project was on women in the work force, and it was for the International Labor Organization. Odd as it may sound, my first relationship then with the subject "women" was this intellectual project, and even then I wasn't really perceiving myself as someone who was interested in women's issues.

CB: But how did you choose to do a project on this subject, then?

JP: I started reading a lot of labor statistics—a field which I used to like, goodness knows why! I began to make discoveries of a new world, and I said, "I need to talk to someone about this, because it is like finding another continent." Recently I saw a woman I had known at the university, and she reminded me of how I was then. She said, "Jacqueline, I always remember you when you said, 'I have to talk to someone.' I told you I had a couple of friends interested in women's issues and that I would introduce you."

CB: What things made such a big impression on you among those statistics?

JP: Three things, really. One was that the percentage of women among the employers was close to zero. Another was the huge income gap between women and men, even at equal educational levels. The third thing was the numbers of women in rural areas that received no payment at all for their work. I realized there was a whole world of discrimination and power beneath those statistics, those cold numbers, that meant a lot.

BS: That there were people there.

JP: Yes, and unequal gender relations. The statistics were talking about inequality that I had not been aware of. My background focused on civil rights and democracy for peoples living under dictatorship with state violence, where people were tortured and then disappeared. This was another world, a new world, and I was very moved.

CB: This was in the early seventies that you discovered active women's groups in Brazil?

JP: Yes, three or four of us women didn't know what to do with this new continent that we were discovering. We started studying and we had assignments to read different things, but we still didn't talk about ourselves. It was an intellectual project: you read this, you talked about that. That was the origin of one of the first feminist groups in Brazil, the group that started my new life and built a new feminist identity.

BS: I am struck by where that all led, especially when I read about your important role in the late 1970s in such things as the attack on the so-called honor defense that provided many acquittals of justifiable homicide for men (but not for women) who murdered out of sexual jealousy or revenge. It was really a courageous thing to be out there on an issue that was so nationally charged and important. How did you become involved in that issue?

JP: When I was very young, five or six, my best friend was a neighbor called Angela. She lived next door, and we used to play together all the time. She grew up to be a beautiful woman, and one day she was murdered by her lover, with six shots to her face while she was sitting for a portrait. That murder in 1979 was a turning point in the history of recent Brazilian feminism. I would have been involved with it anyway, because it was a moment in which women in Brazil got together and said, "Enough of these acquittals." But I was also personally involved since she was my friend. Even though we took different paths and came to live in different worlds, the bonds were there. The case became a big cause, and women like me who knew her, as well as more who did not know her, slept outside the court building and held vigil there, asking for a second trial.

CB: At this time, what were the groups with whom you were doing this organizing?

JP: Actually, there were already a number of groups in the country for whom the issue of violence—including domestic violence and the use of the argument of legitimate defense of honor by defense lawyers to acquit men who murdered their wives—had been a platform for a few years. These groups had stemmed from an important meeting for International Women's Year in Rio de Janeiro in 1975, when we were still under dictatorship and were talking about power from another perspective. We organized that meeting with the help of the United Nations and spent a week discussing women and society in the context of democracy and overthrowing military rule. After that, a number of women at that meeting created ongoing groups. The first official Brazilian feminist organization, the Center for Brazilian Women, started from that; and I'm one of the founders.

Also, since we are discussing leadership, it is necessary to point out that despite the importance of our role in Angela's case, the battle still isn't over. We did manage to get a second trial, since in the first he was acquitted, or rather got a very light sentence. In the second trial, however, he was condemned. Still, as I said, the issue is not over. Only recently, my organization, CEPIA [Citizenship, Research, Information and Action], in Rio de Janeiro had a meeting on "crimes of honor." That is one of the things that it is important to understand about leadership. You always have to be ready to pick up once again the things you thought were already done. They are never done.

CB: How did you move from work with nongovernmental women's groups to become chair of the National Council for Women's Rights? How were you selected and what did it mean to you to take up a governmental and public role?

JP: You're chosen for certain things because, in one way or another, you have made people believe that you're able to cope with them. Maybe you should ask the people who thought I could do the job! I already had some visibility as someone committed to women's causes in my country, although I was working with science and technology as a researcher and at that time was not even running a nongovernmental organization. I had been a professor at the university, but I was so involved with women's issues at the time that I had some credibility in that world.

The other thing was adminstrative capacity. I just recognized that I had that once I became a formal administrator. You don't necessarily think about this ahead of time, but now when I think of myself, I notice that I am someone who is interested in concretizing things. I think very highly of administrative capacity, of being disciplined and organized and making things happen. This is something I have learned by doing.

CB: It was something you probably did in all the projects you've been describing.

JP: Yes, and we did it very well. Even now, I think the experience of the National Council [for Women's Rights] is recognized as unique in Latin America. The amount we achieved in less than five years is unbelievable.

CB: Let's talk about your experience in the National Council for

Women's Rights. You were in a country that had endured a long military dictatorship, and when it ended you were asked to head the council, which meant moving into government after a long time working against the government. What did it mean to you to take that kind of role, so very different than what you had done before?

JP: The first thing about it is that prior to being named to the post, I was involved in designing it. I had earlier discussed the need for such an organ and helped to shape it. We were there working on what this organ should be and not be. So what all this involved was creating a space for ourselves inside government.

What does it mean, generally, to talk about recovering the state, getting the state back? Isn't there a saying, "Women take back the night"? We said, "Let us civilians take back the state. This state has been in the hands of the military for so many years. We own part of it and we have the right to step into it and use it for our cause." I think that was the general feeling. "What is this? Why do we always have to have this divorce between civil society and the state? Why does the state machinery and everything have to be there always to serve others?" So that was the general background.

Women were better organized than any other group in Brazil, I think, at that moment. We dared more. We were the first nongovernmental, civil society group that proposed to use the state—this machinery from the inside—to take what I call that "astronaut's step." So in 1983 we started with the State Councils for Women's Rights, and in 1985 the National Council for Women's Rights. Because Brazil is a federal republic, the democratization process started with some elections for governors, and then the presidential election. Also we advocated the creation of police stations to attend to women victims of violence. This amounted to stepping into police territory.

So I think we women dared a lot, maybe because we have always been outsiders, so we have more freedom in taking steps and knowing where we want to go. So I see all this as just part of the reclaiming of the state, reclaiming it to enable us to use the state for our causes as women. We could do it at that moment, because it was a moment of democratization and change.

BS: In the United States, there's been a lot of discussion of styles of leadership, and the difference between women's and men's styles. Do you have any reflections about your own style and how you view what you did to get things done? That seems to me what you are saying when you describe your administrative capabilities—you are talking about a capacity to make things happen. Could you give us some sense of how you did that? What would you characterize as your own leadership style?

JP: If you want to do something big, it's not just you. You have to have people with you who see the common goal or objective. I think the most important thing in taking initiatives is to make people part of it so that all of them will feel that they are responsible. That is the only way you get things done in my experience. If you personalize too much, you can make an individual person move, but not an institution, not a large cause.

Let me give you an example of the difference I am talking about here. You can put someone in a position, but you run the risk that if that is all you do, the person will "vampirize" the position. That is a very strong word, but I've seen this happen. Individuals vampirize institutions for themselves. They can even reverse the momentum of a larger movement.

As for recognition, I think you get it (and everyone wants some reward, after all) when the institution you are involved with is growing and achieving the wider goals you set for it. But there are proper and improper ways to get recognition. When you vampirize the institution, it becomes empty, and yet for a time, anyway, all the "credit" goes to you. This is not my style. When I get involved with something, I want that cause, or that institution, to thrive overall. I know that if I succeed, I will be rewarded along the way; but I don't want to put it on myself. I've seen this happen, and it's terrible. People take the life blood of the institution for themselves; and they leave a desert behind, where nothing can grow. If you work to make something grow and to share the results with others, then the thing in itself has a life, not an eternal life, of course, but at least it is more solid. So I understand that leadership is related to the possibility of creating solid initiatives that last. You can go away, and the structures or whatever you have created remain, they are *there*.

CB: I think that's a brilliant description. Do you think that there's any way in which women are better able to do that, or not?

JP: I don't like to generalize, because I've seen a few women vampirizing. But I do believe that there's something about the way women are socialized to give to others that can help us refrain from vampirizing. Women are often socialized to be more humble about ourselves, to share more, and here that is an advantage.

BS: Let's move to the issue of education and the possibility of educating women to be leaders. This is an issue of great interest to the Institute for Women's Leadership. You once wrote: "We have to turn to the education system and we have to focus on the girl child. We have to focus on the mechanisms that will provide the girl child with self-esteem." Could you give us a sense of what you think it takes to educate for leadership and to encourage girls and young women to become leaders?

JP: Self-esteem is an important element. More and more, I believe that if you do not see yourself as someone with value, it is hard for you to give others a sense of value. The question is how? It is a problem because in our time, ideas about value in females are changing dramatically. For one generation, the value of women is on her virginity as well as on her capacity to be a good wife. There are different messages, then, about how to achieve female self-esteem, so one issue is what are the grounds of that self-esteem.

With feminism, those grounds are no longer identified as your sexuality—in particular your virginity—or even as your potential to serve others as a wife and mother. The emphasis is instead on your personal growth for a cause, a cause that involves other women. I think this is a big shift, a revolution really. The sense of value, the basis of self-esteem, has changed; the pillars have changed. This is very difficult because the definition has not changed in a homogeneous way. It has evolved as a new cultural value with new messages out there with the old ones, so identity is built on a multiplicity of messages.

I think that one of the main things for helping to educate women is to get them to understand that as adolescents and as adult women they will have to deal with these contradictions and ambiguities and multiple messages. If we give them a model that says "this way only," we are just repeating what has been done to us. So the key is dealing with ambiguity and yet guarding your self-esteem. It is complex.

Education can help women handle the complexity, to see the value in both equality and difference. You become very fragile when you are only prepared to deal with a certain kind of people and a certain set of values. Negotiation skills are very important here, and I would like to talk about them.

BS: Please do, because my next question was going to be, how do you teach leadership, or convey the skills necessary to be a leader?

JP: Negotiation is clearly one of them. What do I mean by that? Well, the whole idea of leadership has to do with building and then preserving something, right? If you want to build something, you have to know how to negotiate; and in order to negotiate, you need clear frontiers about what is nonnegotiable. So you require a certain sense of self-confidence to say, "No, I don't negotiate on this; but yes, I do on that." This gets us back to self-esteem, because you only negotiate when you know you are not losing any integral part of yourself. You can say, "Okay, this point can be conceded. Everyone does not have to think just like me." This is politics. We need to be clear, because the other thing is force, violence, and authoritarianism. A leader can be firm without being authoritarian.

CB: What you are describing is what we sometimes call the "transformative" model of leadership. I think there have always been good leaders who act this way. But so much of the focus on leaders in American society, and I assume in Brazil, has been the macho image of the individual, authoritarian leader (usually male, although Margaret Thatcher has been characterized this way too). I'd like to talk more about the transformational model of leadership—of enabling people to participate in civil society—in the public arena. Your work now is focused on how people exercise citizenship, which is central to leadership, to fostering leadership in other people. I'd like you to talk more about these ideas as reflected in your work, since they are a thread in your activity in the National Council and then again later, when you left government to work on building civil society. How do you envision creating that space for citizenship as the responsibility of the leader?

JP: When I talked about leading with equals, what I meant by equality there was really the old Greek idea of the polis, where you meet among equals. Of course we women, among others, were originally excluded from that polis.

BS: So we need a new polis.

JP: A wider polis, a wider ideal polis. This also includes the idea that the participating citizen can be part of history, can gain a deeper sense of why he or she is here in this world. The idea of transcendence for some is in religion, but for others, myself included, it is in being a political actor. I want to be clear that when I say "political" I mean nonpartisan. I have never had any importance in any political party, and I've never wanted to lead a life in terms of a political party. But I do see myself and my generation of feminists as highly political in the sense that we are all doing politics. And you only do politics by fostering this sense of entitlement and responsibilities for growth in civil society.

In Brazil, we have a saying that we are passing from the culture of "Please do me a favor" to the culture of "I have the right as a citizen." This has been happening to women, who have always been deprived of rights and have always had to ask for favors. This is the big revolution going on, and we are opening new doors.

I like to use the image here of a map of citizenship, as in geography. It can be a map in terms of nationalities, but it can also be a map within one country, where you have different zones of citizenship. For instance,

I think that in Brazil, the recognition of certain rights of women in terms of domestic violence is very advanced, but this is not so in terms of reproductive rights. So there are different frontiers for different zones of citizenship. It is always a challenge to be retracing this map and enlarging the territories where different rights are recognized.

BS: I'd like to talk more about the experience of a lot of young women today who want to be leaders, and tell us so, but who are really afraid of being labeled feminists. They don't see a relationship between being a feminist and being a leader. Can you comment on this? How do we help them understand that *feminism* is not an awful word?

JP: I think that this fear needs to be recognized as the fear of something that is very powerful. You are afraid of being labeled a feminist because a feminist is someone who is seen as very strong. It is not the same as being called a Republican or a Democrat or a Catholic! I don't know about the United States, but in Brazil to be a feminist is often to be placed in the category of denying men and children as well as denying values like compassion. These are the stereotypes.

I have been thinking a lot about this because I have called myself a feminist for years, and today there is talk about people who are "postfeminists," which I don't understand. In fact, I always say, "I'm not 'post' anything; I am still a feminist." To say "post" is to dismiss the strength of the phenomenon. Feminism has also been simplified in order to make it easier to ridicule. All the talk about "burning bras" is something I don't fully understand, but it is part of this effort to make feminists into people who are shocking. We don't have much time to be thinking about the stereotypes, because we know that feminism is not those things. In fact, the beauty of feminism is that it can be something different for Charlotte, for you, and for me. Being a feminist gives you a certain freedom to live it, to read it, and to re-create it.

For the new generation, this re-creation is an important issue, because our generation fought for some things that the new generation is able to take for granted. I think that one of our big challenges is to make them feel that although they are now in a safer world, nothing is guaranteed. They need to understand that the benefits did not come out of the blue, but that they came from political action. They should be prepared to start fighting again for these things, because all the time you can have backlashes.

CB: Is there something you would like to say to younger women about becoming involved in taking action that is feminist, or taking a leadership position in the public world today?

BS: Can you also add your reflections from when you held the Laurie

New Jersey Chair at Douglass College and were working here with the younger generation?

JP: When I was the Laurie New Jersey Chair, I had a very interesting group of students. They came from very different backgrounds and had different questions about the meaning of equality and democracy. Some of them were Cubans, a couple were from Irish backgrounds, one was from an Orthodox Jewish background. All were concerned about issues of liberty, freedom, and democracy, and all wanted to deal with women in these contexts that included their own origins. What I am trying to say is that what made them so interesting to me is that they all were putting issues of feminism, and gender relations, into a larger context of power relations.

In terms of leadership and educating women, I think we're talking about women taking a greater role in changing the world right now. It is important not to lose the connections between the different places women are starting from, their very different backgrounds, and the larger context of global change. What I am trying to do is to keep this connection always, because it is what enables women to understand that larger context and to see how their own particular situations fit into the larger picture.

BS: So this is what you were working on in the seminar entitled "Women, Power, and Social Change"?

JP: Yes, because women, power, and social change are all "macro" issues. As you have said many times, Charlotte, now that questions of gender have power because they have achieved widespread recognition, it is important that they be integrated into *all* issues. "Power," for example, should not be discussed in the absense of a gender perspective. The same goes for "democracy" and for "citizenship." These things cannot be discussed without a gender perspective. Then you can go subthematic and talk about violence, or health, or whatever. These are big things, and they need to be discussed with a gender perspective. This generation, in short, needs to take the next steps in this ongoing activity, by ensuring that deliberation on all major issues integrates a gender perspective.

CB: While we are discussing the Laurie New Jersey Chair as an institution that supports women's leadership by providing space and time for women to develop ideas, I would like to add a personal comment. I know that in my own case, coming to Rutgers and Douglass as an occupant of the chair really gave me the space to develop my ideas about a feminist perspective on human rights. I wonder if you might comment about what that space made possible for you, since it is rare for women to be able to get that sort of opportunity.

JP: Two different things. One has to do with the role of the teacher.

The other has to do with the chance I had to be immersed in the atmosphere of your Center for Women's Global Leadership, of the Institute for Research on Women, of Douglass College, and of the wider community of women at Rutgers involved in women's studies. This was in 1991–92; and at that time there was intense discussion of a whole variety of issues regarding gender, re-creating feminism, and building commitment to institutions that support new visions of society. I used to joke that I was like a fish in good water there, and the environment fed me well.

The teaching experience itself was valuable because most women who chose my seminar were thinking about power and change already. I was able to bring in other people to give lectures; and as it happened, most of them understood leadership in similar ways, as being immersed in a larger process and learning how to deal with that. They talked from their own perspectives about the importance of not personalizing leadership too much, of the dangers of not being able to be a leader of a larger process if you focus too much on yourself. With all this help I was able to convey the fact that leadership is political, that what is important is to understand what is going on by getting out of yourself a bit. There is a danger in all the self-conscious training of leaders, which is that they can become too self-centered and miss what is going on.

CB: Is there anything you would like to say about what, for you, has been the hardest part of being a woman exercising leadership, about being a woman in a public role?

JP: Family life and public life and my relationship with my family, my husband, and my children as they were growing up. Here was this wife and mother of theirs flying around Brazil, often being a continent away and someone they watched on TV. It was hard loving them deeply and not wanting them ever to feel that they were internally abandoned by me as well. Sometimes people say, "Why don't you run for . . . ," and I always say, "No," because now I couldn't possibly repeat the experience of being away from them. You see, when I was in the government, I had to live in Brasília, the capital of Brazil, while my home and my family were in Rio. I couldn't possibly do it again. When I came to Rutgers, I brought all of my children with me.

I hate to talk about sacrifices because you are usually in such a position because it is where you really want to be, it is something you believe in, it's rewarding, and so forth. But there is a cost. It was very hard to keep on going. There are moments in the life of your children that you cannot repeat; they are gone. For me it was a very high cost because I'm deeply involved with my children and they are very important emotionally for me.

At the same time, I had to be there, by myself, and I was often working twelve or fourteen hours a day. My family respected me and understood what I was doing, but it was a high price for them to pay.

The other thing was dealing with power itself. It has a cost. Visibility is rewarding and depriving, because there comes a moment when your face is so well known that you are afraid of being seen in public, or being seen someplace where it might be misinterpreted, so it creates a kind of prison. It is not, of course, like being a movie star, but it is there and it has a cost. Also, it can make you fragile because you might need to be seen, which is something else you have to be aware of. The thing I told myself when I began all this was that I wanted, when I left the National Council, to be like any other person and be able to continue to respect myself. So I tried very hard not to get contaminated with power, because that is very dangerous and it isolates you. Sometimes people don't approach you easily and are shy, while others approach you too much because they're interested in something. Both these things create a certain kind of loneliness around you.

And then, as I was saying, there is dealing with the power itself. My most difficult moments were when I had to confront two crucial issues: racial relations and sexuality. When Brazil was celebrating a hundred years of freedom from slavery, we in the National Council for Women's Rights decided we were going to launch a campaign that was called "Brazilian Black Women: 100 Years of Discrimination, 100 Years of Struggle for Dignity." We put up a tribunal to judge, symbolically, the crimes against black women; and that was considered against national security because racial issues involved national security. We went ahead and did the tribunal. It was very important, but it was also dangerous.

The other moment was when we started our campaign "Women's Health: A Right to be Conquered." The logo was a woman who was in the beginning of pregnancy, and you could see that very clearly. The point of the campaign was that to be a mother is not an imposition, or should not be an imposition, but rather a right involving choice. We were on a campaign for abortion, you see, and it was very difficult.

CB: What were some of the high points that made you feel proudest or happiest in your work as a woman leader?

JP: One of the joys is that in terms of family life, if you have a solid relationship based on love and respect, it survives. Yes, it can be hard, as I said; but I know now that we are together, and happy together, that my worst fears were not realized. My children do not feel that they were "marked" or anything like that!

The other thing is the Brazilian constitution. When I read our constitution, I can see right there something that we were struggling for. It is there, and that is because our constitution, in what concerns women, is one of the most advanced ones I know. I can say that we were part of that, we who were at the National Council at that moment, and we know that we were part of that. This is something that we have in our biographies. Now, the big challenge is how to diminish the gap between laws and realities, and that is a challenge forever. But we know that we changed laws in that country in a certain moment in its history, and that is something nobody can take away from us.

ANNA QUINDLEN

■

IN CONVERSATION WITH MARY S. HARTMAN AND RUTH B. MANDEL

A widely admired journalist, novelist, and social critic, Anna Quindlen was born in 1952 and raised in New Jersey. Before graduating from Barnard College in 1974, she had already begun work as a reporter at the New York Post. *In 1977, Quindlen joined the* New York Times *as a general assignment reporter, and in 1983 she was named the paper's deputy metropolitan editor. She wrote the "About New York" column from 1981 to 1983, created "Life in the 30's" in 1985, and later, until her retirement from the* Times *in 1994, wrote the weekly syndicated column "Public and Private." Quindlen is only the third woman in the paper's history to write a regular column for the Op-Ed page. She won the Pulitzer Prize for commentary in 1992; and a collection of her columns,* Thinking Out Loud *(1993), was on the best-seller list for more than three months.*

Many readers and colleagues were mystified when Anna Quindlen left the Times *to pursue a full-time career as a novelist. Her decision reflected a commitment to spend more time with her family as well as to reach audiences through a different medium with a message about the importance of families and the obligation of the public world of work to do a better job accommodating the needs of women, men, and children. She has written two best-selling novels,* Object Lessons *(1991) and* One True Thing *(1994); her latest,* Black and Blue, *came out in 1998. A feature film based on* One True Thing *has been made by Twentieth Century Fox. In addition, Quindlen is the author of two children's books,* The Tree That Came to Stay *(1992) and* Happily Ever After *(1997). She also wrote the text for the coffee table pictorial* Naked Babies *(1996).*

Quindlen declares herself fortunate to be living and working at this important moment in the history of feminism and of the relations between the sexes. It is this moment, she says, that has enabled her to forge a worldview from a fusion of the personal and the political, a fusion grounded in her experiences of single-sex education for women, the fast-paced world of journalism, and the richness of family life.

Anna Quindlen lives in Hoboken, New Jersey, with her husband and three children.

MARY HARTMAN: I'll begin by asking you about people in your life who made a difference, who helped you become a leader in your field and to make courageous choices—including the one to leave the *New York Times* and pursue your career as a novelist!

ANNA QUINDLEN: Part of the problem is that when we talk about leadership, we talk about it within what I think of as a very male model. We see leaders as CEOs, as members of the United States Senate, as the editors of large newspapers—people in the public eye. Yet if you ask women who set them on the path that moved them forward, many will tell you that their mothers did, or their fathers did. Their mothers may never have worked outside the home, or their fathers may have been plumbers or electricians—unknown in the greater world.

So when we talk about a female model of leadership, in particular, we're not necessarily talking about people who have risen to great heights, but instead people who have sort of sounded a clarion call for something really important, central and pure. My mother, who was not terribly educated or cerebral, was someone who by anybody's lights was a genuinely good person. She did not believe that you had to be gratuitously unkind to be honest. That's a quality of hers that has stayed with me. As deputy metropolitan editor at the *New York Times*, I found the people working with me would respond best to what I'd responded to best as my mother's daughter—constant encouragement, a sense that we were in this together, a sense that we all wanted to do the right thing, as opposed to a sense that I alone know what the right thing is. (I did think of them as working *with* me, as opposed to working *for* me, which I think is a female model of leadership.)

So we have to broaden the idea of leadership and acknowledge the extent to which leadership takes place on a micro level every day in our own homes. To the extent that leadership on a macro level is more like that of families, it is better, I think. It can take us more places that we need to go. I feel that a good family is the kind of model that can teach us everything we need to know about life and that a good organization works on the same principles as a good family. People have roles to play, various roles are accepted, and it's not necessarily hierarchical, although people have different amounts of power at different times. Two purposes are served here. One is that those exclusively involved with families do not feel as though they're doing devalued work, and those doing the supposed great work of the world will do it better if they take families more often as a model.

RUTH MANDEL: Assuming that people who have been conventional leaders in the public world have come from decent family backgrounds, why is there—based on what you're saying—a disjuncture between what they lived with in the family and the way they behave out in the wider world? Is it because the tasks are so different, or perceived to be so different?

AQ: No. It becomes difficult because traditionally we've taken as a leadership model a hierarchy which says one person gets to be the boss and send received wisdom to underbosses, who relay that wisdom to the people. In this fashion, American business has careened along perilously and poorly for a lot of the twentieth century. Finally, people are beginning to say, "How come this model doesn't work very well?" It doesn't work very well for two reasons. One is that a small coterie of guys, and I use that word intentionally, get most of the good stuff. The second is because, in a company, in a country, or in an organization, frequently it's the ordinary people who know the most about how things ought to work. If you want to know what's wrong with the welfare system in this country, I can tell you from experience that the best people to ask are those who have been on welfare. If you want to know how to build a better car on an assembly line in Detroit, the best people to ask are assembly line workers, not some vice president for engineering who comes up with an idea that assembly line workers know will never fly. So, over time, we're learning that a bottom-up management system frequently works better than a top-down one. Yet the way we socialize men, particularly, about seizing and holding hierarchical power positions makes such a new way of doing things very threatening.

One of the things that cemented my feeling that this was true was the study that you all did, Ruth, at the Center for the American Woman and Politics, showing that if you hold steady for ideology and party, women still function differently as elected officials than men. What they do is throw open the doors and say, "Oh gosh, you haven't been heard from in the political process; come give me your thoughts," or "Let's have this meeting open to the public so that we can hear people speak their minds." In other words, women were less invested in the idea "I am the boss here, and I will decide what to do" and more invested in the idea "Gee, I think we could do better all around if we listened to more people." We now have this happy confluence of a necessity for a new way of doing things, because of failures and disenchantment, and the availability of a way of doing things that reflects how women have traditionally got things done. So that when we look at the new millennium, women have a central contribution to make.

MH: I have to come back to the hope that education represents for those children not fortunate enough to have parents such as yours, or mine, or Ruth's. At the Institute for Women's Leadership, we're looking for ways to expand an understanding of good leadership and also to jump-start women's movement into key decision-making roles in many more arenas. With your intense commitment to education, and single-sex education in particular, could you comment on these settings as incubators for women's leadership?

AQ: Well, I feel as strongly as I ever did about education for women, and I mean single-sex education at some point during the continuum. The difficulty is partly a logistical one. When I talked with my oldest child about going to an all-boys' school, he told me that schools just for boys were unhealthy. I happen to agree. I think women's schools tend to reinforce the best things that we want to reinforce in girls, and that boys' schools—I know this is a gross generalization here—sometimes reinforce the worst things about being a man. So how can we put girls by themselves and have boys be with girls? A thorny issue. But I do think at certain times in their lives, and it's a different time for different girls, it is helpful for them to be in an all-female atmosphere. Once I'd spent some time at Barnard, anybody who tried to tell me that women couldn't do anything was in trouble!

MH: Did you go there initially because it was a women's college?

AQ: Yes, I did. I went to visit Barnard and I came home and said, "Well, that's it." Needless to say, my parents were thrilled at the idea that I was going to 116th Street and Broadway for college just after the Vietnam War riots. But it was the best thing that ever happened to me because I had these incredibly strong, powerful, women professors. I mean, I had Kate Stimpson for freshman English. At the end of that semester I just said to myself, women can run the world.

MH: Talk to us about the senior in high school that you were, the one who made the decision to go to a women's college. How common was that among your peers?

AQ: You know, I don't think it was problematic because the Seven Sisters were still overwhelmingly female, and I applied to college the first year that Princeton was accepting women. There wasn't this general sense that if you were a good student, you could go to the Ivies. I think I was more feminist than most high school seniors at that time, and the reason was simple. I became a feminist not to make the world a better place for women but to make it a better place for *me*. I felt that I was smart and capable and that despite that, the guys were going to get all the good stuff, which was unfair. So I did this out of complete self-interest; but I must say I developed a profound sense of sisterhood by the time I left Barnard. That sense only got greater—first at the *New York Post*, where many of the reporters were not only women but generous feminists, and second at the *New York Times*, where a whole group of reporters had been hired in response to the class action suit brought by six of the women at the paper. Now that's what I call leadership, even completely disinterested leadership, because none of those women has ever been on the masthead of the *New York Times*, and some of them arguably didn't have the careers they might have had because of that suit. I know from having talked to some of them that they said to themselves, this isn't going to be so wonderful for us, but it's going to make the world safe for the ones coming up. I was one of the chief beneficiaries of that suit.

At a certain point there is a fork in the road. You can either think of yourself as the smartest little girl who ever came down the pike, or you can think of yourself as the lucky beneficiary of the hard work of generations of women who have gone before you. With that class-action suit so directly affecting my career, I didn't feel I had any option but to go the second way, which then gave me a responsibility to pass it on. I don't think women like me have an option when they're approached by younger women: "Gee, can you write me a letter about how you got started; can you come and talk to a group of us at the journalism or law school?" If I didn't do things like that, well, that's a mortal sin, not a venial sin! I do things like that so that somebody someday will do them for *my* daughter.

RM: As I hear you talk about the class-action suit at the *Times*, and about Barnard, I realize that unlike the women I interviewed ten years ago, who came from a "pre-reemergence"-of-feminism experience, you are speaking as someone from the generation that began to benefit from a feminism in its early stages as a reemerged social movement. But getting back to leadership in a more conventional sense, let's acknowledge that you went to Barnard with a lot of other talented young women and that you're not the only journalist who worked at the *New York Post* and the *New York Times* in that generation. What made you different? Did other Barnard women there with you go on to, quote, "become leaders"?

AQ: There's lots of "name" people who were at Barnard around that time. Ellen Futter [former Barnard president, now head of the Museum of Natural History] was two classes ahead of me, and Ellen practically defines the word *leader* at this point. Mary Gordon was two years ahead of me. Jackie Barton may win the Nobel Prize for chemistry. Barnard turns out leaders with some regularity. But what happened to me, Ruth, was a combination of two things. Somebody said to me the other day that when you ask women about why they've done well, they tend to be self-effacing, and I'm about to do that. But let me preface it by saying I'm good at what I do; that's one of the main reasons I've done well. I can string one word in front of another in an idiosyncratic and interesting way.

I also happened to be at the right place at the right time. My two predecessors on the Op-Ed page, Ann O'Hare McCormick and Flora Lewis, were both women who prospered covering foreign affairs in the newspaper business at a time when to move ahead as a woman in the newspaper business, it was essential that you did not make too much of being a woman. People could then say, "Hey, she's just one of the guys." To some extent that was true of me when I first got started in the business. I had a very free and easy "Cover that? Sure, let me get my notebook and go out." I have a real newspaper personality in that whatever comes up, I'm saying, "Let's do it; let's do it fast; if we don't get it right today, let's get it right tomorrow." That's why I love the business.

By the time that I was doing a column, the tenor of the times seemed to me to make the world safe for a woman who said, "You know what, I think I feel differently about this because I'm female. I have some experiences I want to tell you about that my male counterparts haven't had. There's some issues that they're not as interested in as I am, and maybe it's because they're issues that really affect women." I also think I was good enough at taking the measure of the times—and unafraid enough of what people would say about me—to go full speed ahead. That's why I think some women really responded to my column, and some men too. There was this sense of "This woman is doing something that we haven't seen people do before on the Op-Ed page of newspapers in general and of the *New York Times* specifically. Not only because few women are doing opinion columns, but because she's saying unabashedly some things about her own life and about connecting those things to the political." I mean, I was *raised* on the idea that the personal is the political. I think most people think of great issues in terms of the personal being political, whether it's saying "I don't want to spend my tax dollars on x, y, and z," or "I'm not willing to send my son or my daughter to Bosnia," or "If I got pregnant and didn't want to be, this is what I'd like to have the option to do."

So it seemed ridiculous to me that ordinary people would think about issues any other way. But when you became an opinion columnist, you sanitized your thinking of all of that. I don't think as a female columnist I would have been able to do what I did twenty years ago, and I don't know if it'll be necessary to do it twenty years from now. Yet at that particular moment, I felt I could do it. I think I took the pulse of the time pretty well. I also had a really good role model in Ellen Goodman, who is almost the first person since the revived women's movement who wrote that kind of column unabashedly.

MH: I was not surprised by the validation women everywhere felt in reading your columns; but what did surprise me was that so many men readily admitted to being your fans as well. Men told me they cut out your columns and put them on their refrigerators and that they read them aloud to their friends. It was almost as though they could finally admit to having feelings and thoughts like this since they appeared in the *New York Times*!

AQ: What you find out when you talk to guys about material like I was writing is that a lot of them are in the closet hating traditional standards of masculinity. When I decided to quit my job at the *Times* and do what I did, there was a significant group of men who thought that I'd lost my mind, but there were also these guys who would sidle up to me and say, "Good for you. That's what I always wanted to do and didn't." Now given how most men responded to what I did—thinking I was crazy—I could only imagine how they would have responded if a *male* colleague had done the same thing.

But the other thing is, traditional standards of masculinity ask people to live horrible lives. You read the [Robert] McNamara book, *In Retrospect*, and no matter what you think about why he wrote this book or what he said, it is an object lesson in how lonely and hard and horrible it can be to conform to traditional standards of masculinity. You're not supposed to admit doubt about even the greatest issues. You're never supposed to listen to your heart, only your head. And once you've made a decision with your head, you are never allowed to look back and say, "Maybe we'd better take a second look at that one." You're supposed to do all this within a framework of not having time to touch base with what for many of us is the great solace of our existence, our family life.

One of the things that I learned from the way in which men would respond to the column is that we're at a perfect moment to say "Now it's time to talk about raising our sons more like our daughters." If you look at all this as a diagram, with the way men live over *here*, and the way women live over *there*, what we seem to have been doing over the last twenty-five years is moving the women all the way over to where the men were and not moving the men at all. The whole point of the revolution was supposed to be to create a new paradigm in which women changed certain things about their lives in the public world, and men changed certain things about their lives at home. But the second part of that change has taken up very little of our time and space and thought. It's where we need to go to make things not only better for men, which I'm intensely interested in as the mother of two sons, but to make them better for women, who often are doing two jobs now, the one outside the home for which they get paid and the one at home for which they don't.

RM: That may be because that second part of the change is immeasurably tougher to accomplish. I remember back in the seventies there was an album, *Free to Be You and Me,* that Marlo Thomas produced; and a song called "It's All Right to Cry" was directed at little boys. There was a fair amount of attention in those days to giving little boys dolls to play with and fewer sex-stereotyped messages. If we've made little progress, it's because of the forces that are lined up against that kind of progress. As mothers and sisters, we don't want to humiliate our sons and our brothers and send them out into the world to be laughed at.

Going back to what you said before about the McNamara book, do you think that's part of Bill Clinton's problem, that he's one of those little boys?

It seems to me that what he does is look at his heart more than some others, and that some of the trouble that he has may be due to that. For instance, one of the things that drives me crazy is that he has been hit so much for not being decisive. The stereotype, after all, says you must get up and say what you've concluded, that it's final, it's for all time, and you're never going to change your mind. If you don't do it that way, you can't be a leader. Clinton likes to listen to a lot of people; he's not always sure and may give the impression he cannot decide anything.

AQ: I agree that listening to a lot of people is a desirable trait, but you want to know at base that there are core principles, something the person stands for. When I analyze Bill Clinton, which I do all the time, I always see him as a classic adult child of an alcoholic. One of the prototypes there is the person who never wants to make anybody angry, who really wants to keep everybody happy.

MH: But isn't that something we say more often about women too?

AQ: Yes. I guess I mean that one of the problems with the dynamic for the American public has been that when you come down to it, Hillary has more of what we think of as stereotypically masculine traits, and Bill has more of what we think of as stereotypically feminine traits, and that's what has caused the dis-ease about her in some people's minds.

RM: And what makes it look as if the American public isn't ready to accept that kind of male leader, the kind that he is.

MH: I saw a bumper sticker recently with a message that is to the point here. It said, "Impeach Clinton and her husband."

AQ: That reminds me, I attended a women's ordination conference, where I saw a button that says, "Either ordain women or don't baptize them." I immediately said, "I want one!"

RM: On a related issue, I'm stuck on how we all talk about "different" models of leadership. After working for many years on issues of women and politics, I just don't see any room out there in the political world for these models—not in the way that money is raised, not in the way campaigns are waged, not in the way political institutions operate, not in the seniority systems, despite some changes in recent years. I don't see how the so-called new models of leadership will allow anyone to get in there and lead.

AQ: Which argues for a new way of running campaigns, of raising money, of presenting yourself to the public—which is something that the public dearly wants but doesn't know exactly why. They just know that the system we now have is deeply unsatisfactory.

MH: The people who know that system best are the most discouraged about change. Geraldine Ferraro was the commencement speaker at Douglass College a while back, and I asked her if she would ever run for office again. She said, "I may, but I'm still paying the bills for the senatorial campaign." She doubts that we'll ever change how much it costs to run.

RM: It is just impossible, too, to be unaffected by what it costs you to raise the money the way it's always been done. Yet if you don't, you don't make it in.

AQ: I know; I think that's a huge difficulty, not just for women but for everybody.

RM: But in the corporate arena, too, don't you think that "doing things the way they have always been done" is a difficulty there as well?

AQ: Not necessarily. I think there are more ways to play the angles in the corporate arena, given the women I know who have risen very high up in there.

RM: You think it's possible, for instance, to become a CEO, or close to a CEO, not learning the ropes, not operating in the system, not using the institutional modes that are familiar and that have been handed over? When I think about higher education, which I know better than the corporate world—and Mary and I have sat on many high-level search committees there and in the nonprofit world—here is what I see. You can put people like us on these committees, and yet there are forces of tradition, assumptions, and value systems and credentialing that are so massive, so weighty, that the thought that anyone a little different can get through all that can just disappear in front of your eyes.

AQ: Yes, but increasingly, Ruth, I visit colleges run by women, which would have been unthinkable even ten or fifteen years ago. I have to tell you, when I was in the Barnard search, the most cheering part of the entire thing was how many great women there were out there at levels that made it absolutely simple to think of them as presidents of a college.

The other thing we confront, the question that angers me the most, is: Isn't it true that women are their own worst enemies and that the people who do in women in the public arena are other women? That is such bull. I just happened to be with a woman who is a regent at a large state university that's looking for a president, and she said, "We don't have a woman in the search"; and I said, "Oh, have I got a woman for you!" They're looking at her now. Whatever comes of that, I know we do help each other, we know one another, we look out for one another. That's going to be less true as there get to be more of us, because one of the reasons we all know each other is because there's so few of us, right?

But returning to the issue you raised before about the corporate world, you always climb up the ladder on bodies. The question is: Do you climb it on the bodies of those you have vanquished or on the bodies of those with whom you have cooperated and given help and support, who *let* you step on their backs on the way up? A lot of the women I know who have done very well in corporate life are the second type.

I think the reason I have continuing goodwill within the *New York Times* is that when I was deputy metropolitan editor, I worked hard to say to reporters, "You did a great job on that. What would you like to do for your next assignment?" I already had the job, I had the job title, I didn't need to prove anything about myself, and I didn't look at my colleagues as potential competitors. I looked at them and thought, "We're going to put out a good newspaper." I don't know if that's gender specific. I sure sometimes feel like it is. I ran that desk when the metropolitan editor was on vacation for a month and the turf wars at the *Times* were intense. Other desks would come and say, "Can I borrow so-and-so?" because metro had the biggest group of reporters. You were supposed to say no, no, no. Your bodies were your power base. But that wasn't good for the reporters. When I took over the desk, the line on me was, "She gives away the store."

When they came and said, "We'd like Maureen Dowd to cover the presidential campaign," I said, "Take her. She's going to do a great job, she's going to be really happy, it's going to be good for the readers." But then they'd say, "Gee, she gave away Maureen Dowd. Was she out of her tiny mind?" Maybe there is something in us that wants to make our people happy; anyway I liked making them happy. But as important, I thought I got better work out of everybody when they were happy. They turned out terrific copy, and when they turned out terrific copy, that made me look better.

RM: So there is some other way you keep talking about leadership that has something to do with family, group, or team. Yet women are always given a bum rap that goes: "You don't know sports, you never work in teams, you don't understand how it feels to win for the team, and that's why you haven't achieved, that's why you haven't become leaders."

AQ: That's nonsense. I've been on a team my whole life. I'm the oldest of five children and the mother of three now. I've played shortstop, catcher, pitcher, every sports term you want to use. Not only do I know how to run the team, I know how to feed the team, clean the team, and get the team motivated. That's a nonsense rap on women. In fact, I think we're better team players than men because we're not so invested in being the captain. They can sling around those sports metaphors all they want, and I'll come up with my labor room metaphors and my dirty laundry metaphors. We can play dueling metaphors!

RM: Is that partly what makes you different, that as you said before, when you talked about your column, you're not ashamed to appeal to female experience? Most women, after all, don't get up and do the labor and the women-specific experiences because they aren't valued as highly as the images the guys use of the golf game or the football game.

AQ: Well, I think there's an important part of women's leadership right now that I feel keenly. That is that if you are in a safe place, if you are secure in your job or in your personality, if they need you more than you need them, you have almost a moral obligation to rub their faces in the realpolitik of what women's lives are like and what they need to be like. When you have somebody like me who's not going to get busted down to private anytime soon, you've got to say to them, "Presence doesn't equal productivity, and I'm walking out of this meeting because I've got to relieve the baby-sitter." You can't say, "I have another meeting," because telling the truth makes it easier for women who are not in as safe a place. It also makes it easier for a male colleague to say, "I'm with her. We've been talking about this for two hours, and I've got a daughter with a soccer game."

I think that whenever there's this verboten territory and you're in an ideal position to bring it out of the closet a little bit, you really have to do that. I think that one of the great recent leadership examples has been Ann Richards being so matter-of-fact about her alcoholism—in a way that I'm not sure a male elected official would have been. In a sense she had no choice; but once she had become as popular and beloved as she was, she realized that for her to say "I am who I am and I'm also an alcoholic" was very powerful for people who had problems with alcohol. She was clearly such a wonderful person that it was a powerful leadership lesson. [Congresswoman] Patty Murray has done that when she's talked about the difficulties of being a single mother. Pat Schroeder has been really good about always taking the opportunity to say, "Hey, this is how things are for us." So I think what I am calling "the safe-place effect" is really important for women and leadership.

MH: Let's talk about that safe-place effect in terms of where you are now and where you used to be. When I heard your talk at Douglass, you were saying that the decision to leave the *New York Times* was not as hard for you as many might think. Can you tell us what you did that *was* hard, when you think back on those moments when you made choices about exerting your leadership, times when you weren't in such a safe place? Are there examples of things of which in retrospect you would say, "Yes, that was a very tough thing for me to do but I thought it through and I did it," or has your sense been that you get into a situation and are able to make decisions without a lot of agonizing? You seem to be so capable of sizing up a situation in a hurry and making an appropriate decision that I think it takes a lot of people's breath away. Is it harder than it looks, I guess, is what I'm asking?

AQ: Don't forget I spent my entire life in a business in which we size up a situation over the course of twenty-four hours and put it into print for all the world to read, on microfiche into perpetuity. It sort of comes naturally to someone in the newspaper business. You spend your whole professional life saying, "Okay, we've got five reporters, we're sending them here. This is how we're going to play this story." So that's been a big part of my life. But I think what I mentioned before, [about] when I was deputy metropolitan, is relevant here.

I was the highest-ranking woman in the news department, and I knew that people would be watching me. I also knew that it would be easier in some ways to just do everything the way the guys did, even if that didn't seem natural or sensible to me. I thought a lot about whether I could afford to do things differently. Ultimately it just seemed to me that I had to do it in the way that worked for me and in the way I thought it worked best for the newsroom. I really didn't feel that traditional management standards worked very well for the newsroom. But I thought long and hard about that, and I was nervous. It was a decision that was very hard for me.

I was six months pregnant when I was promoted to that job, which I did for three months before taking a six-month maternity leave. I was not going to be dissuaded from that. Some might say, "Well, if you're going to take on that kind of leadership role when you're pregnant, you ought to cut the leave back to six weeks." But I took the six months and came back; and four months later I was pregnant with our second—happily, intentionally, and despite all the comments about my being Catholic. I thought long and hard about that, too, because I worried that they were going to make me stand for all women, that they were going to say, "Well, we try to promote them and look what happens." I have to tell you, if those guys had thrown up their hands and said, "Oh my God, what is she trying to do?" I wouldn't have blamed them a bit. It's very strange and confusing; and as soon as I got pregnant the second time, I knew I was going to quit when the baby was born. I could immediately see that I wasn't going to be able to hold this whole thing together. So that was something else that I thought long and hard about.

Now, about the decision to leave my column, when people raised their hands at speeches and said, "How could you do this to us?" I was reminded that there's a rich tradition of women being altruistic, whether in giving up their core self to serve a family or in taking on professional roles that don't serve their private selves for the sake of women everywhere. I didn't want to fall into either trap. I knew I was fine on the first one and decided that I was going to be fine on the second, that I would do my best to see that all women weren't tarred with my brush. But by God, I wanted to have a whole mess of little kids, and I didn't have that much time to do it. Once I had them, I wanted to be one of the two pivotal figures in who they would become, and I had to change my professional life to do that.

RM: What understanding or knowledge do your kids have of how well known you are in the world and about these choices that you have made?

AQ: I don't think they experience the full impact of it. It's common for someone to stop me on the street when they're with me and say something, but that's one person. They have never been in a lecture hall filled with people who came to listen to me. They got a first taste of it, I suppose, when I got an honorary degree at Dartmouth not long ago. They said all those things that they say as they're investing you and everything; and the kids were sitting there. It was quite different from what they're used to with me.

My husband and I made a decision to insulate them from most of that. Readers are entitled to the words that I put down on the page; but I don't like it when someone gets right down in my little girl's face and says, "Do you want to be a writer like your mother when you grow up?" I think, "What she wants is to pick her nose and be left in peace."

RM: Has it been hard for your children at all?

AQ: I don't think so, you know, but maybe the time will come. My kids are really interested in writing and they do a lot of writing. At a certain point, maybe being a fledging writer and being my son or daughter is not going to be so wonderful, or maybe it'll be a huge help. You can never quite gauge how those things are going to go.

RM: In a way it's a new dilemma and a new set of choices for women who have achieved so much and become leaders to make these decisions about how they're going to relate to their children on that issue and how they're going to protect them. You see it again in the Clintons with Chelsea.

AQ: What a spectacular job they've done. Here's a kid that everyone agrees is a terrific kid, and I think they have hit the balance perfectly. Having visited that house, which is sort of a cross between a Southern mansion and a federal penitentiary, raising a kid to be able to go to soccer, spend the night with friends, and grow up healthy and grounded—whoa! I have to applaud them for that.

RM: It must take a lot of effort to be sure that she's not in the public eye all the time.

AQ: It really does, and the public has kind of collaborated with them. I think there's backlash against the unveiling of every foible and blip on the screen for every public figure.

But there *is* part of myself that's out in the world that I don't want to insulate my kids from, especially the boys. I like my sons to know that I have strong opinions and am not afraid of airing those opinions, particularly not because I was born female. You know, the number of words that just apply to outspoken women is amazing. I was just going to refer to myself as "mouthy." No one uses that term for a man. They don't use "bossy" or "feisty" either. All these are words that denote women doing things that we covertly don't believe women should do: speaking out, taking charge, trying to lead things.

You know, I've never for a moment wanted to be male. I wanted to be a woman with all the rights and privileges of a human being, which is what I think being a feminist means. To the extent that I've said that publicly in a variety of ways in print, I like my kids to know what I do. I just don't want them ever to be in a situation where they feel that they're adjuncts of me or that they're there to take the edge off, like, "Oh, you know she has been very strong-minded about the war, but look at these three nice children." You know, the celebrity who has her kids on the cover of the magazine to show that "Gee, I did this and that, but look! I also gestated." I find that offensive because it asks us to prove our bona fides in a way that we shouldn't have to do and that men don't have to do.

MH: Someone once asked about the basketball net that we put up in the backyard of the dean's residence at Douglass, which is located in the middle of the campus. The person was told, "Oh, that's for Dean Hartman's son"; to which he replied, "*She* has a *son*?" as if somehow this known feminist must be physically incapable of producing a male child.

RM: Do you see in your sons any difference because you're their mother? (This is picking up on that challenge that Gloria Steinem has thrown out about concentrating on our sons.)

AQ: I have tried to raise feminist sons from day one. They recognize sexism. There'll be an ad on TV with a woman talking about fabric softener, and they'll say, "That's sexist; it assumes only women do laundry." You know, simple, basic stuff. All of our children are going to be different, though, because they see so many role models around them.

My favorite story about my guys is about one of my good friends, who for many years was their pediatrician. We were driving home from her office in the car one day, and Christopher said, "You know, Quin, I think when I grow up I might like to be a doctor." And Quin said, "Oh, don't be ridiculous, Christopher; only girls can be doctors." And I thought, "My god, now there's a sea change." They *do* have this sense that, "Oh yeah, there was a woman on the Supreme Court, and then there were all those women in the Senate, and then there was this woman who ran this company, and then there was my mother who was a columnist, and then there were these women editors she worked with." I think that that will make them different.

But asking your children to be different is the hardest thing you ever do. That's why it's difficult to raise feminist sons and to say to them, all the time, "You know, you might want to marry somebody who would work outside the home and you would stay home and take care of the kids." I do the lion's share of child rearing and domestic affairs around here, so that if they get their cue by watching what's going on, then they get the cue that women do that. Quin said to me once, "I think women can do every-thing, I mean, look at you; you write your column and you take care of us all the time." It sounded like a really nice thing, but when I deconstructed it, I thought, "Uh, oh, this guy's going to go out and look for another woman who can do everything." So we've had to talk a lot about it.

I think that's the key to it all. We talk all the time about sex-role stereo-types, about why people do what they do, about how satisfying child rearing can be but how society doesn't value it enough. They do have one set of friends whose father is the one who cares for the kids and does the cooking and cleaning and the mother works outside the home in a pretty high-powered position. I think that's been a good thing for them, and I can see in some essential ways they're different. They're different in the way they see men and women and in the way they see blacks, whites, Latinos, and Asians. They have more of a melting-pot mentality than I ever did. They go to school and live in a neighborhood with people of color; I went to an all-white school and lived in an all-white neighborhood.

MH: Let's pursue that one a minute. You've been talking about change and how rapid some of it has been in one generation. I've had similar ex-periences as you describe. The coed school my son goes to has kids of many colors and backgrounds, and I also went to a school where kids were all one color.

I once heard Eleanor Holmes Norton comparing the challenges around race with those around gender. She said that if we put our minds to it, we could solve the challenges around race in about twenty-five years. The gen-der challenges, she said, are tougher and will take much longer, perhaps a century or more. I'm interested in your views on how long you think it's going to be, for example, before we have women in equal leadership positions in our key institutions. When will we have a woman president; and when we do, will our homes be transformed as well? Are you writing about any of this in your next novel?

AQ: Yeah. I'd say over the next hundred years we're going to work through a lot, but it's going to take that long, and even then it won't be done. I wouldn't even blue-sky the woman president thing, and that's not a good measure anyhow. The measure should be how commonplace misogyny is, how sanctioned it is, and the kind of one-on-one rapprochement we've reached with our male colleagues, at home and at work. I think the big challenge of the next twenty-five years is going to be this piece of bringing men along to some middle place in this new paradigm. But that's hard. Changing hearts and minds is harder than making legislation; and one does not necessarily guarantee or presage the other. So that I think that one hundred years is what we're looking at. But when we think of how huge the change has been in the last twenty-five, it's astounding. All our assumptions about how we live have changed in twenty-five years, which is nothing in the grand span of history.

MH: Yes. I've always been so grateful to be part of this particular set of years, to have witnessed and participated in so much positive change for women.

AQ: People have said to me, "Are you angry?" I say no, I've been *privileged* to live in the most exciting time to be a woman. If I had had this personality fifty years ago, I don't know what would have happened to me! It would have been horrible. That's what I'm writing about, Mary. I'm writing about women—and men, too—over time, but I'm writing about those sometimes pernicious ways that women have exercised power because the system was set up to forbid them to exercise it in more direct ways. I am writing about ways women exercised power over their families, power that was sometimes crippling, and also those ways in which men feel like women. I wrote about a man who feels his life is totally controlled by women—his secretary, his wife. He says he feels women have cornered the market on tears, leaving men with nothing but a deep and abiding sadness that they can neither acknowledge nor understand. I really think some men have this sense.

There's another man, later on, who says he keeps hearing how men run the world, but he thinks women do. Women in his life decide what chairs are in his house, what dinner's going to be on his table, what time he's going to get up in the morning. You know, men might have what we think of as the big power, but that little power over the details of daily life is completely controlled by women. Now, is that real power? We might say no, but it is real in terms of how life is lived day to day and how men often feel, as though in some odd way their lives are beyond their control. That is why men say, "Where's the salt?" when they know perfectly well where the salt is. A woman asked me the other day, "What do you think is the biggest difference between men and women? Just oversimplify." I said, "Learned helplessness." Learned helplessness gives the sense, for lack of a better term, of impotence, that can make men very angry. Some of that is what I'm writing about—different kinds of power. Subtler, more traditional kinds of power, I guess.

RM: I was following in this direction to the so-called angry white male phenomenon, including the angry recent response to affirmative action. But the image you have about the next century is really optimistic. I keep saying, "But Anna, it's harder than this and it's tougher than that," and you keep coming back with, "Look, there are women here and there; there's so much positive change." Yet we're at a moment when messages from all directions are saying men are threatened, cornered, and angry. I've heard them interviewed on NPR: "I'm not going to let my son go through this kind of experience," and so on.

AQ: His son won't *have* to go through that experience because what happens is that once you've had an assumption of privilege and you lose that assumption, you confuse it with being underprivileged. Somewhere between assumption of privilege and being underprivileged is the reality of life for the embattled white man now. That is, that he used to be able to make certain assumptions about his stature in the community based on nothing more than an accident of birth, just as we women used to be able to make certain assumptions about our *lack* of stature based on nothing more than accident of birth. It's having to change those assumptions that's been difficult and painful for men. I'd be angry too. But the son of that man is going to grow up without such an assumption of privilege and, therefore, without the same anger, since he won't feel as though he's lost anything. If he looks at it carefully, he'll find that he really has gained something, because while his father bemoans the loss of 100 percent of a certain kind of pie, he'll wind up with only 70 percent, which is is better than you deserve, no matter how you slice it! This is a critical moment in the life of this country in terms of attitudes about fairness. With any critical moment you have people who are angry, who want to go back, and who think that they're getting a raw deal. But we're going to move beyond this, and very soon.

RM: Ten years of this agony is what you as an optimist say we're going to have to go through on issues of fairness.

AQ: Ten to fifteen years, and it won't have the same level of bile that it has now.

MH: Given that you've already stated that we need to spend a lot more time looking at young men and what we're saying to them, what kinds of things do you think we should be saying to young women? I've now seen several generations of women students at a college for women, and I think that they are finally coming out of a long period in which they wanted no association with the term *feminism* into a period in which they are much readier to call themselves feminists and, far more important, to act on feminist goals. At the same time, I get the sense that they're beginning to feel a little sorry for young men. I'm seeing this and I'm wondering, how big a trend is this? It's a very difficult issue to address, because you want to strengthen young women's goals, interests, abilities, and courage. At the same time, you want to tell them that it's all right to be supportive of their male friends. Something to celebrate in this generation of young women is that they have lots more male friends than our generation ever did, and that's likely to help them tremendously. But it's a tough balancing act. What do you think is going on?

AQ: Well, I think young women already intuit something I tried to talk about in a speech when I mentioned the letter a friend wrote to Paul Tsongas when Tsongas found out he had cancer. It said, "No man ever said on his deathbed, 'I wish I'd spent more time at the office.' " I think young women understand that their range of choices still allows them more of a life outside the office than men's, which will mean none of the kind of regret that is summed up in that sentence. Their male friends are still less open to those choices. It's only when they look back on their lives, or perhaps when their fathers look back on their lives, that they say, "Why did I spend so much time running in place and so little time with my children?" Over and over you read encomiums from older men who either say, "I didn't spend enough time with my children, but I'm spending it with my grandchildren," or "I didn't spend enough time with the first set of children, but now that I have a younger wife and am getting a second chance, I'm doing it right." To which you want to say, "Hey, I'm one of the first set of children; I'm not so happy about your epiphany here."

When I realized I was going to be part of a generation of women living this rich life in the world and yet spending a good deal of time also raising children in what seemed to be an impossible balancing act, I was angry that the guys weren't stepping up to the plate. I think I went through all the stages of terminal illness: anger, denial, and at a certain point, a sense of sadness, because I can tell you unequivocally that when my time on earth is done, I will not only have done everything I wanted to do in the world, I will have done everything I wanted to do in my life with my children. I think lots of men still can't say that, and to me that's the greatest failure. It makes my blood run cold to think of looking at my children and thinking, "Well, I blew that one." So I understand why young women have this kind of sympathy for the men that they know. I think they intuit some of this.

But you've got to communicate to them that no one's going to give them anything. It's going to be a fight every step of the way. Some of the fights are so silly and petty that they're not going to be worth pursuing, and you should probably pass on them. Some are going to be really important, and you're going to have to find a way to fight them without losing your soul. A friend told me the biggest bill of goods a women's college sold us was the idea we would be taken seriously. But it wasn't such a bill of goods, because it taught us inner strength. You pull that strength out of your pocketbook as you're doing what you have to do. I think that's the thing that we should say to young women, that there's still plenty of guys out there who, covertly or overtly, think you're second-rate. You're going to have to deal with that by proving yourself first-rate—often even better than your male colleagues. You are going to be competing in time, energy, and ideas with men who will have lives you do not because they have wives and you do not. You're going to have to find strategies to deal with that. Also, whether or not you call yourself a feminist—and I don't care what you call it as long as you do it—we are serious about this choices stuff.

If you look at your first baby and think, "The job I really want, and that I can afford, is to raise this child to full man- or womanhood," we're behind you on that, but what we want you to understand, if you're counting on your husband's income to make that possible, is that men leave, and that men die. The most important thing you ever do for your children is to be able to take care of them emotionally, spiritually, psychologically, and financially. It's hard. It's all going to be hard. It's all been hard, from beginning to end. And yet for me it's all been so great that I wouldn't trade my life for anything.

RM: You talk a lot about your decisions around children. What about your relationship with your husband? I don't want to pry into anything; I wouldn't be able to get away with it with you, anyway. But did you magically meet someone where a meeting of the minds and hearts and values made it work this way for you, so that it's not a struggle?

AQ: Oh, no, no, it's always a struggle. Do we know anybody who's married and it's not a struggle? I don't. My husband and I met when we were very young, so we grew on a lot of these issues together. Luckily, what he saw was what he got. It wasn't like he had this sweet, self-effacing girl who suddenly turned into Madame Curie. I was always like this. I think my husband is often as confused and embattled as any man coming of age under this changing of the rules, and I also think that he's more aware of being a beneficiary than many are. The question of an egalitarian marriage is complicated for us by my being a kind of public figure. We still don't have a way of dealing with the man who is married to a public figure, as opposed to a woman being married to one. Still, I don't think we would have lasted three dates if my husband weren't a feminist and didn't take me seriously.

RM: So are the two hardest parts, as you've just suggested, struggling to find that balance and this issue of the husband of a publicly recognized and acclaimed woman? What's the hardest part of that? Just being in public with you, or what?

AQ: Yeah. Being called Mr. Quindlen, which bespeaks a whole range of ego things. Having the sense that you're supposed to be the front person. I remember one day, a guy called. He was doing a poll and he said to me, "What does the head of your household do?" And I said, "There are two heads of household." He said, "I can only take one." I said, "Then I'm not doing the poll." There is still that mindset that there ought to be one head of household, and when you have two people heading a household who are as outspoken, strong-willed, and smart as the two of us are, and one of them gets to be very publicly that way, it's tough for the other one. Frankly, it would have been as tough for me if it had been the other way around, but the world wouldn't keep telling us all the time that we had kind of a weird little thing going on here, which is what it does now.

I can't remember which conservative radio talk show host said, "The man in America that I have the greatest sympathy for is Anna Quindlen's husband." My mother-in-law said, "I wanted to call him up and say, "He eats better than any man you've ever met.' " I said, "Ma, it's okay, calm down." But I take that to heart; it's hard. Having said that, my husband is the oldest of six boys, so I was like the first girl that he ever spent a lot of time with. It's pretty amazing that he's as egalitarian as he is, but my mother-in-law's a really smart lady who ran that whole thing with a VW bus and a loud voice.

RM: I'm married to someone now who, when we go somewhere and when they have neglected to ask, the nametags or the dinner table cards are made out for him as Mr. Mandel. He's not Mr. Mandel. It's usually an event I've been invited to and he's coming along, but the thing about it is that it doesn't bother him at all. I don't understand; I don't know where that comes from. It goes against everything that you would expect.

AQ: Well, Mary, how did *your* husband deal with . . .

MH: Extremely well, and he's had some real moments, I'll tell you.

AQ: Listen to the way we're talking: it's like saying, "Oh, he helps so much around the house," or "My husband's home baby-sitting"; I love that one. It's like anything they do—my husband would change a diaper and his mother acted like he had parted the Red Sea.

MH: The first year I was dean at Douglass I was actually *acting* dean; and Helen Meyner, our former governor's wife and a congresswoman, was at the college for a reception or something. My husband, Ed, was chatting with her when somebody else she knew came up. She immediately said, "Oh, you may not have met Dean Hartman's wife here." Ed said, "Ahem, Congresswoman Meyner," and she realized she'd said something that was not quite right. "Oh, I'm sorry," she said, "I meant *Acting* Dean Hartman's wife." My husband still tells that story all over the place. He loved it.

AQ: I was just at Denison, and I don't know if you know Michelle Myers, who's the president of Denison, but her husband's name is Gale. There's a total absence of ego investment. He's sort of happy to be seen as President Myers's husband, and it was really notable. But he said, "Let me tell you, my name isn't Gale; it's President Myers's wife Gale." There's no blueprint for these guys, and some of the old blueprints they don't have to follow. For example, I was talking to the president of Colorado College's husband. He was saying, "You know, Catherine's predecessor's wife was expected to do a whole array of social duties that I'm just not expected to do. Or conversely, *she's* expected to do them because she's a woman. She has the president's duties and a little bit of what were the president's wife's duties." We're really in uncharted territory.

MH: Is there anything we have *not* asked you about this subject that you'd like to talk about related to leadership or to education about leadership? Since we're in the process at Rutgers of defining some of the things that we will do at this new Institute for Women's Leadership, I would be interested in your ideas. Sometimes yet another conference seems pointless. If we could reconfigure our activities in a better way, perhaps we could realize sooner our dreams about helping to level the leadership playing field. Do you have any ideas for enhancing women's leadership potential, or for making scholarship in this area more accessible to people who can benefit from it?

AQ: I'm the only person you're likely to get this one from. It's sort of appalling to realize that only about a third of the people who go on-line on computer networks throughout this country are female, that overwhelmingly the on-line world is male, which means that overwhelmingly men are controlling what will probably in the twenty-first century be our primary means of disseminating and collecting information. Networks on the Internet are the easiest way for busy people to communicate about subjects of substance, not only as themselves but anonymously, and they're wonderful ways to share scholarship. I think women really have to move full speed ahead into the world of the new technology.

I'm already involved in a couple of different networks, and someone was saying to me the other day, "You know, I don't know very much about being a DES daughter, and I'm approaching menopause." I said, "There's a great chat board on the Internet, with a whole bunch of us who are DES daughters. Doctors don't know bupkes about DES at this point, but we know everything."

RM: What's your thought about why so few women are on the Internet?

AQ: I think the first people to get serious about computer communication were the ones we stereotype as math and science nerds, and as we all know, these still tend to be overwhelmingly male. While, at Harvard, a bunch of women were working on their first novels, Bill Gates was dropping out of school to start Microsoft. It's going to get better as more women continue to go into math and science. The other thing is that it's a very hands-off form of communication, and women aren't as crazy about hands-off forms of communication as men are. That's going to change, too, as we understand how important this is, and as we get a sense of how valuable it can be to all of us. It's like talking on the phone to your girlfriends every morning except your girlfriends multiply by about ten!

RM: I was ready to ask you all kinds of questions about your mother and father, but . . .

AQ: I have the standard configuration; I'm my father's oldest son. My mother died when I was nineteen, which is the seminal event in my life, and my father is a classic man in that he will stop strangers on planes and tell them that he is my father; but when he tells me how proud he is of me, it's always in a letter because God forbid he should say to me straight out, "I'm very proud of you." But I think there's a huge sisterhood of girls of a certain age who were raised as their fathers' oldest sons, raised in a gender-neutral way. This was not for any political or praiseworthy reason, but because we were the oldest children. My father wanted a son, which was foolhardy because he does not deal as well with men as he does with women. He got this baby, so he went, "Well, let's go; let's build it from the ground up—the perfect man." I hear that again and again from successful women.

RM: It may be more possible for a father who wanted a son to do that at this time in history. What I thought of when you said that was Elizabeth Cady Stanton's autobiography, which opens with her father wanting her to be his oldest son but knowing she couldn't be, since she was a girl. He was so disappointed, and she spent a lot of time trying to prove to him that she could be his best son. She studied Greek and rode horses and more; and he said, "That's wonderful you can do all that; too bad you're not a boy."

AQ: There's two kinds of kick-ass women that I've met, two configurations. One is the ones raised as their fathers' oldest sons, and the other is the motherless daughters. There's a lot about this in Hope Edelman's book [*Motherless Daughters: The Legacy of Loss*]. I happen to be both, which means we're going nuclear here. But there's a certain kind of woman I meet, and I'm talking to her, and I think, "Oh, you're one of the sisterhood." I understood about the way Madonna is when I found out her mother died when she was nine. It's like, "Hey, you know what? I am my own invention. Where do I come from? No place. Might as well be the Immaculate Conception. Where I come from is finished, gone. Boop, I am the grownup, I am the woman, I am the eight-year-old woman, I am the twelve-year-old woman, I am the sixteen-year-old woman, I am the twenty-year-old woman." It's really powerful, the people I meet whose mothers died relatively young and who just felt free to create this life. With Gerry Ferraro, it's her father, who died when she was really young. I saw a lot of it in her, the "I gotta get out there and do what needs to be done."

Hillary Clinton's her father's oldest son. You talk to her, and it's all there. There's no suggestion of weakness at all, none. I hate to keep being the eternal optimist, Ruth, but I have to tell you, when I'm giving a speech, if I need an applause line, I mention her name. For all the people who hate her, there is a hard-core group of people who think that she walks on water. Anybody who's ever seen her and heard her speak—oh my god, she's the most amazing person. I wish she gave speeches more often. Her feelings about social responsibility are—I don't want to say conservative—but she has strong feelings about how nobody's going to raise your kids but you. Nobody's going to say no but you. She says we've got to talk more about working, because even though we need and want to work, we need the mother. She does a lot more of that than people think, but she expended a lot of capital making policy in the first eighteen months. It wasn't worth it.

MH: I think that she can't do what she can do best in the role of First Lady; it's a very ambiguous position.

RM: I just feel that so much of this is so difficult. It's not that you're a total optimist and I'm a total pessimist, but I do feel it's been unfair, because of who she is and what she's got and what she's capable of. It's such a grotesque distortion that's emerged of her.

AQ: I think history will be kinder to her. And perhaps history will be kinder to the rest of us mouthy women, too!

NAFIS SADIK

■

IN CONVERSATION WITH CHARLOTTE BUNCH AND MARY S. HARTMAN

Nafis Sadik, executive director of the United Nations Population Fund (UNFPA), was born in Jaunpur, India, in 1929. A Pakistani national, she received her undergraduate education at Loreto College in Calcutta and earned her medical degree from Dow Medical College in Karachi. She has also studied at the Johns Hopkins University and was a fellow at Queens University in Kingston, Ontario. Before coming to the United Nations, she was a civilian medical officer in several Pakistani military hospitals, with responsibility for women's and children's wards, and also served as director of planning and training of the Pakistan Central Family Planning Council. These positions gave her the foundational experience with women's and reproductive health issues that have since been the focal point of her work. In 1971, Nafis Sadik joined the UNFPA, where she served as chief of the program division from 1973 to 1982, and as

assistant executive director from 1982 to 1987, when she became the first woman to head a major U.N. program.

Since her appointment, she has worked tirelessly to bring women's issues to the forefront of the United Nations's agenda. She has promoted many qualified women to administrative positions; and as a result of her efforts, the UNFPA has become a model for other U.N. agencies, as more than 40 percent of the professional staff are women. She also sees women's issues as fundamental to concerns about international population, a position she affirmed as secretary-general of the International Conference on Population and Development in Cairo in 1994. Sadik argues that substantial change in the world population outlook requires a major rethinking of sexuality and reproductive methods, one that transcends cultural barriers. She is persuaded that awareness of the issues is the necessary first step in creating an international dialogue. Most important, she says, is women's full participation in both the educational and political processes, so that women's needs become central rather than peripheral to an ongoing discussion about population management. She also advocates children's rights and parents' responsibilities, a political position she practices in her own family.

CHARLOTTE BUNCH: Our group decided that we could learn best about what is happening with women's leadership at the turn of the twenty-first century by having some conversations with key women leaders such as yourself, women from a variety of backgrounds and experiences. We want to discuss your own path to leadership, your experience here at the United Nations, your views on the prospects for women in leadership, and your advice to the young women whom we also hope to encourage to brave the world of public life.

MARY HARTMAN: Let's begin with your observations on your family background and the people who inspired you to achieve and ultimately to move into leadership positions.

NAFIS SADIK: I come from a family that would probably be labeled conservative, except for my father, who believed strongly in education for his daughters as well as his sons. I was fortunate that I had that support, and I wanted to have a career from an early age. But I still worried whether I would be allowed to, because in our family, girls generally got married quite early. I told my father I wanted to go to medical school, and he said, "Yes, you will go." Against the opposition of many family members, I did go to medical school. Even in the last year of school, my mother would say to me, "Why don't you leave and get married now, and I'll give you jewelry and clothes." She knew I loved jewelry and clothes!

MH: By that time, were you tempted to turn back?

NS: In truth, my father was so strongly in support of my career that there was no active opposition. In any case, I was quite happy, doing all the things that I wanted to do! At about that time, I met my future husband, who was in the army. During my last year at medical school, he came to propose for me. My father said to him, "Well you know that my daughter has very definite ideas about a career and about working." He said, "Well, don't I know it. She has made that quite clear." My husband in fact supported me strongly, though in the beginning of my professional life, I followed him because he was in the army. When he left to go into business, I also followed him wherever he was posted.

I was offered many international jobs before the U.N., but I wasn't particularly interested in any of them. When the U.N. job was offered, I was a bit interested and my husband said, "Well, let us make the decision, since you followed me all your life, I will now follow you." So it was a conscious decision on his part. I think that I would never have taken a job and moved my family without his support. That provided me the opportunity to come to the U.N. It is true that from Pakistan I'd been active in international programs and spoken at many conferences, but that was not the same thing as coming to the U.N., where I would have the chance to manage international programs.

I came to the United Nations Population Fund in October 1971 as a technical adviser, to try out whether this arrangement would work with our family. My husband got a job with the company he was working with in Pakistan, but soon after, they moved to Boston and he had to find another job. I meanwhile joined the U.N. and was lucky that the executive director of the Population Fund, who came from the Philippines, also gave me a lot of opportunities. I recognize now that in the beginning, I was being tested in many ways. Soon after I arrived, he said, "Will you go to Yugoslavia and see if you can raise some funds from them?" I thought that very odd; but in retrospect, I see that he wanted to find out how resourceful I was. He asked me to organize a conference with the other population organizations. I had a bit of a difficult time, but I did it. I think now that he was being very supportive, but I didn't see it at the time. I was given opportunities that others senior to me were not given, which was very advanced of him to do. Of course, it is true that I was one of the few people in the organization with actual experience with programs.

I also knew a number of international programs—not just Pakistan's—because I'd been an adviser in Thailand, Tunisia, Egypt, Kenya, Ghana, and elsewhere. I knew the difficulties and constraints you encounter in this work. So I was promoted to chief of the program division within just a few years of coming to the U.N. As such, I made proposals for reorganizing and expanding the organization, most of which were implemented. But I must say that I also found discrimination in odd kinds of ways.

CB: I was going to ask you about the obstacles you encountered.

NS: You come to a western country and you think that everybody accepts women, but that's not the case. In fact, I was very surprised to find that I have more acceptance in Pakistan in the level of my job and in dealing with people. Once you're in a position, people don't question whether you're a man or a woman in Pakistan. True, there's a lot of gender discrimination in who gets to go to school and who has opportunities for higher education and all that; but there doesn't seem to be discrimination once you're in a position. Here, when I first came and was organizing a seminar with a small steering committee, no matter what I said, people didn't pay any attention. It became quite irritating, and I had to become quite aggressive. When they accepted an idea when a man said it, I said, "Well, you know, I said it first." I think I sounded quite petty, but I had to do it. I was quite surprised that many Europeans and Americans just sort of ignore women as if they don't exist. For me, the treatment was like, "You're very decorative, you wear a sari, and you're attractive, or whatever"—that was my place and that was where I was supposed to stay. It used to irritate me a lot, and I became more aggressive than I ever would have been. I realized that I had to be firm, even strident, to get my point across. It was unpleasant.

The fact that I had support from the top helped a lot, though. In the end, I had the program to manage almost by myself, with a deputy director who oversaw it. We had some difficulties in the beginning because he resented it that I took into account the personal situations of staff in making assignments, that I would consider problems of spouses or of children. He would say, "That's *their* problem." When I became executive director, I think that the former secretary-general [Perez de Cuellar] was courageous in making the appointment, as there were several candidates who had a lot of political support. I was pleased when he chose me that he announced publicly that mine was the best appointment he ever made.

MH: Had you made it clear to him earlier that you were interested in the position?

NS: Oh yes. It happened rather suddenly that the former executive director died. No one wanted to scramble for the position at first, of course, and in fact I initially assumed I would simply be selected. Then many contenders presented themselves. I asked advice about whether I should tell the secretary-general I was interested and was told by people I trusted to do so and also to ensure that my government supported me. I first asked what my government had to do with it but realized that it is a sort of political appointment.

My government *did* support me, and when I spoke with the secretary-general, he asked lots of questions about what my vision was for the future of the organization. All this went on for about two months, during which I got calls from many developing countries about job candidates, so I realized I had support from many places. The secretary-general told me of letters of support from U.N. agencies, from various organizations, and from university people. Shortly before the appointment, he announced that it would be a woman, and since there was another woman in the running, everyone assumed it would be she. Another high-ranking official in UNFPA, who wanted the job and was keen that I not get it, had earlier suggested to me that if I saw the secretary-general about the appointment, it would look unseemly. Meanwhile, he himself went to see the secretary-general. I told myself that whether it was unseemly or not, I did not want to lose the position by default.

CB: Many women find it hard to put themselves forward in this way.

NS: I just wanted to register that I was interested and that I had the experience, that I knew what the issues are. I explained that the issues are very much related to women's needs, to their status and to their situation—that I could be a solid spokesperson for those issues. As I recall, I said, "I can make a better case than most other candidates for this secretariat, which requires advocacy. I am not scared of anybody because for me, when I speak about the substance of an issue, I'm not taking positions on religion or culture. I'm saying that individual rights and needs have to be respected and that for me, any cultural tradition that denies rights is something that has to be done away with. You cannot really support cultural traditions that oppress a group of people, in this case half the population in most societies." When he asked about the church, I said, "I don't have any quarrel with the church; the church is an individual matter for people, and the pope or whoever it is can preach to the people. It is the individual who must decide in the end. What I am going to do is talk about the problems and make recommendations based on scientific knowledge. Then individuals can make the choice."

I followed that throughout my tenure as executive director. I denied I was having a confrontation with the church, saying that any woman in any country who wants to plan her family by abstinence should have the very best advice we can give her. We should also tell her the pros and cons and ask her if she has control over her own decision to abstain. If she does not, which is the situation in most of our societies, then she's not going to be very successful in this matter. With the church, also, I said that unless you can preach to men that they must respect the views and the needs of women, your recommendations are not going to succeed. Anyhow, my appointment came as a surprise to many people, though a number, including the majority of the staff, supported me. A few did not.

MH: What happened with your chief rival?

NS: The secretary-general said he wanted to announce my appointment at the next meeting of the ACC [Administrative Committee on Coordination] which is chaired by the secretary-general and consists of all the heads of the twenty-four or so U.N. organizations. He told me this on a Friday and said the meeting would take place in Rome the following Monday and he wanted me to attend. I knew that the other candidate was planning to attend that meeting and said, "No, I don't want to start off by making him look bad, so why don't you announce my appointment after the ACC meeting?" The secretary-general said he did not think that the individual would be so generous to me; and in the end, I don't think my gesture was much appreciated. He did go to the meeting, having already been informed ahead of time of my appointment. Then he rang me from Europe, acting as though he had just learned. In six months he was gone, as he was simply unable to accept me as the head, and we had many differences over personnel matters.

In fact, he put in his resignation without telling me, hoping to embarrass me with the Governing Council of UNFPA. I made known my displeasure with his timing just before a council meeting, but I let him make a statement there. That first year with the council was difficult; but by the second year, the members were very supportive. There was another high-ranking executive who also wanted my job. He said to everyone that he was going to succeed me and that I was there just as a sort of spokesperson, while he was the real manager. I took this up with his government, and also with the secretary-general.

MH: Since you've raised the issue of the culture of the United Nations and what you have been doing to change it, I'd like to ask more about your reputation for moving and shaking there. One of the things that you have done as director of UNFPA is to name more women to positions of authority there than in any other agency.

NS: The U.N. has lots of political pressure in the hiring and firing of personnel, especially hiring. I made the rounds of all members of the Governing Council to start, all our donors, and then others, to say I wanted this to be an efficient, effective place. I asked them not to request me to hire specific people, telling them that I was putting a distance between my role and the candidates by establishing a hearing panel that would interview and recommend qualified candidates, with only a shortlist coming to me for final selection.

We are not a large organization, but any organization depends on its staff and their morale for overall effectiveness. If staff feel that political considerations matter more than performance, why should they contribute? Many people work very hard because they have a responsibility and they are committed, but they need to know that their commitment will be recognized, that they are contributing to an organization with some vision. It took me time and effort to get rid of some people who were not performing; it is especially difficult in the U.N. since you have to inform governments and so on. In time, I stopped getting the calls about appointing individuals, since I just kept saying, "Thank you very much, the name will go into the pool to be considered by our panel." We now have an excellent staff.

In this process, we paid particular attention to the situation of women. We had a task force on how to integrate gender issues into our programs. I asked the members to make recommendations, which they did. They were not very far-reaching. I accepted them all, including 50 percent women by the year two thousand and something and 20 percent in managerial positions—really modest. Since in this and other fields now, many more women are available, I was dismayed to find that when I went to different countries, women were reluctant to apply and were convinced that they were not going to be considered. I then sent out letters to all my field officers and said this is from me and I am interested in names of good people in your countries and your programs. I want the word out that women are as welcome as men to apply.

Gradually we got a number of applications. I never eliminated men and went down the list, but whenever there was a woman on the final list, my preference would be for her, all things being equal. Also, I didn't accept common views that this or that country couldn't have a woman. I said, "Why not? Half the population is female." "Oh, you can't have a woman in Country X," they would say, "Oh, you can't have a woman in Country Y, or in blahblahblah." I said that is totally unacceptable. Now already we have 46 percent women, and I am sure we'll soon be at 50 percent, much before the year 2000.

MH: And you've done all this in less than a decade. Congratulations.

NS: In top managerial positions we are over 60 percent, since four out of eight division chiefs are women, one of my deputies is a woman, and I am a woman. So for the past two years now, we have had six out of the eleven senior positions.

CB: Have you run into resistance from other parts of the U.N. to this reorganization?

NS: We're used as an example by the secretary-general. In the beginning I must say that "in house" I got some representation from men, who said to me, "Are you never going to promote us now?" I said, "I'm not saying that, nor do I wish that. If two people are equal, I will promote a woman, and if I'm recruiting from the outside, I will look for women as well as men—you know as well as I that governments always send men." The secretary-general also has this problem on senior-level appointments in areas like peacekeeping, where they're not running military operations but instead doing negotiations, which women can do as well as men. But women aren't usually named. I am especially looking at middle-level positions, where we still have too few women, because that is how we can ensure that there will be more women available later on for senior-level promotions.

We have had less success in getting enough women into field positions. Only about 35 percent of program officers are women, although a majority of the field staff—our national program officers—are women. It's interesting that we did not go out actively to do that. It just happened that they have been appointed by the local offices. So overall, 70 percent of our national program staff are women, and these are professionals. Women just began to apply to us, excellent women—so many that we are having to turn good applicants away. I'm always sending names to other U.N. organizations.

CB: What has your own experience been like as one of the few senior women at the United Nations?

NS: At first, I was the only woman on the Administrative Committee on Coordination [ACC], which consists of the heads of all the agencies. In the beginning, the men didn't know how to act, and some very old heads of organizations always would compliment me on my clothes and say things like "We look forward to seeing what sari you will be wearing at the next meeting." I used to joke with them that they might look forward to what I would be wearing, but they probably didn't look forward to hearing what I was going to say! "Oh no, no," they would reply politely.

When they complimented me on my saris, I returned the compliments on their suits or their ties, or I mentioned how nice they were looking. Or I would say things like, "My, you're looking very young!" They really got very shocked by this, and I must say I didn't at first do it deliberately, but rather just as a way of saying something nice back to them. But to men, it comes as a great shock when they're complimented on their looks or their clothes, and it doesn't come as a shock to me; I'm quite happy. Some westerners used to ask me if I minded being complimented, and I would say, "No, I quite enjoy it. I would mind if you said 'What a terrible sari you're wearing' or 'How awful you're looking.' I do not want to be told that."

These compliments and joking about how we looked actually helped me in introducing more serious gender perspectives on many issues, including family planning and the rights of women. Gradually I noticed a change in the way the men were reacting. In the beginning they used to be very embarrassed when I talked about contraception. I remember one day making a presentation about the Eastern European countries, especially the former Soviet republics, and saying that we had a special mission there, since the conditions for women were really terrible as far as choice was concerned. I explained that they had no decent methods and then said something like, "The condoms are so terrible they are like rubber tires, and the IUDs are inferior and often crumble." Well, the men were shocked, and they didn't know where to look. I was just straightforward in describing the situation, explaining that women have to resort to abortion as the only method and that some women had had ten, twelve, even fifteen abortions. There was pin-drop silence, and the secretary-general then said loudly, "Well, thank you for this wonderful account." He was very nice. Then someone else said, "Well, we've never had this kind of statement in the Administrative Committee on Coordination before."

I suddenly realized that these were not the sorts of issues usually talked about in high places. But it was quite fun, and I noticed very soon that whenever these men gave presentations, they were likely to say something about the women in their organizations or in their programs. They would then look at me as if to say, "Did she notice that I mentioned a woman who works in my agency?" But all this is changing now. We have three other women in the ACC—the head of the World Food Program, the high commissioner for refugees, and the executive director of the UNICEF.

CB: Does it seem to you that a critical mass of women is emerging, then?

NS: I don't know. We had a recent experience at a senior meeting in which a man presented a paper on reform at the United Nations that was not very good. Now no one said anything right afterwards, so I spoke up and said that I wasn't sure the paper should go out, that it didn't seem to add value or say anything. Then all the other women agreed and added their own comments. No man said so, however, even though I later learned that all of them agreed with what we women were saying. After the meeting, they said to me, "Oh, you have demolished So-and-So." I said that that was a mean and cruel thing to say, that I was not personally against the individual. I was talking about a paper and an issue, and I might have demolished the paper but not the man. I added, "If you don't like something I present, I don't take it personally. I take it as your advice and your opinion. I might try to defend it if I feel strongly, or I might start to agree with you."

Some men then said that all the women had ganged up on this poor man. I said, "Are you saying that women should not show themselves to be strong? I think men don't have the courage to speak out about issues because they feel that somehow they will have labeled themselves or attacked someone, but the only way you can deal with difficult problems is to talk about them. You have to be more frank and open and not think every time you say something, 'Oh, So-and-So's department is going to be involved, or this or that person will be upset.' " Otherwise, I said, you can never talk about reform or change.

I was quite irritated by this experience, and I thought this might be an area where women and men just do differ and that women may be more at ease discussing such problems. But it may not have to do with gender but instead with a mindset. I gave them an example of when I was preparing the International Conference on Population and Development, the first document for the Program of Action was done by my staff and was really bad. Still, it was very much in line with the U.N. language then, so I got a group of experts convened by the Rockefeller Foundation to review it. The expert group said, "My god, this document is like a dead body talking. It's awful." I said to these men, "You know, I might have sat there and said, 'My god, how dare they; they're attacking me.' " But they weren't attacking me, they were attacking a document, and I wanted to know what an outsider would think about it. I went through fifteen drafts in the end before we presented the document to that conference and to the intergovernmental body where there was a discussion. To present the material in a way that would provoke a dialogue and at the same time keep the substance of the argument we were making intact required a lot of thinking.

MH: You managed to achieve that while at the same time saving the face of your staff.

NS: Right, because I couldn't say directly to the staff that their document was terrible. I had to find a way to do it that made us all feel that we were sort of helping ourselves along. I think we came out with a good document, and the process helped the staff be more comfortable with criticism and outside assessment. I took the criticism myself, too, and told the staff that it was my responsibility to have given them better direction.

CB: I want to ask you a question or two about the International Conference on Population and Development in Cairo. For many people, you became visible as a woman leader there, when as the secretary-general for the conference, you stood behind a woman's right to control her reproductive life in the face of considerable opposition. There was a lot of admiration for you. How did you experience the conference, and how did it affect your view of what women should be doing now in the world generally with regard to population issues?

NS: The Cairo conference agenda is really something that was always my agenda, but there I had a chance to present it to the international community and have it articulated more openly. My own personal experience, you know, is that most women have no authority, no power—that their status is low in our societies. I think that control over fertility by society, by religions, by imposition of authority of all kinds—especially by men—is one of the chief ways in which women are controlled and kept powerless. Motherhood may be, what you call it, "idealized," but women are not really supported in *that* role either. It was designed to capture them and make a mold of the stereotype of what a woman should do, of her subjugated role in the family. But in family planning there are so many other issues, such as this issue of imposition of authority by the men close to home, that women don't consider enough. They talk about domination of the West or the South or the North.

I wanted to get these issues out in our Cairo program of action, and it took me many, many rewrites on the whole question of male responsibility. The chapter would somehow disappear when I submitted it, but I would say, "You know, this is what I want to say, that men have a responsibility to promote the status of women, that issues such as violence in relationships and the declining self-esteem of girls as adolescents are things we know about and must make recommendations about." In the begininng there was not much interest from the international community in this conference, because the Rio conference [U.N. Conference on Environment and Development, 1992] was going on, and all the interest was there. In fact the women's groups were for the Rio conference and very hostile to family planning.

CB: Some of them were, anyway.

NS: Yes. They felt that population control was being used by the North to suppress the South, and I had a lot of work to do with women's organizations that were very antagonistic to us and to our programs. In the beginning we weren't going to have an NGO [nongovernmental organization] forum because we didn't have one in the first population conference in Bucharest, Romania, or in the 1984 conference held in Mexico City, and there was no provision for a forum in the intergovernmental decisions for Cairo. Then the NGOs started to agitate for a role, and I explained that our secretariat was extremely small, although I did think they should have a role. They got some money from foundations to set up a secretariat, and I also got money from some governments for a small NGO unit. We agreed that there would be an NGO forum, and I said I would be pleased to get suggestions from all groups—they are a wide spectrum from extreme environmentalists to population control groups to extreme feminist groups as well as many in-between groups, all the health groups, and the women's leadership groups and so on.

I decided we had to plan for four expert groups discussing four topics agreed upon by the member governments, but in addition I decided to organize many roundtable discussions on issues of concern. For example, we included gender issues and their relation to fertility, ethics, and values and their relationship to population issues, and so on. I invited lots of NGO representatives to those roundtables and urged them to draft recommendations that I could use as part of the program of action, remembering that that program of action could not be a huge document with every single recommendation included. I also urged them to recall that we were working in an intergovernmental situation, so that abortion was going to be a very hot subject.

CB: Turning to the future and the question of women's leadership in the world, what would you want to say to young women, and where do you think they should move?

NS: One of the things that I think happened in Cairo was in part due to all the preparatory visits I had made around the world. Governments were more disposed to look at women's needs and women's issues as part of mainstream problems. The conference was not a conference about women; but every leader, every person who spoke there, spoke about the status of women, the empowerment of women, their positions, their needs, their health status. It became more than a women's conference because we were ministers of planning, prime ministers, and others not really dealing with women's issues, but nonetheless talking about those issues. The half a million women who die each year from maternity-related deaths became a rallying cry throughout, and I think that happened because of the massive movement of NGOs and individuals from all over the world.

Now what we need in the next generation is to continue that process of education and outreach, because that is the beginning of getting international acceptance on the critically difficult issues that will make all the difference in every area, including women's leadership and more opportunities for young women. What we are trying to do is to keep the momentum going, keep these support groups informed and trained, and get many more people at leadership levels to speak out—not just the women. One of the things I do now, having talked about women in general to everybody, is to make it a special point to talk to leaders. I say to them, "Now I know you agree with the fact that women need to have this or that; what have you done to speak about any one of the particular issues? Have you talked against sexual violence or rape? Have you condemned the practice of keeping girls from attending school in so many places? Have you picked out issues involving discrimination against women that you regularly address publicly?"

Many people say, "I don't believe in such discriminatory practices," but unless they speak out and condemn them at every opportunity, these things will remain the social norm. Laws don't change behavior; laws set some parameters, but to change attitudes and social consciousness, you need condemnation of behavior that is discriminatory and oppressive to women; you need attacks on stereotyping, or whatever practice that is negative to women. So that is one of the things I think young women have to do: they have to get more directly involved in addressing these issues themselves, and they also have to urge their leaders—men and women alike—to speak out in behalf of the upcoming generation.

MH: Do you think that the atmosphere is going to be receptive to this next stage you are describing?

NS: The atmosphere is very good now for this. I think we have an opportunity and we should capitalize on it immediately, because I also think there is going to be a backlash. There is already an attempt now to denigrate women who are supposedly being too strong and aggressive toward the poor men. All that is a kind of preparation for an assault on the gains that have been made. One of the things I caution staff about is that in our own advocacy, we must be very clever in getting the support of groups we need while trying to deflect antagonism. We also need to be prepared for whatever antagonism is bound to come out anyway, in local situations at least. These are, after all, very profound changes we are calling for in attitudes and in the general thinking of society.

Second, I feel quite strongly that women have to get more political power. To make change happen, you have to be in the political decision-making process. You cannot always be lobbying from the outside; you must be inside. So I think that not enough attention has been paid by women leaders and organizations to getting more women into the political process. It is very important that we strategize about ways to make this happen, that we consider such examples as the recent Indian decision to have 30 percent reserved seats for women in the Parliament. This is a big step, and it is going to change the whole status of gender relationships in India. It won't happen overnight, but things will change dramatically. We need to press for more political representation for women, in industrialized societies as well as in all the developing countries.

A third thing we must do, all of us, is to get girls into school and keep them there! The content of education, the curricula, the discourse in schools, and the ways we teach our children must somehow give girls more self-esteem. I think that during my own growing-up days, I never had to bother much with that. We went to girls' schools and never had to confront male pressures on us. But I see young people in the United States and in many other countries where the situation of girls changes in high school. They start to do badly. You look at all the research, and you talk to young girls, and you can recognize this problem. I went to the YWCA once, and girls there said that the boys didn't like them, that they said they were too clever, things like that. I think unless girls have more self-esteem and more vision for themselves—unless they place more value on themselves—they will never be able to do all the things that they should do. I think there is still a lot of blackmail in the sense that girls or women who are professionally talented are made to sacrifice having children or even to remain unmarried, since somehow a family and a career are seen as incompatible. I believe that is a terrible thing to happen.

Also, and this is my personal view, I believe that every child needs parents who are there for him or her. I think society must start to think more about that. When two people make a decision to have a child, they also make a commitment to a person who is now their principal responsibility. They have to decide when they have had their own opportunities and when they must turn to providing the child with his or her opportunities.

These views were reinforced in my own background; for in my family, my mother used always to say, "Once you get married and have a child, you must remember that the child has only you, that his or her future is dependent upon you as a parent." I have always remembered that. When you have fights, you need to think that this child is the one you have brought in as a witness, that this child is going to reflect your past and your future. I think this was wise advice, that somehow in providing for individual rights and freedom and all that, there needs to be a certain balance that we make, a certain self-sacrifice to fulfill the obligation to every child that is born. Children are not toys; they are not something you own; and too many parents try to claim rights as parents. I don't think there should be rights of parents; I think there should be responsibilities of parents.

I also think that for women who want to get ahead, there must be some commitment to work on the highest of principles. Women must learn to be courageous, to make their views known in many different kinds of environments and situations without losing the chance to persuade by being too confrontational. The point is, never lose an opportunity to make your point! That is the lesson that I have learned in life.

MH: That is a wonderful point on which to conclude a fascinating discussion.

PATRICIA SCHROEDER

■

IN CONVERSATION WITH RUTH B. MANDEL
AND MARY S. HARTMAN

*The former Democratic congresswoman Patricia Schroeder is cur-
rently the president and CEO of the Association of American Publishers (AAP). Born in Portland, Oregon, in 1940, Schroeder
graduated in 1961 from the University of Minnesota, where she supported herself by drawing on her expertise as a licensed pilot to adjust aviation insurance claims for an insurance company. Schroeder
then entered Harvard Law School as one of only fifteen women
among more than five hundred men in her class. Earning her J.D. in
1964, she moved to Denver with her husband, James, who prompted
her to challenge an incumbent Republican for Colorado's First Congressional District seat in 1972. A mother of two young children at
her election, Schroeder went on to serve in the House of Representatives for twenty-four years before leaving Congress undefeated in
1996. During her tenure in the House, she became the dean of con-*

gressional women; cochaired the Congressional Caucus on Women's Issues for ten years; served on the House Judiciary Committee and the House Post Office and Civil Service Committee; and was the first woman to serve on the House Armed Services Committee. As chair of the House Select Committee on Children, Youth, and Families from 1991 to 1993, Schroeder saw the Family and Medical Leave Act and the National Institutes of Health Revitalization Act to fruition in 1993.

Patricia Schroeder was an early supporter of legalized abortion and sponsored legislation making it a federal crime to obstruct access to abortion clinics. She was also active in military issues, expediting the National Security Committee's vote to allow women to fly in combat missions in 1991 and working to better the situation of military families through the Military Family Act of 1985. She was never a single-issue candidate and has always been a strong advocate for education and free speech issues, commitments that she continues in her leadership of the AAP. Schroeder has long considered herself "a minority in a majority," having been a woman in an overwhelmingly male institution and remaining a liberal when that term had gone out of style. Her broader goals have included putting her critical and sometimes adversarial faculties to work in changing the nature and terms of debate in modern U.S. politics.

MARY HARTMAN: You're one of the most prominent women on the political scene in this country, and you will always be sought after and quoted. Can you talk to us a bit about how it all began—your family, who they were, where you were raised, some of your youthful experiences?

PATRICIA SCHROEDER: The quick study is that I was a child of World War II, born in Portland, Oregon. I probably would have died there except that there was this thing called Pearl Harbor, and my dad got called up. My mother was a teacher, and we moved everywhere you could think of. At the end of the war we were in Texas. Dad then went into aviation insurance, and we moved to Ohio. Then he started his own insurance company in Des Moines, Iowa, and later Denver, Colorado, so I lived in an awful lot of places. It was a very different lifestyle for both of my parents, who had been born and raised in Nebraska on farms.

RUTH MANDEL: Did you have siblings?

PS: Yes, I had a brother who is younger, still do. I got into politics in a very ad hoc way. At Harvard Law School I had been interested but never thought I'd run for anything. Then all of a sudden in 1972 my husband was on a committee looking for someone to run. There was a Democratic candidate running, but nobody was enthusiastic about him because he was thought too far to the right. There was a Republican incumbent who everyone assumed was going to win, so nobody else wanted to take on the primary. My husband came home one night and said, "Guess whose name came up? Yours." I said, *"Mine?* I've never run for anything; I don't get this." His attitude was, "You'll never win, but you know you really ought to carry the flag; somebody ought to discuss the issues." I think they thought it would hurt me the least to do it because I didn't have some big job. I had part-time jobs at that time because we had two little kids. So I did it. It was about that casual.

MH: We need to go back further before returning to your political career. Why did you choose the University of Minnesota, and what did you study there?

PS: I studied history, and I went there for several reasons. My father always felt that you ought to pay your own way through school, and it was difficult then to figure out what you could do beyond a minimum wage job. Luckily, the U. of M. was in Minneapolis, and you could get a higher-paying job there. I also had a pilot's license and knew a lot about aviation insurance because of my dad's company, so I was able to get a job adjusting aviation losses. I also could rent planes from the university for ten bucks an hour and use them for my job. I actually made so much money my first year that I bought a Lincoln!

I was able to finish in three years because Minnesota also let you take twenty credits a quarter if you passed the Minnesota Multiphasic exam and weren't going nuts. I graduated in 1961. My generation was in a hurry, though I'm not sure we knew where we were going!

RM: Then you went straight to Harvard Law School. Talk about that, about what made you decide to go to law school, about why you chose Harvard, and about what it was like getting into Harvard for women ▪ at that time.

PS: Well, I didn't know what I was going to do, and I thought law school was the most generic of the degrees because you could teach it, you could practice it, you could use it in business—it was broad based. Since I didn't know where I was going to live, I thought I should probably go to a national law school. I didn't know much, but I thought, "Well, I've heard of Harvard. That's a national law school." So I applied.

MH: Was anyone at the University of Minnesota or in your family prodding you to do this?

PS: No. I originally wanted to do aerodynamic engineering, but I had one of those classic counselors who screamed at me, "No, no, you can't do that. You'd just be wasting your parents' money." I tried to say, "It's not my parents' money; it's *mine*."

RM: But you were not discouraged about applying to law school? Plenty of women were.

PS: It was such a huge university that it never occurred to me to ask anybody's permission. I just applied. We're talking about a university at that time of forty thousand students. When I graduated, I hired an undergraduate for thirty-five dollars to go through the line to get my diploma! My friends and I sat up and watched it. We were detached.

RM: Even then, Pat, you clearly had a lot of self-confidence!

PS: Either that or it never occurred to me there were barriers. I had always gone to public schools. When I got to Harvard, I realized there was another world out there. There were all these people who'd gone to sex-segregated schools all their lives, both men and women. There was just a handful of women, fifteen or so in a class of five hundred and some. A lot of them had gone to sex-segregated schools and were as nonplussed by the whole thing as the men were. I remember thinking, "Who *are* these people?" I'd never met anyone like them.

RM: Were your parents impressed that you went to Harvard?

PS: Not particularly. My mother was actually depressed. You know, "Nobody will marry you, and now I'll never be a grandmother." My dad's attitude was: "This is not fair to your younger brother; what's he going to do?"

RM: What *did* he do?

PS: Oh, he went on to law school at the University of Iowa. At that point, my thought was, "Hey, it's my money, and that's what I want."

RM: So you had enough money put away from your aviation career to put yourself through law school as well as undergraduate school?

PS: Yes. That reminds me that in the middle of all this at Minnesota I got nominated for making the most dangerous landing. I was in a little plane coming into Pipestone, Minnesota; and the winds we were going into were so high that the plane literally couldn't move forward. Nobody, including me, figured out how I got the plane on the ground, but I did.

RM: I was at another public institution, Brooklyn College, in those days. It cost only seven dollars a semester, plus books; but I worked in the summers for other expenses. Most women students were preparing for marriage and majored in education so they could teach until they had children. I majored in English, which my parents thought impractical, although it was considered nontraditional for women then. Yet no one was flying planes or announcing that they were going to Harvard Law School. That would have been extremely unusual.

MH: What about your peers at the University of Minnesota? They were stunned by your achievements and your airplane feats, no?

PS: I was in a sorority and they loved me because I always had high grades, so I kind of kept them from getting into trouble. I was also in student government and a lot of other things. They found that they liked me, but I was different. They thought it was very weird that I was studying Chinese, which I did for two years, and that I flew; but they thought it was fun, too. I became their academic mascot.

RM: In the early years, how did you think of yourself? Did you imagine a future in public life? You said you chose the law for flexibility. How did you see the future back then?

PS: I just had no idea how it was all going to be packaged. I was thinking, "Okay, I'm going to graduate, but I'm not ready to go out into the real world yet. I want something else punched on my ticket, so what can I do that will give me the most choices at the end?"

RM: From what I'm hearing, you also had little sense that what you were doing was unusual for a woman. I mean, it was common to be in a sorority, but not to fly a plane. It was common enough to go to college, but not to go to Harvard Law School. Other than the counselor who discouraged aerodynamic engineering, did you run into any gender bias?

PS: No, Minnesota was a really wonderful school that way. Oh, you'd run into pockets of it, but basically the school was as progressive as any at that time. It was a mature campus; a lot of students lived at home. It was a streetcar place, different from your traditional college.

MH: That was true in some ways for the previous generation as well. My mother went there, and her home economics track was essentially identical to the premed track. She took every single science course that the premed students took.

RM: Did you meet Jim in law school? And when the two of you married, did you go to Denver because he had a job there?

PS: No, we just sat down and said, "Where do we want to live?" He was from Chicago and didn't want to go back to Chicago, and I didn't particularly want to go back to Des Moines. We didn't want to stay on the East Coast, either.

RM: So you went to Denver, lived there for a number of years, and then entered that race for Congress. Just what happened when he came home and said, "We need you"?

PS: This was April 1972, and the organizing caucus was the first week in May. In Colorado it's a very convoluted process. You had caucuses, and then you elected people to go to the convention, and then the votes at the convention decided what position you had on the ballot. Then you had a primary in September, so it was layer upon layer. When I agreed to run, I said, " I will do this only if I get top line at the organizing convention." They said, "Okay," since nobody else was available. I then won top line, and it was like, "Oh no!" But it was clear I couldn't get top line and then say, "Hey, I'm not going to do this."

We were in the primary. I never thought I would win because we were so outspent. My opponent was the minority leader in the state senate. I went to Washington once for support from the Democratic Congressional Campaign Committee, and they literally threw me out. So I went back and won the primary, and once again it was like, "Oh no!" Now we were in the general election, which was six weeks later, and all I could think was, "Oh my god, this'll be over, this'll soon be over." I kept my jobs. I was teaching, and I was also a hearing officer for the state of Colorado. I was almost insane. And then I won! Only a handful of Republican incumbents were beaten that year. It was absolutely bizarre. So I gave up my two jobs, though I had to keep them until December 31st. We had swearing-in on January 3rd. My life was just the biggest nightmare; and it kind of hasn't ended!

RM: Do I remember correctly? You furnished your new house in Washington on the phone? You bought the drapes and the carpets and everything on the phone?

PS: Yes. I had not given one minute's thought to what I would do if I won. I never thought it possible. I just thought, "I have to keep focused on this campaign; it will soon end; and then real life will come back." When the campaign was over, I had papers to grade, decisions to write—I was seriously backlogged just in my work. Suddenly I thought, "I've got staff to hire. Jim has to give up his job, and he never thought that was going to happen. My children are two and six." It was just nuts.

RM: Those were the days when reporters always asked women elected officials about their children and families. What were you saying?

PS: Oh, we were very clear. Jim would say, "Of course we'll move to Washington." I would say to reporters, "I notice you never ask the *men* what they're going to do with their families. What do you think I'm going to do, freeze them?" I just brushed it off. It was so dumb.

RM: So you moved to Washington, they all came with you, and you moved into this house.

PS: We're still there.

MH: Let's talk about your first impressions there. I recall that when you spoke at Douglass College several years ago, I was blown away by your candor about the men's club that is Congress. When you first entered that culture, what was it like, and how significant was change over the years? You've been quoted saying things like "Even when we Democrats were in the majority, I was in the minority."

PS: I don't know how you answer that question. It's not like you have a thermometer and can say, "Well, it's fifteen degrees warmer for women." It clearly isn't as bad now; 1972 was a nightmare. And it wasn't just the men. I remember the call from Bella Abzug, whom I'd never met: "I hear you won!" she said. "I hear you have little kids." I said, "Yes." "Well, you can't do it," she said. This was America's premiere feminist. I also remember Shirley Chisholm saying, "I don't think you can do this." So there was no support then from men or women. You could have a career or you could have a family; but if you had both, you had to wait until your family grew up. Everybody accepted that, including the women's movement.

I was a founder of the Women's Political Caucus in Colorado, and they would not back me. They backed my opponent. Hello? They didn't back me for the next three races, either. They thought it was too early for a woman to run. They wanted me to run for city council or for school board. By now the difference is that more women are ready to be supportive. We're not there yet, but we're better. The men still really don't pay much attention. They just wish we'd go away. Our cause is not their cause, though they know they have to pay lip service to it. That things have changed with women is certainly a big help. And obviously some men are better than others.

RM: So when you got there in '72 and you showed up and were sworn in, you found a very chilly climate. Where did you find your strength, where did you find your support?

PS: You know, I never even had time to think about those things because every day the issue was, "Are you going to get through this? Are you still going to be on your feet? Are the kids still going to be alive? Is the house gonna be there, is the marriage still gonna be here?" You know the old saying, "It's good that a dog has fleas because he forgets he's a dog." I was so busy swatting fleas that I didn't have time to think about anything else.

RM: What was your commitment?

PS: I think my first two years were positively miserable. There are no words to describe how miserable they were. Yet at the end of the two years, you think, "I cannot step down now because then people will say, 'We had a woman once, and look, she didn't even run again.' " So you run again. At the same time, with Watergate, you did have reason to hope, because of all those things that were going on. And things did get better. In '74 we had the Watergate class come in. They were a lot more activist, with lots more soul mates, philosophically, among them. So that was an easier time. I think after the next two years, I began to feel that there were just so many critical things to do, I became overwhelmed. The place was so nuts.

RM: Beyond your sense of obligation to women—so that it wouldn't look as if women were wimping out—was it the issues that held you?

PS: The excitement of the times. You figure you roll the dice and hope.

RM: So then you stayed for twenty-four years altogether.

MH: When I read the stories after you announced you were leaving Congress, I was amazed that so many people said things like, "Oh, she's disappointed because she won't get committee chairmanships, with the Republican victory." I must confess that *my* question was, "How did she manage to hang in there so long?" With many others, I'm sure, I could relate to your annoyance about those who said, "Well, I didn't actually vote for you, but I was so happy you were there." Or, "You have no right to step down, even after twenty-four years."

PS: You just shake your head and say, "What *are* they thinking?" You know, in retrospect, I do wish I had quit two years earlier.

MH: But only two.

PS: Yes, it was a good run! I almost wore it as a badge of courage that the leadership of my party never asked me to go on any trips or to participate in any of the other perks. They thought I wasn't paper trainable, which I think is good. Both sides really only want women to be cheerleaders, and it just frosts them when you ask them questions; it makes them furious. You see young women coming in, and they get so conflicted: "How do I get to be a player?" My question is always, "Why do you want to be a player? What tune are they playing that you want to be part of that band?" I don't look at the place with this warm, wonderful feeling. I look at it as a place that constantly needs to be hammered at.

RM: I'm so interested in your comment that the leadership of your party never asked you on a trip or anything like that. Are you saying that throughout more than two decades in Congress, you were not acknowledged, encouraged, or connected to your party's leadership?

PS: Yes. It was interesting, too, because if you asked a lot of my colleagues when I was there, they would say, "Schroeder gets all this good stuff because she's a woman. She gets all this press attention, you know; and it's just not fair. She gets everything, and she won't share with us." I'd always say, "Really? Isn't that interesting, because we have lots of other women here; what do these guys mean?" As for the leadership itself—the speakers, the majority leaders—they always have their troops and they have their little bennies and pork chops that they hand out. Obviously, I set them off very early, right after Wayne Hays and his little girlfriend got into that big hoo-ha over her being on the payroll in a phony job.

We put together the House Fair Employment Practices Committee after that, and of course the leadership on both sides went nuts. They preferred the place as a plantation, thank you. Why didn't I understand? Well, we got over a hundred members together on the issue. The leaders knew they could kill our legislation, but our going ahead and setting up something voluntarily was really offensive to them. That was rubbing their noses in it. So they wouldn't even put the committee on the directories that are by all the elevators. They wouldn't give us a phone; they wouldn't give us office space or anything. We had to run the committee out of our offices just to make it work. Those things were going after the club. You don't do that.

RM: So you were perceived as the person who was thumbing her nose at the club, naming it and challenging it, and therefore never being asked to join.

PS: That never bothered me!

RM: What were you proudest of in over twenty-four years in the Congress?

PS: Survival. I mean it. When I think of the people that I have seen that came there and got hammered, chewed up, and spit out—the people that lost their families, and all the other things that happened—just surviving looks like an amazing thing.

RM: So you're personally proud for surviving with humor and resilience and a family intact. What about the legacy in Congress? What makes you proudest from those years?

PS: I suppose I'm proud that I tackled all sorts of things in Armed Services which you weren't supposed to do. I did an awful lot on women, children, and family issues, although those were not seen as big power issues. I did a lot of challenging the institution, trying to bring it into the twentieth century. It didn't want to come. It liked being where it was.

MH: When you visited Ruth's graduate seminar, one of the students asked whether you missed the power that you had in the Congress and whether you enjoyed exercising it.

PS: Yes, I told her I don't miss it, because I don't think you'd have much in this Congress. You don't have to be a rocket scientist to figure out our agenda's going nowhere. You can introduce a bill, stand in front of a mike and talk about it, and give a press conference about it. But you're probably not going to pass it. I really was about passing things and getting things moved to the "out" box. Do I miss the power? I guess I never felt I had internal power. I mean, I could introduce stuff, but then I spent most of my time trying to figure out how you got pressure from the outside on the body, because it was always fairly clear to me that the bills I had were not ones the members were waiting for. "Oh, family leave! Why didn't I think of that? Finally! Sign me up!" Instead, I thought, "We need family leave, they aren't receptive to families, so what do I do?" So I'd think, "Okay, go to the press. Look at *their* ages, look at *their* lifestyles. The press will understand family leave. Can I get them interested and use it as a platform?"

I just never had the kind of power that walked around and people said, "You want me to jump? How high?" But I never really wanted that kind of power, either. The guys who wanted everybody to stand up when they walked in—well, that was just not me. (Some women were like that, too; this is not totally gender specific.)

MH: How did your office work *around* the power?

PS: If you looked at my staff, it was not so different in some ways from most congressional staffs. But in ways that mattered, it was. Most had been there from the day I came, and we probably had the longest-serving and highest-paid staff on the Hill. Average Hill staffers stay a year and a half, and an awful lot of money gets used for leasing automobiles for the member and paying for drivers. I drove myself and I did my own phone calls. Everyone would call me by my first name, which stunned people. They were professionals in their own right and we dealt with one another in a very horizontal manner. I figured we were really more of an ideological think tank.

I ran for political office in order to change some things, and I selected some pretty serious things, such as work and family issues. A poll of Congress contained important news for those of us interested in legislation grappling with those issues. That poll came in and said to me, "Now we know why you are having so much trouble. When you look at U.S. society, only one family in ten looks like Ozzie and Harriet, but when you look at Congress, only one in ten doesn't look like Ozzie and Harriet." So the Congress was the reverse of the country. When it came to issues of women in the workplace, these guys did not have a knowledge base and they didn't want one. When we passed family leave, they were still saying, "Oh my gosh, maybe my wife will go to work. Or maybe if you make the tax code more equitable, that'll push the last woman to take a job, and then no man will ever have a warm meal." So getting back to staff, I knew I had to have people who were well grounded in serious issues like these, and I wanted their skills to be used in making outside contacts rather than in carrying me around on a silk pillow.

RM: Where do you think campaign finance reform is likely to go?

PS: There's absolutely no reason for it to happen. I don't know what's going on with Americans. They seem to have turned into the biggest bunch of wusses I have ever seen. I fear Congress will pass some awful bill and call it "campaign reform." Then two years from now the public will discover that nothing's any better, and maybe it'll be worse. You just keep feeding the cycle of cynicism. I'm very pessimistic right now.

When campaign finance reform was passed before, the idea was that people disclosed where they got their money. That was supposed to be all we needed. There are beginning to be studies of the links between the donations, their amounts, and the influence wielded in government. Yet it is shocking that people have mostly been too lazy to go and connect the dots. The way things are, every member knows that to get reelected, you have to collect x dollars every day, depending on your district. Your campaign manager tells you the amount, so how are you going to spend your days? On the damn telephone, that's how. You're not going to be calling ordinary people, either. You'll be calling fat cats, who then will be saying to you down the road, as the votes come up, "By the way, Charlie."

The problem is, once you get elected that way, you're fearful you can't get elected another way. You kind of lose your self-confidence. And these fat cats probably belong to nice clubs. They play golf, they have football tickets—all that kind of stuff. So if they become your friends, it's certainly a lot more fun to go to those places than to the union hall picnic at the amusement park, where we're eating hot dogs.

RM: How did you raise campaign dollars?

PS: My average campaign contribution when we first got elected was $7.50; when I left, it was $32.93. You can imagine what kinds of fundraisers we had. They were not thousand-dollars-a-head dinners, and they were not golf tournaments. We had a family night at the Natural History Museum, we had kite-flying picnics, and we had pancake breakfasts. I honestly think that's how you ought to run a campaign. Then you're talking to real people. The other way gets to be very incestuous. It's cozy, and those folks soon become the only group that you're getting your information from legislatively. That was also one of the reasons I never felt I had power, since I was not inside that group. I understood that group, and I understood that my issues were not that group's issues, so I knew that I had to do something on the outside all the time to figure out how to make an impact inside.

MH: Returning to your comment on Americans as wusses, I'm mystified by the paradox of journalism and political science departments throughout the country turning out scads of majors—with more women among them than ever before—while the constructive anger and critical consciousness raising you are talking about just don't seem to be happening.

PS: You know, I sometimes wonder what people are teaching them. I know they are not teaching students how to be effective citizens. They are teaching about polling, and they are teaching all this conventional crap about writing to your congressman. When I was at the University of Minnesota, we were blessed with Hubert Humphrey coming to campus all the time. He used to do what I still like to do, which is ask college students, "What would you do if you were upset about *x*?" The answer I most often get is, "I would write a letter to my congressman." I say, "That is a third-grade answer and deserves an F." They are stunned. How do we teach people what kind of power they really have? No wonder they're wusses. They have tremendous power in our system, and they don't even know how to use it.

RM: In my class we talked about the considerable changes for women in leadership through electoral politics in the last quarter century, and we got into a discussion about what makes people act. We were talking about women in this case but were posing the question of what prompts people to change things. My response was that if you look at your own family and at your own life and think about what it takes to really change something, it is not very surprising that people don't very often act to make changes collectively.

PS: I guess I'm kind of stunned, though, that people don't know how to do it better. Take the letter issue. Why not write a letter to your representative, you ask? Okay, you're me, and you get this letter. Now you don't have to be very smart to figure out this person is mad. So you can waste your time and write back, or you can ignore the letter. What is the average reaction going to be? "That damn Schroeder. I pay her salary, I can't stand what she does, and she won't even answer my letter. I'll show her, I won't vote." I guess I just grew up as a terrorist because I sat around all the time thinking of things that could make more of a difference. Never write a letter. If you have totally run out of ideas, at least sit down and make a creative poster: "Wanted: Pat Schroeder. This creep does dadadadada." Send it to me, and then add a note saying, "I just made a thousand of these and I think I'll put them in the menus wherever I eat, and I'm going to hang them in the laundromat, too, because I am really mad." Wow, now you have my attention. You just realized you have some power. But as long as you keep it in a little envelope just between you and me, forget it. Now, there's three hundred other levels you can go to. Why does no one know that? That may be the difference between now and the sixties. Then, at least, Americans thought they could make a difference; they thought government could be changed, and they saw themselves as change agents.

MH: Why is that no longer the case, in your opinion?

PS: What happened to progressives? I don't know. I spent my last two years of Congress wondering what happened. The first six months after we were all beat up, I thought, okay, they're in mourning. After the next six months, I notice there's still the same six to ten people speaking out; and after eighteen months, the same thing. Finally I say, "I don't need this." I don't need members of my own party saying, "Why are you out there attacking Newt Gingrich?" My theory always is if you pat a dog on the head and he bites you, I feel very sorry for you. But if you keep going back and patting the damn dog on the head and you keep getting bitten, I finally say, "You know what? You're not real smart. You don't learn."

Getting back to your other question, Ruth, about why people act. Here too, I figure people don't act unless they really think they have some power and a chance to make change. If there's an alcoholic, most people say, we can do an intervention. But unless he or she is ready to change, we won't succeed. But in another situation, you might make another judgment, a judgment that if you try to intervene, you could make a real difference. You kind of pick your fights. Yet I think we need first to recover the sense that we can do this, that we actually do have the power to be agents for important change.

RM: You were in Congress from the early seventies to the mid-nineties. A lot happened then for women in our society that we wanted, and a lot did not happen. From your vantage point inside the system with the "Ozzie and Harriet" guys and the world they controlled, what was it like to have a few more women come in with every election? Did it matter at all? It took until 1992 to double the numbers of women in the House, but even now we are talking about only 11 percent or so. Did the addition of more women make a difference?

PS: Well it did make a difference, expecially for women's issues, which would be nowhere otherwise. The men just don't think about them. It's not malfeasance, it's just nonfeasance. They don't think about it, and they don't hear about it either. One reason has to do with what we have allowed these Ozzie and Harriets to do. Harriet goes home a lot; maybe she stays at home or maybe she's home all summer. Women's groups are naive about power and will invite Harriet to come and speak for Ozzie. That's where you hear about work and family issues, child care, family leave, women's health initiatives, breast cancer, and so on. If I flipped scenarios and decided to send my husband, Jim, to talk to the men's groups, they would say, "Bring him along to lunch; but you're the one we want to talk to, you're the one who votes." Men's groups are clear about this. They talk to the one with the power. What happens when most of these issues are confined to all-female groups is that the members themselves can give you a perfectly genuine reaction: "No one ever mentions this issue to me." Well, you look at their calendars and you understand why. They're at the Kiwanis Club, the Optimists' Club, the Chamber of Commerce, and the golf tournament. No one ever mentions these issues in such places. So having women there in Congress—because women do hear these things directly—brings the issues to the table and forces a different chemistry. Women there bring up things the Ozzies otherwise don't hear and wouldn't deal with.

RM: So women are helping to shift the agenda and change the issues?

PS: Yes. Just look at putting mammograms in Medicare. I don't know how many times we passed that on the floor. It'd come up for a vote and sail through. Then it would come back out of conference, and it was gone. What happened? When it went to conference, there wouldn't be a woman on the committee, and it would be the first thing missing on return!

RM: They would get rid of it in conference. You don't consider that malfeasance?

PS: Yes, I do. There's obviously a long way to go. The moderate Republican women did try during the Reagan and Bush years, but those years were very hard on them. Many of them joined the bipartisan women's caucus and supported bills like family leave. But Reagan and Bush never met with the caucus during their entire twelve years. Never. They met with the black caucus, and they met with the Hispanic caucus. We had a stack of letters that would fill this room, signed by Olympia [Snowe, Republican of Maine] and me. Olympia was a Bush supporter, but they wouldn't meet with us; and as you know, Bush vetoed family leave. For the moderate Republican women, it got harder and harder to explain why you were in a caucus when you could not get the president whom you had supported even to listen to you explain why your bills were important. So these women became extremely uncomfortable.

MH: Are congresswomen still taking bipartisan actions in the current partisan environment?

PS: After '94, of course, there were more conservative Republican women who came in. There had already been rumors that at the end of the

103d Congress, Newt called in the Republican women and got on their case for staying in the women's caucus, the largest bipartisan caucus on the Hill. The first thing he did when he took office was to change the rules for caucuses, which trimmed their effectiveness. Until then we'd been able to take a percentage of our staff salaries and assign it to one pool so that you could have some dedicated staff and space and phones to enable you to track certain issues. He took away that ability and moved everybody off the Hill, so it's much more difficult and costly. The real message to the Republican women was that they did not need the caucus. After that, Connie Morella stayed, but that was about it. The women's caucus limps along, saying it's bipartisan; it's really not.

RM: Let me switch to another category of women's political leadership. You are one of a handful of women in our history who not only considered running for the presidency but took some steps to do so. In our time, in the two major political parties, there are Margaret Chase Smith, Shirley Chisholm, and Patricia Schroeder. Smith wanted to run in 1964, but didn't campaign actively the way that Shirley Chisholm did in 1972 and you did in 1988. Talk about considering the presidency of the United States.

PS: Well, my situation was probably unique because I had started out to be the cochair of Gary Hart's presidential campaign. As a consequence, I'd cleared my calendar, I'd traveled all over, and I'd monitored all the other candidates for that purpose. When Hart's candidacy blew up, there I was; and I had real dissatisfaction over how the whole contest was going at the time. I remember looking at the visuals on TV and imagining how women across the country would look at them. I recall seeing all those candidates actually shaking hands with babies; and I said to myself, "Only Jesse Jackson looks at all comfortable with children." So I thought, "Well, this is very hollow. I don't like the fact that none of these important issues is being discussed by any of the candidates, so let me test the waters." I was also realistic that it was very late and that there were six or seven people already out there who had been organizing like mad. Where would I get the money? I knew that people don't give money because they think you are nice. A lot of them want to be ambassador to such-and-such, and they're looking for someone they think can win.

MH: But you raised a lot of money in a hurry.

PS: We did, which was amazing, because it was summer and I had only announced in May. But I decided that I had the summer either to do it or not. By September it had to be decided or I would jeopardize the House seat, so the campaign had to be very condensed. It was exciting. We worked like fiends, and people were unbelievably wonderful. But I also came away with the feeling that there were parts of the country that could not get over the novelty of a woman candidate. *Time* magazine ran a poll in which I came out third, and my read of that was I would always come out third. I did the best of all of them on "Which candidate do you trust the most?" But still people weren't ready, especially in the South.

At that time there were hardly any women in major public office down there. Most people hadn't even seen women in city council, so they're going to think about one for president? That is a real leap of faith. We didn't make what I thought was enough money to be competitive; and while you can go into hock, I just wasn't prepared to do that. So I backed off. But I kept thinking about whether there was any other way to have an impact on issues in the election without being a sacrificial lamb. I decided that the way to do it was this Great American Family Tour, which we then did through the primary states in '88. It worked very well. Suddenly we saw all the candidates running off to daycare centers. It was very funny. They had no idea why they were there or what the issues were, but they were going, and we all tried to keep a straight face. If you remember, we even had George Bush coming out for family medical leave, though as I said earlier, he later vetoed it as president.

RM: Would you think about running for president again? When I interviewed Margaret Chase Smith some years ago, I was fascinated to learn that she had been dead serious about a run for the presidency. I knew the history of her name having been placed in nomination, but I had not realized that Margaret Chase Smith imagined herself as president, had relished it, really tasted it. Is that something you identify with?

PS: No, to be perfectly honest.

MH: When people twenty years your senior set out to become president, as Dole did, it obviously can't have anything to do with age! There are other reasons for you.

PS: Yes, it's just too discouraging to look at it right now. Do you really want strangers staying in your house all the time for fund raising? Do you want to spend your life doing that? I figure I've sacrificed so much of my life to public service as it is, why in the world would I do something like that? That's just about as blunt as I can be. Now if they ever clean up the system, that might be different. But I'm not real optimistic they're going to do that. I also know that the party would go nuts. It's still such a guys' club. Think of all your visuals coming out of the White House and everywhere else. It's all guys.

RM: When you say you've given up much of your life to public service, are you saying that you see public service mainly as a sacrifice?

PS: No. I think you have to be able to segregate it, to separate it; and I think I've done a better job in that than almost anyone there. I'll be really brazen about that. I remember when I first got elected, Liz Carpenter, who was writing for some women's magazine, asked me, "What would you do if you were president?" I said, "For starters, I wouldn't live in the White House." She said, "No, no, no, you *have* to live there." I said, "Why would I live in a museum? Why would I do that to my family? What would I do with my spouse? He doesn't want to sit there and have his little projects. He's got a life. No."

It is a real problem for women, because the First Ladyship is so built in. The teas and all that. It used to be that presidents of universities had teas, or their wives had teas. In most of the rest of society that's cleared out by now. There's still a lot of that in the White House. Then you add to it all the other stuff. I was proud of myself that I found a way to run without doing all that—the kowtowing and special-interest stuff and the Washington PAC stuff. I just don't know how you do that at the presidential level. So a lot would have to change for me to consider that run again.

MH: Let me ask another question then. When you were contemplating where else you'd like to be other than Congress—leaving aside what you're about to do as head of the Association of American Publishers—what kinds of things did you consider as options for what Pat Schroeder ought to be doing next, or would love to be doing next?

PS: You know, I really didn't think about that. I have just never been a person who sat down and planned her life out ahead of time. It was just that I knew I was getting very close to the age when I'd be a lifer in the Congress, and I wouldn't have a choice.

MH: They announced on television some time ago that you were considering the presidency of Haverford. My son was about to go there; and I thought, "Terrific!"

PS: I figured I should look at a lot of things. Anything that came over the transom, I was willing to sort through. But in twenty-four years, I have not given much thought to what was next, not really had an agenda. Even when I left, I hadn't focused that much on what was next. Unlike most people who quit, I was really involved right down to the day I walked out the door.

MH: I understand you are developing some projects for the Institute for a Civil Society in Boston that will involve topics of special interest to women. Tell us more about the institute.

PS: We call it an out-of-the-box think tank. One project is putting together an interhemispheric conference on domestic violence with the Inter-

American Development Bank. No one has ever gotten a bank to deal with this problem as an economic and health issue. So we hope to do some culture cracking with that one! We are also involved with a group of African-American professors from Harvard who plugged in with the churches in Roxbury and came up with a program for rebuilding the community. It's really grassroots. We're seeking ways to rebuild the fabric of the civil society, not just study it some more. We're also doing some work on corporate responsibility. The writer Phyllis Katz has published a book about the feminist dollar in which she rates all eight hundred American corporations by the numbers of women on their boards, the numbers of women in upper management, the quality of their work-and-family policies, their corporate philanthropy, their community outreach, and more. What an interesting model for measuring equity for women!

I've also been intrigued to follow the work of my friend Laura Liswood, a remarkable businesswoman from Seattle who decided to film fifteen women who ran their countries for nine months or more and present these interviews at the Beijing conference. It is very powerful just to see the visuals of these fifteen women, alive on the globe today, who led their countries, and it puts the issue of women in leadership into a "new-millennium" context. To see how different they are—with the unique mother-daughter story in Bangladesh, and our friend who ran Nicaragua with her son the Sandinista and the son who wasn't—trying to do family dinners with them every Sunday and run her country at the same time! One of the most profound comments was made by the prime minister of Iceland, who said, "No woman on this globe would ever think of forming a government without including men."

I think we've had too much of this What is a leader? question. It prompts all the images of male leaders, which is why I think it is so powerful to see Laura's film with all those women. What we usually think of, after all, is the white shirt and red tie, the unbuttoned collar with conversations on the phone. It's about busy-ness, it's about image. When you peel it all away, these guys usually don't know what they're doing; they just know they want to see their picture and they want to be in the bright lights. There was a great film called *The Candidate* with Robert Redford. The whole thing is spent on all the PR of the campaign, the maneuvering of this guy's handlers to get him into office. When he finally wins the election, you see him asking kind of plaintively, in the last frame, "Okay, what do we do now?"

Then there are the types who think they know exactly what they are supposed to do, and their stories all run like this: "Okay, now I'm a congressman so I need to be a subcommittee chairman and then I want to be a chairman, and then I gotta have a big office and more staff, etc." For them, it's all about the accoutrements of power. I think the reason I hate the words *leadership* and *power* is that they are words we use without thinking about them enough. Do you want power *over*, or do you want power to do something, power to make something important happen? There is a huge difference.

If I want power, it is to do something. Do I want to lead the world? No. I don't have any place I want to lead it. That kind of leadership scares me to death, anyway. What people need to be aware of, finally, is that in our system *they* are the ones who have power, if they will only use it and use it well. One way to use it well is to use your head when you choose the people you call your leaders. The bottom line is, any institution is never any better than the people running it. If you've got good people running it, they'll find a way around bad rules, or they'll change the bad rules. If you've got bad people running it, any number of good rules won't help much. Americans need to understand that the core principles of the people they elect are more important than anything else.

MH: Whatever you do next, you're going to be fascinating to watch.

PS: Well, I don't know, I hope I survive it all, right?

RM: We aren't worried.

PS: I keep saying that whatever this life is, it's not a dress rehearsal. At some point you have to figure out what it is you really want to do. I probably have had more fun than most people, and I plan to keep on figuring out what it is I want to do. Right now, I think working with book publishers is going to be really, really interesting.

MH: You're going to shake it up, wherever you go.

PS: That's one of the things I like to do.

Ruth J. Simmons

■

In Conversation with Alice Kessler-Harris and Cora Kaplan

Ruth Simmon's appointment as president of Smith College in 1995 marked a historical turning point in women's education, as she be-came the first African American, and only the third woman, to head that eminent institution. The daughter of tenant farmers, Simmons was born in Grapeland, Texas, in 1945. She was raised there and in Houston, where she distinguished herself as an outstanding young scholar. With her parents' encouragement, she won scholarships that allowed her to attend Dillard University in New Orleans, where she earned her B.A. in French and graduated summa cum laude in 1967. She attended the University of Lyons in France as a Ful-bright scholar, then earned a Ph.D. in romance languages at Har-vard University in 1973. Simmons took her first teaching job at the University of New Orleans, later becoming assistant dean of the Col-lege of Liberal Arts there. From 1979 to 1983 she served as assis-

tant and then associate dean of the graduate school at the University of Southern California.

Ruth Simmons next accepted a position as director of Butler College at Princeton University in 1983, serving as acting director of Afro-American studies there from 1985 to 1986. She found this latter position enormously rewarding, succeeding not only in increasing the program's budget but in hiring stellar faculty including Toni Morrison, Nell Painter, Arnold Rampersad, and Cornel West. She then served as assistant and associate dean of the faculty from 1986 to 1990. After a stint as provost of Spelman College in Atlanta, Simmons returned to Princeton in 1992 as vice provost, where her special report on race relations earned her national distinction. In 1994, she became the unanimous choice of the presidential search committee at Smith. There, she is working to enhance not only Smith's focus on multicultural education but its national role as a leader in women's education. Simmons remains committed to preserving Smith as a women's institution and to maintaining the college's emphasis on the liberal arts as the basis of a sound education.

ALICE KESSLER-HARRIS: We're interested in exploring ideas about women's leadership with you. We would like to know what, if anything, the term *feminist leadership* means to you. Also, do you think women lead differently from men; and if so, does that matter?

CORA KAPLAN: Let's begin with the comment you made a few minutes ago about believing in social justice as a child, and how that relates to the development of your notions of leadership, as rooted in your personal history.

RUTH SIMMONS: I'd begin by saying that I am not sure that leadership is anything more than achievement. In terms of one's outlook as a child, if one grows up believing that there is opportunity for achievement, the effect on what one does is great. I happened to grow up in a time of intense discussion of civil rights, and in particular of achievement of rights previously denied to African Americans. As a child, I anticipated that the outcome of those struggles would be to the good, because it seemed only logical that in the end, this country would recognize that you cannot impede peoples' success simply on the basis of race. Because the signals in society confirmed I was right, I was able to continue to work.

It didn't much matter to me that in the very immediate future I couldn't see the rewards of my efforts. I was going to school and working hard. Yet as I was doing all those things, I was still going into back doors. For example, I was not able to go into some department stores and try on clothing, and I was still not able to go to some restaurants. So there was this dichotomy in my young mind, because while I was working hard for success on the basis of my achievement, I was living a different reality every day, in which my color determined the places I could go and things I could do. My optimism was based on the hope that my people could hold out and that things were going to change.

Often enough I have imagined what my life would have been like if I hadn't believed in the promise of the future. In a sense, I see that in the older children in my family, whose decisions were quite different from mine. I am from a large family in which the age spread between me and the oldest child is twenty years. The result is that many of the older children were making decisions based largely on the options available to them in rural East Texas, where our family were sharecroppers when I was very small. Three of my brothers went into the military. One of my sisters married quite young, which was typical then; and another sister dropped out of school and went to work. I often wondered if they made those choices because they could not imagine finishing high school and going on to college. Becoming a college president would have exceeded anybody's expectations.

AKH: How much of that achievement, do you think, comes from your own determination, as opposed to your location in the family and the different messages at different times from the outside world?

RS: There's no question that some of it, at least, has to be messages from the outside world. I do not believe that I am the brightest of the children my parents had, nor the hardest working, nor the most articulate. Why would such success come to me? The generational difference clearly played a role. If my oldest brother, for example, had been born twenty years later, who knows what he would have achieved? Societal messages to children about what is possible for them to achieve are very powerful forces.

It is similarly true for women that the messages they receive as children affect what they are able to do. Those messages can determine whether women step off the path to high achievement and decide that they are going to do something easier, because they believe the path leading to the highest achievement is simply not realistic. Most people, after all, want to be realistic; they don't want to be disappointed in their lives; so they try to make plans based on what they think they can achieve. Most adults encourage their children to be realistic, and few say, "Just imagine anything you want to be, no matter how foolish or unrealistic, and try to do it anyway!"

In addition to the promise of the civil rights movement, then, the second important thing that happened to me was the harsh reality of being part of a family that was virtually without means. It is hard for people today to understand what a sharecropper's life is like; it may sound exaggerated or even romantic, I suppose. But the truth is that the sharecropper system was nothing less than an extension of slavery, due to the way tenant farmers were held on the land through debt structures. The system prevented them from getting the means to become independent of the plantation owner. Growing up in that system was extremely hard for children, who were taken out of school to work in the fields at very young ages. Those large enough to do serious manual labor were forced to work like adults. The irregularity of their encounter with learning was extraordinary, and many were unable to finish high school. Luckily for me, I was never brought fully into that system since I was able to go to school when I was six, and about a year later we moved to the city, where I was enrolled in schools on a regular basis through high school.

All this meant that I never paid the price that the older children in my family paid. Instead, from an early age I encountered teachers who showed me something different both about myself and about the possibilities for this country. That made all the difference in the world for me, all through school. That is why I believe so strongly that both for minorities and for women, encounters outside their own experiences—outside the limitation of what their families and their own psychosocial circumstances allow them to imagine—permit them to see the breadth of possibilities open to them. Here I was, the child of a very poor family, having teachers constantly expose me to different outlooks, sometimes through books, sometimes through advising, sometimes through firsthand intercultural encounters.

CK: Were your teachers themselves energized by the political moment and the times?

RS: They may have been. My guess is, however, that when I started school in 1950, it was too early in a small town for people to believe that the kind of revolution we have seen was possible. I think they were just doing what they did for every child: they were loving that child and trying to make survival possible in a harsh environment. By the time I reached high school, I encountered teachers who fully believed they were preparing me for access to more than they had ever had; but in the early days, I think it was just good teachers doing what good teachers do.

AKH: Wasn't there also something about the fifties that sustained optimism? The possibility of living better than one's parents is the thing that is always said about the fifties, so it may be that those years that encouraged a sense that everything is possible helped set the stage for the expansion of particular opportunities with civil rights.

RS: That may be, except that I don't think that optimism was so characteristic of the African Americans who remained in the South. Remember, there were waves of black migrants who moved away from the South, and there was certainly much hope and excitement among them about the future, mainly because they were escaping the pernicious Jim Crow and sharecropper systems. For those who stayed in the South, there was little evidence of potential for change. Recall that Emmett Till was lynched in the fifties. There was ever-present danger to Southern blacks during the fifties; it was a terrible, terrible time.

AKH: What about the impact of B*rown v. Board of Education* in 1954?

RS: I think people make much of that decision because they know its historic importance today. I don't think many people at the time thought it would matter. After all, when in our lifetimes had the federal government really stood up to Southern segregationists? Never. My parents could not have had confidence that the law would have the impact that it did. They had seen lynchings throughout their lifetimes; they had seen the reign of the KKK. How could they have believed that the federal government would one day protect their rights? That, arguably, is a fairly recent phenomenon.

AKH: Yet for your growing up, did Little Rock matter in 1957?

RS: It mattered in the sense that we were aware that things were happening in the country, but it was still not clear where we were headed. One way to put this in context is to recall the reaction to Martin Luther King. Many African Americans thought he was crazy, that he was risking people's lives when everyone knew things were not going to change in this country. True, there were also those who thought King was too much of a moderate, but we tend to forget that it was his idealism that frightened lots of African Americans. They worried that he didn't understand how dangerous his opponents were. When you watched TV and saw the dogs and the hoses, what you thought was "How could anybody put people through that?" It was not as idealized as it has been depicted in recent years.

It's odd to me, but I have not been able to remember what it felt like when I was finishing high school not to have the college options that African American students have today. I know I didn't contemplate the idea of going to college in Texas because of the racial situation there. I remember applying to Iowa but thinking that I would have a better experience at Dillard, where I went—a safer experience than I thought I would have in a white institution. I recall making that decision, or being helped to do so by advisers; but I don't remember a feeling of disappointment that the next cohort of students from my high school would likely have many more choices. So my guess is that I was hopeful as a result of the 1957 decision without having that intensely hopeful feeling you might read about now.

CK: The movement gave you hope, then, but also heightened the sense of danger?

RS: Absolutely, because of the brutality you could see on television.

AKH: All your teachers had been African American until Dillard. Was there any contact with white teachers?

RS: That would have been inconceivable in Texas at the time.

AKH: Talk a little about your first contact with white faculty and how it felt.

RS: It didn't feel a particular way. Let me explain. In Texas, although I didn't have contact with white teachers, I had contact with whites. What people forget about the South is that we lived in close proximity to whites and had close relationships with them, even during the days of segregation, although the place of blacks was severely circumscribed by the Southern caste system. Segregation just meant that blacks could not aspire beyond the level set for blacks. So could blacks go to church with whites? Absolutely not. Could they live next door to them in most areas of Southern cities? No. But close friendships arose. Black and white children played together. Some of my close friends when I was small were white. That's a curiosity that the history books don't capture very well.

It is also true that when we moved to Houston, my mother would occasionally do what was called "day's work" for extra money. On a Saturday she would sometimes take me with her, and I would help her with the cleaning and such in white homes. For me, there was no mystery concerning interacting with whites and no fear of whites who were in certain positions. So having my first white instructor when I got to Dillard didn't seem odd to me at all. Many of my instructors at Dillard were white because historically black college faculties had many white members. These colleges were segregated from the standpoint of the students but not from that of the staff or faculty.

CK: I want to circle back a little and talk about your consciousness of gender as you grew up, whether you thought that girls' futures were going to be different from boys'.

RS: With African Americans, it's extremely complicated. I'll just free-associate a little and talk about some of the influences. First, I grew up in a family completely dominated by males. There were seven brothers and, of course, my father, who was a typical Southern parent in most respects, though not all. He was dictatorial, although I say that lovingly because it was thought proper for the head of the household to be that way. My mother served him as one would have in the old days. We all paid homage to him in this very typical African American Southern household in that time. Girls were expected to be of service to men. They were not expected to have independent lives. It was not proper to harbor goals independent of what our husbands wanted or independent of what the men of the family dictated. All the emphasis was placed on the boys, on what they did and what they could achieve. Girls were expected to get married and raise a family, but little more than that. The expectation was that we would preserve our place in the social order and support our men.

In a large family there is fierce competition among siblings, so as girls we understood right away that what was being forced on us was patently unfair. We understood that our brothers got more—including more freedom to go where they wanted and make their own choices. My older sister resisted these notions, and because of her, the rest of us developed strong independent streaks. Having sisters helped, because we supported each other and we fought back. My mother saw her task as supporting her husband, and she did a perfect job of that. She was not able to impart to the girls in the family any notion of ourselves as individuals with talent and with goals.

But here's what we *did* get. My mother was a person who was very wise in her understanding of the human character and of human possibilities. What she was able to teach us was about the challenges we would face in life. She would tell us stories about the past, about my grandmother and her experiences as a woman trying to survive; for her husband died when the children were very young. Her education of her children was in a sense the gift my mother gave us, because she taught us about life, about wisdom, about respect for people, about how to place a value on what we encountered, about what mattered in life and what didn't. Without her knowing it, her life inspired us and fueled our independence. Every time we saw her have to take a back seat, or have to serve or to do all the things that women of her generation did, we were angry for her, because we knew that it was not just.

Now as an African American family, very close to the Baptist Church, there was the additional complication in that the church imposed certain strictures on women. That was even more oppressive in some ways than what was happening in the home. In those days, the African-American church dictated that a woman's role was to be a helpmate to a man. The church used biblical mythology to underscore the limitations placed on women, not just in the church but in the home. Because in Southern culture, social life centered around the church, the church was able to inculcate these values in young women. It's fair to say that in school this process more or less continued. It was the expectation that men should naturally be at the top of the class, that they should naturally achieve more, and that girls would have fewer opportunities.

AKH: How did you transcend that expectation?

RS: I transcended it mostly by being open to other worlds. This openness came primarily through my reading. I was an incredible reader as a child. My brothers and sisters say I always had a book in my hand! What reading allowed me to do, and what school allowed me to do, was to understand that there was a reality other than the one I was living. When I went off to college, I gravitated to languages because I was always fascinated by other cultures. I wanted to understand something about myself, and I must have surmised that in order to do that, I had to gain distance from my own culture. So I studied languages. I think I understood at an early age that my own culture, wonderful as it was, should not be the limit of my experience. I understood the problematics of the education I received at home, but I also loved it because ours was a close family, with a moral education unequaled by anything I have had since. I think, though, that education helped me understand that I could maintain my ties to that culture without being limited to it for all time. That is why I believe in multicultural education. I know what it does, and I know how it transforms your life. I know how it teaches you to understand the limitations of your own society and culture and the positive attributes of other cultures.

AKH: I want to segue into a comment you made about your year at a college for women having transformed your life. Do tell us more about that.

RS: Let me pick up on what I said about the culture of which I was a part. Some of it is Southern, and some of it is distinctly African American. When I went to college, I went to a coed school where the whole notion was that it was more important for men to succeed and achieve than women. It was clear in my college that men were being prepared for something special and that whether in academics or extracurricular activity, it was appropriate for men to dominate. I had learned as a child to defer to men—to their wishes and to their goals—and I carried that with me into college. While learning about my own possibilities, I was not internalizing those as yet. I was just able to store all this information from other cultures and other peoples' lives. I can still remember the men who graduated with me in high school and how I thought of them as much more brilliant than I or other girls. In fact, one didn't use the term *brilliant* for women, and I certainly didn't think of myself as brilliant, even though, as I look back, I was one of the brightest kids in my class. In a way, I suppose I thought back then that I did not deserve to be called "brilliant."

When I went off to college, this thinking continued because it was the same cultural context. True, I was active, I was outspoken, and I was seeking chances to expand my understanding of the world. But I was still deferring constantly to men, who I thought were more important than I was. I did well in my first two years and was a decent enough student. But I would still say there were no glimpses of a truly gifted mind then. It would be interesting to talk with my teachers to see if they agreed.

The first time that I understood that my intellect mattered was when I went off to Wellesley on an exchange program from Dillard and sat in classes where I began to see the higher expectations for women there. That's what awakened me, and I think it was primarily because there were not men present. It was impossible there to defer to the brightest boys in the class and assume they were going to raise their hands and give the answers. It was up to us to do that. I once went to a French teacher to explain how lost I was, because unlike at Dillard, the classes were taught in French. When I sought out the professor to tell him I needed to drop the course, he just said, "No, you'll get it. Just stay with it, and one day you'll begin to understand the French." The fact that he expected me to make it helped me to apply myself anew, and he was right.

At Wellesley, there was no question of *whether* you could do the work. It was the hardest thing that I ever had to do, but I was able to master French because somebody said, "Yes, you can learn it because you are bright, because you are at Wellesley, and because we know you can do it." That transformed my thinking about what I could achieve.

I have been told many times that I was spinning my wheels and would never achieve a senior-level position in a distinguished college. I remember people telling me at Princeton, "You're doing very good work, but of course you should not aspire to be president of a place like Princeton because it's not realistic. So you ought to leave and go someplace else and do something you can do at your level." These are messages women hear all the time. Minorities hear them all the time, too. How do you get beyond that? You do it because someone has helped you to understand that you can achieve. For women to achieve in this country, they had to tune out messages from people who said women could not achieve on a par with men. Sometimes you can't afford to listen.

CK: You've worked at a lot of different institutions—public, private, historically black and geographically distinctive. What would you say about them in terms of leadership?

RS: We have many different models of leadership. We know about how people who have been successful in leading organizations, or even countries, have come to those tasks from many different routes. There is no single formula for leadership, nor a single path to leadership.

My enduring interest in academic life in this country has made me want to know more about what has worked and what has not worked. I wanted to know what it would feel like for me as an African American woman and an academic to be in a large public institution such as the University of Southern California [USC], to be at Princeton, to be at Spelman, and now at Smith. What guided me has been my interest in what higher education offers young people, and I've wanted to understand better precisely what those things are. What I've discovered from my personal odyssey is that these institutions are at once more different from one another and more alike than we imagine. People often ask me how I could go back and forth among such different types of colleges, but all have one thing in common, after all: they educate young people. In fact, they educate them for exactly the same things. Students who leave Spelman go to Harvard Law School, or Harvard Medical School, or they go out into the workforce. Princeton students do the same thing. Although we imagine a great difference in terms of educating students, I think the basis is largely the same from institution to institution. There are some differences that derive from geography, from the ways in which faculties are selected, from the different missions in terms of research and teaching, from the various cultures that predominate at these institutions. So a school like USC is profoundly southern Californian in every way.

CK: The Barbra Streisand Chair?

RS: Exactly. The popular culture, film culture in particular, dominates in southern Califormia. When I first came to Princeton, I found it much more conservative and more rigid in terms of perceived opportunities for women. However, that did not continue to be the case in subsequent years. Princeton was extremely good for me in that it brought out my leadership skills in a way that other institutions did not. It probably happened at Princeton because the challenges and need were so great there, and because there was not an easy means of making headway. There were many women at USC working hard in the administration and very active in trying to do more. There was very little of that at Princeton when I arrived. I think often you develop leadership skills because there's a need and a vacuum, and it gives you a chance to work at something that has not been done before. I had a chance to explore ideas that I had about transforming Princeton. I came to believe that change was needed on a fairly significant scale and that change was possible. I came to believe, moreover, that I could play an important role in bringing about that change.

CK: One of the wonderful things that you did at Princeton was to build the Afro-American studies program. I wonder whether being associated with that initiative helped or hampered your career, given that people often see a contradiction between the special set of interests associated with such programs and being able to undertake the kind of role you have assumed since, administering an entire institution and all its programs evenhandedly.

RS: It's interesting that you ask that, because when I was asked to take over Afro-American studies, everyone on campus who knew me and was concerned about my future asked me not to do it, bcause they thought that it would mean that I would be severely limited in what I could do afterward. The conventional wisdom was that I would be pigeonholed, that I would be doing something outside the mainstream that would not lead to anything. I did not believe that. Well, that's not quite true. I didn't care if it was so. I thought the job needed to be done and that of those available to do it, I stood as good a chance as anybody of doing it well. So I undertook the directorship knowing that most thought it was a serious mistake if I was an ambitious person.

Now, how did it happen that I did not get stereotyped in that role? First, because the effort was immensely successful. Princeton is a place that treasures quality above all else, and the fact that we were able to recruit extremely able people to the program attracted attention. I think people believed that I understood how to judge quality. Often in Afro-American studies, or women's studies, there is a misperception that what we desire is to make a political statement rather than to engage in critical inquiry. When you do first-rate work in those fields, some are startled and even overly impressed. Second, because I was successful in recruiting in an area that had been difficult for some time, the assumption was that I might have similar success in recruiting for the entire university. I was not taking a risk in leading Afro-American studies because it was something that I was committed to, something I very much believed in, and something to which I was prepared to give every bit of my energy! I was not looking at where it would lead my career; I was just doing what I had been taught to do by my mother: work hard, be honest, respect people!

AKH: It does suggest, though, a kind of faith, not only in the capacity of institutions to change, but in the power of institutional change to transform society, to achieve some measure of justice.

RS: Absolutely. I thought that trying to do something significant in Afro-American studies would help to change Princeton. I was working for transformation on a much broader scale. It's unquestionably true that the best things one does are rooted in that kind of passion about one's work. In terms of achieving leadership, one is not always seeking to play a visible leadership role, because sometimes the best leader is acting invisibly to bring about change. What I did in Afro-American studies was to unify a lot of people in a common effort. I was able to convince people that Princeton could do something few thought it could do. A number of others were with me behind the scenes trying to facilitate our success, but what I was doing was hardly widely known at the time.

AKH: Could you imagine yourself doing the same sort of thing in women's studies?

RS: Sure. It happened that Princeton had a very strong women's studies program; but if I had been in an environment where that had been the need, I'm certain I would have been called to address that need. I think that throughout my career, I've been attracted to particular places because there was an opportunity there for change.

CK: I want to move to affirmative action. I'm interested in your assessment of the current climate, whether affirmative action can continue, and how you think affirmative action relates to women's leadership and to leadership and achievement for minorities.

RS: I feel strongly that when we talk about affirmative action, we must begin with where we are now. Whatever the issues, whatever the emotions, we have to begin with where we are. And where we are, as you know, is a place where women do not earn what they should compared with men. You can assume that is based somehow on men having been in the workplace longer, or on any number of things. But if I am working in an office where many departments are sending me recommendations for hiring, people will still send two names forward for the same position—a woman's and a man's—with the same educational backgrounds, but with two different salaries recommended. Women in executive positions are earning less—not because they are getting smaller increases but because they start lower than men. How would you address that without some program to make sure that people are conscious of continued inequity and discrimination?

Affirmative action requires us to look at pay scales and to compare how women are being paid relative to men. Where isolated or systematic disparities exist, we are required to address them. That says to me what affirmative action ought to be doing. We need to know what opportunities there are for minorities and for women, and we need to make sure they have a fair chance. It is not an issue of promoting these groups beyond their qualifications or beyond any other group; it is an issue of equal opportunity. Where we still have evidence that fairness and equity are not applied, we must be prepared as a nation to seek justice by instituting actions that address the wrongs being done to people. To abandon all aspects of affirmative action would say to me that we are prepared to live with inequities. What I worry about is that if we are prepared to say to young people that we are going to live with these inequities, it will have a serious deterrent effect on their desire for achievement. It is true that we do have to address the widespread perception that women and minorities are advantaged at the expense of other individuals and groups. But in doing that, we should certainly not rid our country of the only effective means it has in place of achieving more equal opportunity for all.

AKH: You have made the wonderful point that the children of alumni in our educational institutions get "affirmative action" and have done for years.

RS: Yes, but nobody mentions that; nobody really cares about it. I am not even suggesting that such preferences be eliminated. I'm saying that we ought to acknowledge that in fact we do not have a true merit system. We probably cannot have a true merit system, because there will always be devices that we use to give some people a better-than-average chance. If at any time we learned, for example, that men were systematically paid less, and systematically excluded from certain professions, I think there would be swift agreement that a program was needed to remedy that situation and that it should be kept in place until equality was achieved.

AKH: On the one hand, you are saying that affirmative action is consciousness and ideology, and on the other, that affirmative action is structure with rules and guidelines. Separating the two makes it quite apparent that what men are complaining about now is what minority kids and women have complained about for years: that there are some limitations out there on their aspirations. But what the white males are *really* complaining about is not the loss of an equal chance but instead the loss of the unearned edge that they have long had in the job market, by virtue of the accidents of being white and male.

RS: Yes. I think one of the things that people are very reluctant to say in the current environment is that in the future many people are going to be living with less in this country. That is a fact—this loss of the presumption of privilege on the basis of birth. It is a frightening thing for people to contemplate. I think that is where we ought to be, however, since we aspire to be a place where there is true equality of opportunity. That does not mean we are going to succeed in any realm that we select, that we will become the CEO of any company we choose, for example; but it does mean the opportunity to compete. What affirmative action was remedying was that people did not have an opportunity to compete, for goodness sakes. They couldn't get into particular schools, or they couldn't get into certain companies. They couldn't possibly have a way of learning the ropes and moving up through the ranks because they were prohibited from core areas of the company, just by virtue of their race or gender. That is what affirmative action was remedying; it was opening up areas for competition. Of course, it was also remedying past discrimination in some instances, by paying people who may have been underpaid for many years in a job. This is an important tool to deter employers from future discrimination.

CK: Now you're at Smith College, a place that has been an elite leader in women's education since 1875. What needs to be changed there?

RS: It isn't so much that things need to be changed here. In this case it is more taking advantage of Smith's opportunity to be a catalyst for change for women in this country. What I long for even now is more rapid progress for women. I really do. It seems to me that although in some ways women have got in the door, we all know that it is just not happening at the leadership level to the extent that we would have expected. I think myself that women's institutions are in a unique position to prepare women for leadership, not just for careers, but for leadership in their professions. What women's institutions do better than others is to instill in women the expectation that they will be successful, that they will achieve, and that they will do that at the highest level. These schools say to them, "The fact you are a woman does not impede in any way your chances of success," and that is not a message that women readily get in many institutions.

I want to intensify here at Smith the kind of messages delivered to young women who have an opportunity to play leadership roles in this country. Princeton is known as a place that sends leaders out—CEOs, judges, secretaries of state, and so on. An institution can promote advancement and leadership, and I think that Smith has done that in the past. I think that it can do that even more in the future; and I want to concentrate on what we are doing to enhance women's chances of playing important leadership roles in the nation. I also want to have a chance at Smith to help other colleges and universities understand what they ought to be doing in educating women. I'd like for us to be able to export some of the skills we have in doing this to institutions that don't know enough about how to support women. I think it is Smith's obligation to be helpful in transforming this nation, so I actually see our mission as being beyond that of just educating the young women who are fortunate enough to come to Smith. It is to stand as a model for the country, showing what we can be doing to make this society a truly equal one in which women can be supported in their aspirations.

AKH: So the public role beyond the institution is one you welcome.

RS: I welcome it because I think Smith has so much to teach the nation. What the students and faculty and staff at Smith believe is that we have a secret here; we know something about what it takes to prepare women for leadership roles. The country doesn't know about that. We want the country to know. So my mandate as president of Smith is to try to share that message, to try to find ways of getting Smith into the public consciousness a little more, into boardrooms and into government. It is to try to talk about what everyone needs to be doing for all of the young women coming through the educational system. It is they who will increasingly be responsible for leading this nation, and we need to help them be ready for that role. I think it is a wonderful opportunity for women's colleges, and of course for Smith, to carry that message forward.

CK: What about preparing women to live and work in a multicultural world? Is that something that Smith needs to do more?

RS: Most at Smith would say yes, absolutely. I think it is a difficult area, yet I find it truly amazing, given our history, that we understand so little about how to do it right. I have thought a lot about why that is so. It seems to me that we are so poor at it because we have worked so little at it. Multiculturalism and all that it implies is every bit as complex as any other challenge we are facing, and yet the extent of what we do, too often, is silly little things like having people come together and chat. This is merely placing tokens strategically through various areas of our lives, such as having a week in which we talk about what women have contributed, or Native Americans or Asian and Pacific Islanders. We trivialize the importance of an undertaking that in my view is among the most important that we confront if we are to ensure that our society endures.

Rather than continuing to function at such a trivial level, we need to recognize that true multicultural preparations call for deep thought, for expertise, and for the formulation and articulation of fairly complicated ideas. How can we do a better job? For one thing, I would like to see more work in the academy on a very serious intellectual level. Faculty at Smith, for example, along with faculties on other campuses, need to help bring greater understanding to the issues. I am surprised that the departments and faculties that would seem to have the best head start in helping the rest of us understand how we should proceed, such as the language and literature areas, have not been leaders in the multicultural debates.

Let me use myself as an example here. I grew up in circumstances that were quite segregated, and when I went to college I realized that one way for me to escape the boundaries of my own culture was to study language and literature. That is why I selected these areas. I can still hardly believe that I did this, but at the end of my sophomore year, at the age of eighteen or nineteen, I went off alone to Mexico to learn Spanish and live with a Mexican family. I have often asked myself what might have impelled a person from my narrow background to do something like that. Certainly it was the desire to know more and understand better how to relate to different people; but it was also the fact that study of language and history and culture helped me understand the worth of other cultures as well as the worth of my own. I believe that language, literature, and history faculties should be leading this development and participating intensely in the many multicultural debates.

CK: But those faculties often don't think so!

RS: What they have been doing for their own students is precisely what they need to be doing for all students in the area of multiculturalism. I very much regard myself as an example of what we are seeking from multiculturalism. Here I was, a child growing up and seeing throughout my life the terror wreaked on my family by Southern whites. There is no particular reason, based on my experience, for me ever to want to associate with whites, other than the fact that I was permitted to understand the historical, social, and cultural contexts for what was taking place. I was able to learn about how these factors influence cultures over time, over long stretches of history, and I think that fundamentally that is what all children should be learning. That is the only way that they can move beyond the kind of biases that are otherwise inevitable in societies.

Perhaps unknown to them at the time, or perhaps not, the people who were teaching me French, or Spanish, were teaching me something about multiculturalism. The result of that has been that I have been able to live a life that is completely infused with different cultures. So when people ask me how I could work at Princeton, for example, and then work at Spelman, the answer is that it is just as comfortable for me to be in a black institution or a women's institution as it is for me to be at what people perceive as a very conservative white institution. That is the impact of a multicultural education. And that is an understanding that I will continue to work to develop better here at Smith, and I will also collaborate with others to strengthen multiculturalism at other colleges and universities.

AKH: What I hear you saying throughout our discussions is that what leadership constitutes, really, is courage—the courage to face these and other challenges instead of walking away from them.

RS: Courage seems a little self-inflated. But I'll tell you how I think of it. I don't think of it as being courageous as much as having the capacity to see a need and to take responsibility for it. At a certain level, I think we should be teaching every individual in this society to take personal responsibility for contributing something, for bettering society in whatever way possible. I take this view largely because of what my mother taught me as a child. She said that if you see somebody in trouble, you can either wait for someone else to come along to help or you can help the person yourself. What she taught me was regard for other people.

We think of leadership as something on a very broad scale, but it really isn't. In the end, it is something on a tiny scale, because what you are looking at, immediately, is the opportunity to do something that will probably make an immediate difference in only a small arena. What I thought I was doing with Afro-American studies was unifying people around a goal of improving something. Rather than what you were describing, I think of leadership as beginning with a small idea and a very intense desire to do something useful, something worthwhile, and something significant. That is what sticks with me.

I find it perplexing, I have to tell you, to be at a point in my life where I am leading an institution such as Smith, since when I look back to try to understand how it happened, I can't see it! I can't explain how it happened, because at no point in my life did I imagine anything like it. What I see instead is a whole series of individual things that I have endeavored to do. There was being a parent, which has been day to day, moment to moment. There was my role at Princeton, also day to day and moment to moment, looking for opportunities to do things that would contribute to what I fundamentally believed Princeton was destined to be. People have often asked me how I survived at Princeton for such a long time, because there tends to be such a high turnover of people of color and of women there. How did I continue believing in Princeton and believing that what I did there made a difference? I always said that it was because I was not thinking about the present but about the future. I was thinking that what I was doing, every day that I was there, was transforming the place by being there. Every time I had an encounter with someone, every time I had an opportunity to contribute something to help a program flourish, I was doing something to transform Princeton.

So often for women and minorities, it isn't helpful to think about what we're actually achieving now, because you can be discouraged about the many barriers. But it is awfully helpful to think about what the future is going to bring. So when I was building Afro-American studies and everyone was saying, "Forget it, you'll never get Toni Morrison here," I was saying, "Yes, but if she were here, what would it feel like?" So that is what was before me: what it was going to feel like with someone of that quality being able to encounter students at Princeton and what that was going to do to Princeton. That's what I was thinking about.

In a sense, I think it is still true that with Smith, what I am thinking about is beyond Smith. I interact with alumnae, faculty, and students; but what I am thinking about is way beyond that. What is Smith going to be twenty-five years from now? What statement is it going to make to women around the world about what women can do, working together? What statement is it going to make about whether an African American woman can lead an institution that is predominantly white?

Students ask me frequently what I consider the most important things to remember if they want to make a difference, if they seek to be leaders. I think they are often surprised by the answer, because I always say that you have to have regard for other people first if you want to be a good leader. That is one of the things women bring to leadership, I think—an intensity of feeling about the people for whom they are responsible. Beyond concern for other people, I think there is no single path to leadership. I tell students that what I believed in, always, was my capacity to move beyond where I was, to get better at what I was doing. I worked on that, and it seems I always knew that hard work counts for a lot. But there is no magic formula that says you must study calculus, or you must spend five years abroad—that doesn't exist. What does exist is a prevailing idea that whatever you do matters, so you should try to bring your very best effort to each thing you choose to do. Young people come to understand these things after they have worked for a while, but it is hard for them to see it immediately.

AKH: What do you understand by feminist leadership? Do you think of yourself as a feminist leader?

RS: I am not the one to judge that, but I'll tell you what I expect of other women whom I would like to think of as feminist leaders, and then I will leave it to others to judge me. I believe that for better or worse, we have been born at a time when women and minorities still do not have the full rights to which they are entitled. I believe further that because of that, each of us has a special responsibility.

My expectation of feminist leaders is that they will care deeply about women's needs and that they will not betray the true goal of equality in any way. That is a very simple answer, but I think that is what feminist leadership is. Now, that doesn't mean signing every petition that comes your way. That is not what it is all about. Feminist leadership is about advocating fair opportunities for women in everything that you do and demanding in every conceivable way the respect to which women's abilities and intellect entitle them. It is understanding and supporting the particular challenges that women who are trying to raise children face. It is having the fortitude and the wherewithal to remember constantly where we are in time in terms of women's rights and what we must all be doing to advance society to a place where all women will be treated on a fair basis. That is what I envision as feminist leadership. It goes without saying that if someone regarded me as a feminist leader by this definition, I would be honored! I would be the last person to say that I have already achieved that status; but it is a goal toward which I strive every day that I live.

CHRISTINE TODD WHITMAN

■

IN CONVERSATION WITH RUTH B. MANDEL
AND MARY S. HARTMAN

Born in 1946 into a prominent New Jersey family, Christine Todd Whitman was raised in Oldwick and attended Wheaton College in Norton, Massachusetts, where she earned her B.A. in government in 1968. She put her education to work immediately, taking a job, fresh out of college, with the Republican National Committee, where she created the Listening Program to open the party to the concerns of traditionally underrepresented groups, including students, senior citizens, and minorities. After teaching courses in an English as a second language program in New York City in the 1970s, Whitman entered New Jersey electoral politics in 1982, winning election to the Somerset County Board of Chosen Freeholders, to which she was - reelected in 1985. During her five-year tenure as a county free- holder, she served as both deputy director and director, implementing numerous projects including the establishment of a shelter for

Somerset County's homeless persons. In 1988, Governor Thomas Kean appointed her president of the New Jersey Board of Public Utilities, where she emphasized ethical responsibility and won the respect of many constituents, including union leaders.

Whitman set her sights on an elective post again in 1990, entering the Senate race against popular incumbent Bill Bradley. In a strong showing, she came within two percentage points of Bradley; and the campaign gave her statewide recognition. In 1993, Whitman was able to unseat then-governor Jim Florio with her message of a 30 percent tax cut and a balanced state budget. She delivered on this promise in two years and became a symbol for the new movement for fiscal responsibility in government. A popular and visible figure as one of a handful of women governors, Whitman was reelected in 1997 in a surprisingly close race. She is a leading moderate Republican whose name has often been mentioned for a top spot on a national ticket. Her wide range of interests includes education reform, the environment, women's health and rights including a pro-choice stance on abortion, and programs to enhance workers' education, skills, and earnings.

MARY HARTMAN: We'd like to start with some brief questions on your family background. We're aware that much information is already out there, with several recent biographies of you as well as accounts of your parents and their prominent role in the Republican party.

CHRISTINE TODD WHITMAN: In fact, I read in the *National Review* about how the sins of my parents are visited upon me. I don't fit their conservative model, so they're coming after me. It's all because of bad genes. My father was for Wilkie, so what can you expect? They actually say that!

MH: Well, we're interested in your own take on that family background, so here's an opportunity to talk back. We'd like your sense not just of the major, formative figures and influences while you were growing up but also of what turned you on to political life. Were there particular individuals aside from your parents, and do you regard your mother as more important than your father as an inspiration and role model?

CTW: It is much the way most of the published things have it. There's no question I was lucky to be raised within a strong family structure, and my parents were the dominant influence. In my youngest years, my mother was more of a factor than my father because he was commuting into New York, although they worked so closely as a team that it's hard to separate their influence. We children did many things that they did. What we do now with our own kids is like what my parents did then—making sure that every summer we get away together as a family to do something. Dad was certainly a part of all that, but it is also true that I was in a rather unique situation. I'm the youngest of four, by eight years, so I grew up almost as an only child. My parents had had all the experience with the other kids, so they certainly knew what they were doing. But they'd also worn out their discipline on the older ones! Mother raised me more on her own, and she used to say that while Dad was the disciplinarian with the others, she was able to keep him at bay with me!

What I remember especially was the conversation around the dinner table, just Mother and Dad and me. It was on their favorite subjects—government and politics, what was happening in the world. I was treated as part of that because we had dinner together almost every night, except when Dad, or both of them, would be out politicking.

RUTH MANDEL: No TV.

CTW: I didn't get to watch much TV, although we had one. I remember when it came.

RM: But you didn't watch it at dinnertime.

CTW: Not at dinnertime. No, no, no. Those family dinners together obviously steered me—those plus other experiences I had with my parents. Dad was older, and he had retired from his New York business and come to focus more on politics by the time I was a teenager. He wasn't commuting any longer by then, although he still had an office in New York. He was state chairman [of the Republican party] and really focused on that. Mother was very involved in politics, too, so I went to a lot of things. My earliest memories are going with Mother to count paper ballots in Oldwick until two in the morning. I was allowed to stay up late on election night, and I loved it.

MH: Did your parents talk to you at all at that stage, or later, about going into politics? Did they ever say, "What about you, Christie, you might be interested in this kind of thing"?

CTW: No, never.

RM: What were their expectations of you? In a way, what you're talking about is like the family store—politics as the family store. I grew up with a father who literally had a store, and he would have liked me to work in a similar business.

CTW: They were enough of a different generation that that didn't happen. For example, I was expected to go to college, but if I got married and didn't go, that was no big deal. Dad said, "You've got to learn secretarial skills." I said, "Over my dead body, because if I can answer 'yes' to that question Can you type? I'll never go beyond it." I refused to learn how to type. Mother's message was more: "You can do whatever you want."

I think it took Dad a while after Danny, who was the next oldest to me, left the state for Washington after serving in the New Jersey legislature, to recognize that I was the one who was going to be in politics here in New Jersey. But he wasn't opposed to it, because he also thought I should get a law degree. So it wasn't "Learn secretarial skills because I expect you to be a secretary," since he also said, "You've got to go to law school because then you'll always have a career." *I* was the one who said, "I don't want to be a lawyer, so I'm not going to go to law school. I'm not going to waste my time doing that." I think they were very pleased that I did get involved in politics from the very beginning, right out of college; but they never pushed that as a way of life. It never was Dad's primary way of life, or Mother's either. It was a paramount interest always, but it wasn't their life.

RM: I've heard you talk before about how theirs was really more an ethic of public service, as opposed to political life as a career.

CTW: It was never their career. It was an ancillary but very important interest, actually more so for Mother than for Dad. I didn't see her in that role, since she was older by the time I really focused on it; but both she and her mother were seen in their youth as barrier breakers. She was a very active woman in politics, and although never an elected official, she was always a force behind the scenes.

RM: Do you remember any fantasy or moment of dreaming about being in public life? I remember once standing up at a Mother's Day tea in college when all the students were asked, "What do you want to be twenty years from now?" and hearing myself say, "I want to be a 'lady ambassador.' " I don't know if I ever thought about that at any other time; it just came out at that moment. I knew that I didn't want to do the secretarial thing, and the peer pressure was to get an education degree and teach—which I didn't want to do. What were your dreams or images of the future?

CTW: For a while I wanted to be a surgeon, but I got into this Bio 101 class and had to learn all about the sex life of the mossy fern! I figured, "That's it. Not exciting enough."

MH: Did you picture politics?

CTW: Yes, I really always did, from about the age of thirteen on. I recall asking myself whether I was really a Republican, or whether I was a Republican just because my parents were. You have to understand that I grew up in a somewhat rarefied atmosphere in the sense that Mother and

Dad were within the party structure—behind the scenes, but high enough that they were doing important things. Mother was chairman of the program in 1956, when I was ten, and she had an organizing role. I went to my first convention that year, and I was able to see all the people everybody else was talking about. Later in my teens, I recall being a page for Efrem Zimbalist Jr., who was on *77 Sunset Strip*; I was madly in love with him! It was glamorous and a lot of fun; but I also did a lot of the stuffing, stamping, sealing, and sending. I also did door-to-doors, which I loved. I was fascinated when a person once shut the door in my face, saying, "It's my right not to vote."

So I was early plunged into politics at a level most people don't get to until they have slogged through the vineyards a long time. My parents did the slogging, and I was able to ride their coattails to an extent. I did plenty of grunt work, as I said, but I was also able to see the excitement and the glamour parts of it. I loved meeting all the people, and I knew I wanted to be involved in government for a long time, even though I didn't know what I would do. I wasn't committed to elective office, but I interned with [N.J. Republican senator] Cliff Case the summer between my junior and senior year in college, and I had a ball. He did a good job with his pages, and I wrote a speech for him that he gave on the floor of the Senate. That was a lot of fun.

RM: In addition to family history and childhood experiences that gave you the immense advantage of knowing how it's done, so to speak, you also came of age in a particular historical moment. As you look back now, I'd like you to comment on the importance of the social and political context of the women's movement and what began to happen for women and politics in this country in your early adulthood.

CTW: Timing is everything.

RM: At least it is very important. How do you perceive the influence of what was happening? I recall when we formed the Bi-partisan Coalition for Women's Appointments during the Florio-Courter race, you were sitting in the drawing room of the Eagleton Institute with the rest of us. You were then chairing the Board of Public Utilities. How did that historical moment influence the choices you made and the directions you took?

CTW: Obviously, the women's movement opened a lot of doors. It made more things possible, because people were beginning to accept . . . well, they *didn't* really accept women. Deep down inside, most of the guys still didn't think women belonged in politics, but they were harder and harder put to explain why there weren't more women there. If a qualified woman came and said, "I am interested and I want to get involved and I'm willing to do the scut work to get involved," it was harder for them to keep her out, so that helped.

One of the things I should add is that when I went to college, I majored in international government and never took a domestic politics course. I stayed away from American politics out of youthful arrogance: "I know as much about this as anybody is going to teach me because I've been out there doing it." What I didn't know about was the international political situation. I took all my courses in that in order to broaden my horizons and because I was always interested in the field. I thought I'd like to be an ambassador. I also considered the State Department and thought about being a foreign service officer, because I'd lived abroad as a kid. I spoke French, and at that point I spoke Spanish pretty fluently, too. So I looked at several things, but finally it was the determination that I wanted to be involved that made the difference; and I do think that the women's movement played a role in that.

We had Millicent Fenwick in Somerset County, who was a big role model for everyone, a trailblazer. I also still had the very personal role model of my parents, with Mother being someone who was in the forefront in areas where women weren't usually taken seriously. Dad deferred to her opinion on many things, and he'd always push her rather than himself when people started talking about running for public office. They appealed to him several times because he was known as being absolutely dead honest and a person all sides could deal with; but he'd always say, "No, Eleanor's the one. She's the one who should run." He very aggressively tried to push her at the point when [N.J. governor] Tom Kean was able to appoint someone to replace [Senator] Harrison Williams. Dad really, really pushed him to put Mother in there. He would have stayed in the background to get her to do things, but she was always doing the opposite, saying, "You know, Webster, you've done all this work, you should get the attention and the rewards." So they were very much a team, and I was used to seeing that.

In fact, a lot of what I was doing came out of ignorance, because I didn't realize I *shouldn't* be there, or I *shouldn't* speak up at that meeting, or I *shouldn't* have a place at the table with the guys. After all, I had seen it all my life—that back-and-forth between men and women—so I figured, "Hey, that's what you do." That there was also so much happening everywhere else for women made it seem even more natural. I remember when I was down in Washington in the late sixties or early seventies, a friend of mine was very close to Bella Abzug, who at that point was really leading the movement. I went to a meeting in her office involving strategy for the movement. Abzug wasn't sure who I was or why I was there, but she knew

I was coming from the wrong side! I can remember being absolutely fascinated by how she was working the other women who were there, who were clearly neophytes in the political system. She had the agenda, she knew what she wanted to accomplish, and she had them just completely wrapped around her little finger! They were saying, "Yes, yes"; but their vision was over here, and her vision was over there. Hers was the practical vision. She knew exactly what it took to make politics work, while they were looking at the broad, idealistic, everybody's-going-to-be-happy-and-be-together side. She was so pragmatic, and they didn't see that at all. They missed entirely what she was doing and how she was using them—not in a bad sense but in a good sense. It was absolutely fascinating to watch.

MH: Speaking of your youthful career, I was fascinated too, to learn that early on, you were already the declared moderate Republican, supporting Nelson Rockefeller's candidacy for the presidential nomination in 1964 and again in 1968. In Vienna not long ago, at a conference on women and democracy in central and eastern Europe, Ruth and I heard the American ambassador to Austria, Sewanee Hunt, introduce Hillary Clinton by recounting that the two of them had something in common back in 1964: they were both out there ringing doorbells for Barry Goldwater! And there *you* were for Nelson Rockefeller.

CTW: Yes, that's part of that *National Review* article, too. I was clearly destined for doom because I was a Rockefeller Republican!

RM: Let's jump far forward, to here and now in New Jersey. You are, after all, the first woman in this state ever to win statewide office. This is an enormous achievement, and it took until 1993.

CTW: I would say it was a big achievement to be the first person to defeat an incumbent governor. That's always overlooked, and I keep saying, "That's sexist." What everybody says is, "You're the first woman governor." That's true, but I'm also the first candidate to defeat an incumbent governor in a general election since the new constitution in the forties.

RM: Do you think that's a more important achievement historically?

CTW: I think no, but I like pointing it out because everybody gets so hung up on the sex. There wasn't much I could do about the sex, but defeating the incumbent I could do something about!

RM: The Center for the American Woman and Politics regularly issues fact sheets with the percentages of women in the fifty state legislatures. New Jersey has always ranked low. In 1997 we're thirty-eighth in the nation, and we have only one statewide elective office in addition to the Senate seats. In 1993 when you became governor, it was still hardly inevitable that a woman would be elected statewide. How did it happen?

What were the most important conditions or circumstances that made this historic event possible?

CTW: It was, first, the guys being willing to have a woman as a sacrificial lamb against Bradley. I never thought I was going to win. I looked at it this way: The one opportunity—and there aren't that many here in New Jersey to run statewide—was for the United States Senate. I said, "I'll take it on, I'll do it." They were very willing to have me do it because they didn't think there was a slight chance—any chance at all—that I'd win that election. So they didn't stand in my way for the nomination. They tried when I ran for governor, but I made too good use of the intervening years, and I did too well in that race. They couldn't dismiss me. It was the party organization's worst nightmare come true, because they hadn't supported me. They gave lip service but they didn't give me money, they didn't campaign for Whitman save for a few exceptions—Chuck Haytaian was there, and there were a few others. But for the most part, they didn't.

MH: Bush didn't come into the state.

CTW: Right. Bush wouldn't come into the state; he would not come into the state for me because he didn't want to tick off Bill Bradley. He stopped at an airport once after the race, and when he came in, I thought my husband was going to kill him! He came to a fund-raiser for the party, and I sat on the dais having just run that race and come within a hair of beating Bradley. They had me up on the third tier of the dais, way off in the corner. George Bush came in and talked about new faces, fresh faces; but never mentioned me. He was talking about legislative races. Finally he came up and gave me a kiss at the end, but he never, never ever once mentioned the Senate race. Never once mentioned it.

MH: How large a piece of this was your being a woman; how large were other issues?

CTW: I think a lot of it was my being a woman. Obviously with the governorship being the only statewide elected office other than the two senators, there's a lot of competition for this job. So naturally, it doesn't matter whether you're male or female; there's going to be a lot of resentment if you go for it. But that Senate race was the key. I spent that summer of '90 really going after the Republican bases, showing up at every one of the counties and at all the Republican events to say, "I'm alive, I'm here, and damn it all, I'm going to fight this!" Then I took it in the fall out to the general election. We had less than a million dollars, so obviously we couldn't do much.

But at that point the issues started to fall my way, and Bradley was utterly stupid in the way he handled the campaign. I was waiting every day for him to blow me out of the water, which he could have done with one statement. He just never did it. So we come back to the adage that luck is what happens when opportunity meets preparedness. I was lucky, but I also happened to be prepared; and then I was given opportunity. By doing as well as I did, I became a national story, so they couldn't deny that I existed. Then I knew what I wanted to do in the interim. I spent those interim years party building, just going out and campaigning for every candidate, no matter what they were running for—mayor, local council, freeholder, or sheriff. I was there for them.

MH: But that was your own game plan, right? You had little in the way of backing.

RM: That's what I remember as so striking. After the Bradley race in 1990, you went out on your own. It appeared similar to what we'd seen in other places—that is, women organizing outside their own parties. In your case, however, it was particularly striking because you had such a background, such a history with the party. Yet even you became one of those women who, acting like mavericks, were forced to organize outside the party in order to be accepted. One would have thought it would have been different for you, that you would have been the party's golden girl after the Bradley race.

CTW: I was a threat to everybody who wanted to be governor, because they knew perfectly well that that was where I was going. That threatened them, that's the power base, that's where it's at. So they weren't going to be there for me.

RM: You knew all along it was the governorship that you wanted? Because in 1990 you could have won a seat in Congress. You didn't have to challenge Bill Bradley in a Senate context; you could have won an open House seat in a Republican district.

CTW: What actually happened was that I was president of the Board of Public Utilities at the time. It was a wonderful position and I was delighted to have it, but I couldn't wait to get back to elective office. Appointive office just didn't offer the same connection to people; it was too much layering between you and the public in that office. I knew I wanted to get back into elective office. That was the year that [Congressman] Jim Courter said he wasn't going to run. Everybody expected me to go for that seat, and I would have won the seat. I would have won the primary, and I would have won the seat. But I really didn't want to go someplace where I was going to have to run every two years. The minute you get there you start raising money again, and I knew who my opponent was going to be because the Democrats had already ceded the seat, since once again they saw it as a hopeless thing for them. So they gave it to Marguerite Chandler because she had her own money.

I knew I was going to have to raise at least a million dollars anyway, because she had promised to spend that much of her own money. I thought, "Why? I'm going to have to raise all this money." I was going to have a primary because Dick Zimmer was going to go in. I was confident I could beat Dick in the primary; but I said, to myself, "Look. I'm going to have to have a primary, I'm going to have to raise a million dollars; I might as well go for the statewide experience. Why go for something I'm going to win and use that as a stepping-stone to be governor? If being governor is what I want to do, I should focus on that." So I chose to do the statewide race, because I wanted that experience if I were going to run for governor.

RM: One last question about that, so I'm clear. You came close to defeating Senator Bradley, and so you were seen as more of a threat. Other people wanted the governorship, which is especially competitive in this state. But you also loomed as a promise as well as a threat, no? Here is someone who almost beat this enormously well-known, presumably highly popular senator. So wouldn't it have been likely that had you been a man, a huge base of support within the party would have shifted in your direction, notwithstanding the fact that there were other people who wanted the position?

CTW: Well, maybe so, if I'd been a man. But I wasn't. That put me perforce a little outside the system. And also, in fairness, I think part of it is who I am. I haven't had to depend on the party apparatus, I've never had the IOUs, and that makes me very threatening in and of itself, male or female. To have somebody in this job who doesn't have all these IOUs out there is very threatening.

They were the ones who made the mistake. They hadn't backed me in 1990 in the Bradley race. I had been able to raise a little bit of money; and we had enough, even though, as you say, we did it more on our own in the first governor's race. But remember, too, this isn't my whole life. I've got a family, and I can survive this time if I don't get reelected. Now, I *want* to get reelected, no question about that. But the point is, I can survive, and I will have a life. It's not the power trip that turns me on about being governor. I think that showed, because I wasn't so desperate that I'd do anything or promise anything. They didn't have any hooks in me, and that was threatening.

MH: That's a good lead-in to a question about what you found once you got here. Were there surprises? What has been easiest, and what has been hardest about being governor?

CTW: I don't know about the surprises, in the sense that I had a pretty good understanding of what was involved and of the responsibility of the governor's job. Frustration, perhaps, has been the hardest thing. Always having to overcome who I am, always being told that I don't understand people and stuff like that. Then there is the frustration of not getting the message out about all that we have accomplished in this administration beyond that 30 percent tax cut. That cut was important, in its substance and also for being a promise made and a promise kept. But there is so much more.

To cite just a couple of examples, we're national leaders in welfare reform and in environmental water-quality testing. If you look at the scope of the kinds of things we've focused on, you realize a lot of the states are looking to us to see how to get things done—everything from technical things like electric restructuring to the big, wide-ranging, politically sexy things. It is also frustrating that everyone expects that with a Republican legislature, everything should be a piece of cake. It shouldn't be, and it's not; and that is probably good. But every once in a while, it's frustrating that people expect that it should be so much better. As I look on this campaign, the fact that I'm being attacked for not having solved auto insurance and property taxes when we've been number one in the nation in auto insurance costs for nineteen of the last twenty years and property taxes—

MH: Now it's all your fault.

CTW: Exactly, and it goes with the territory. I know that, but there doesn't seem to be much understanding out there. I think we're victims of our own success. Perhaps because I've kept so many of the other promises, it's easier to say, "Why didn't you do this? You've done the income tax, why didn't you solve everything?" Property tax increases have been going down every year for the last three years. I don't know what they'll be this year, but for the last three, they've been going down. Property values meanwhile have been rising. Under the last administration, property tax increases were going up, property values were going down, and every other tax was raised. We've done it, even with lowering taxes; but that message is not out there. I'm saying it, but it's not getting heard.

One thing that you might be interested in is that when Art Weissman was doing the research for his political biography of me, he came in and said, "You know, you have a reputation of being harder on female reporters than on male reporters at press events." I said, "I do?" He said, "Yeah, do you think it's because they ask tougher questions?" And I said, "I think it's because they ask more adversarial questions. They are also much more challenging on supporting women, especially if it's a women's-type issue and they don't think I'm a thousand percent there. They will just hammer away at it."

I have always thought that that's part of our problem as women supporting other women. We demand that women excel at everything. We're willing to cut men breaks because we're so used to the kind of leadership they've provided. Because women represent us and there are not that many of them out there, the ones who are there have to be the absolute best, which means we don't cut one another much slack. That's a problem that we'll just take time to mature out of, I guess, when we have more women in office.

RM: Because all this is connected to a larger social movement for women, with ideological imperatives, and occurring in a period of great change. Over the years, I've seen a number of women who were, so to speak, "outside" go "inside." I've watched them being squeezed by the inevitable constraints and compromises and realities of operating inside systems while also dealing with the high expectations of those outside who want a magic person to go inside and turn things around.

CTW: The compromise part doesn't bother me that much in the sense that life has always been a compromise, whether you're on the school board or whatever. If you have a partner in life, you're going to compromise at times. There's nothing wrong with that as long as you're still focused on the right goals and moving toward those goals and not compromising principles. You may compromise the purity a bit, but life is not nice and clean and pure anyway. So that's not where the frustration has come from. It's come from convincing people to do things for the right reasons overall. There are a lot who will constantly say, "What's in it for me, and how does this benefit me?" I want to say, "How about we talk just once about getting something important done?"

Take the bond issue, whether you like it or not. The day of the vote, I would have been much happier if a single person who was concerned about his or her vote had come in and spoken to me about the merits of the bond issue as a bond issue, as a fiscal action, and not about "What can I get" or "What's in it for my district?" If just one of them had said, "Hey, let's talk about the wisdom of this bond issue. I don't like bond issues." If just one person had wanted to pursue the fiscal nature of the issue we were discussing, instead of saying, "Well, I'll vote for it if you make this person a judge and that person something else, and if you give me x, y, or z." But that's what it was all about.

Every once in a while, out of frustration, you just want to take people and say, "How about our doing something just because it's the right thing to do? You all admit, don't you, that it's the right thing to do?" One guy said to me, "I've been asking people to tell me what's wrong with this for months, and no one can tell me." Sure, it's the role of a legislator to protect his or her district, but every once in a while you'd like to say, "Come on out of your district. Representatives are also there to look at the broader picture."

MH: As you're thinking about your next administration, how would you like to focus some of these people's attention on those broader issues? If you were to pick out the major problems for New Jersey that you'd like to address and solve, what would they be? How would you like to be remembered in your role as governor of this state?

CTW: I've done some thinking about that, because to run for reelection you've got to think about that. What I really want is to leave office and have people proud to say they come from New Jersey. I would love that. I'd love them to be proud because they know there are good jobs that will enable them to support themselves and their families with dignity, proud because they know the school system is the best in the nation, proud because we're protecting their environment, proud because they know their cities and streets are safe.

Those are all the underpinnings of the pride that go very much to what government can do, and should be about doing. Overall, I would like to be remembered as someone who worked to give people many reasons to be proud to say they come from this state. *Not* embarrassed, *not* apologetic. *Proud*. We've had a wonderful history that most people don't know enough about. We're also making history every day right now. We in New Jersey are on the cutting edge of problem solving, setting examples for the nation.

RM: How do you do that?

CTW: For one thing, you build on what we've done thus far. I believe that people are beginning to feel more of a sense of pride in the state, that they do see that New Jersey is a happening place. People get a perverse pride, if I can use that expression, when they realize others are looking to *their* state for how to get a job done. And that is happening more and more these days. We need to keep taking that message out, to keep doing things, and to keep reminding people, "Hey, that was a national study that said we have the best ocean water standards in the world—not just the nation, but the world." What I look for is third-party reaffirmation of what we're doing. When you have other organizations saying these things, it's not just us. When the federal government comes to us and says we're one of only six states that we sign the NEPPS [National Environmental Performance Partnership System] agreement with, that's outside validation, because New Jersey's doing it right. We're one of only six out of fifty states. You have the national leaders on workfare efforts say, "We'd like to take credit for the corporate partnership, but New Jersey is out front; they've done it." Those are the kinds of things that we should build on.

RM: It's a great challenge: how do you make any human being proud of who he or she is? You are right that in this state it is a special challenge.

CTW: Yes, but communities are beginning to feel more positive. There are noticeable changes in attitudes. It's not that people suddenly say, "Oh, gee, now I have pride," or "I know where this pride I am feeling is coming from." Instead, it is something that grows gradually as people begin to feel better about themselves because their communities are getting better, because crime is going down, because more jobs are available, and because they're not as scared as they used to be. If you think about four or five years ago, everyone in this state either knew someone who had lost a job or had lost a job themselves. They looked around their communities and saw so many houses for sale and people moving out because they couldn't afford to stay. There's less of that now, although it hasn't gone away. There are more opportunities to work, and people know that. Even if they don't have jobs yet, they know people who have. It's different.

RM: Let me ask you something about being proud. I will long remember sitting in the Assembly chambers as you rose to speak during the swearing-in ceremony for Deborah Poritz as chief justice of the state supreme court. You are smiling now, as you did then, with a special gleam in your eye. I can't recall your exact words, but I observed you getting an enormous kick out of appointing this woman as chief justice. You have a striking record of appointing women to key positions. How deliberate has that been, how do you think about it, and is it special among the achievements in your first term as governor?

CTW: Yes, but we haven't done nearly enough, either with women or minorities. Once again you talk about frustration. The reality is that a lot of the appointment process is senatorial courtesy and getting support from the party. I would beat them over the head when they would come forward with lists of all white males. I'd say, "Go back and try again. I want a woman, I want a minority"—at the same time being careful to ensure that we get qualified people, since the other thing they'll do is to throw a couple of women's names at you. They know they're not qualified, but they think then they've done their bit.

The reason we have done as well as we have is that we really have been a pain in the butt, going back in many instances and saying, "No. I want a woman, I want a minority. I want a woman, I want a minority." We've appointed lots of white men, and I have nothing against white men. I'm married to one, I love them. But if you don't really push to get the women or the minorities, it simply won't happen. The more I'm in this job, the more I see that. Also, [Chief Justice] Debbie [Poritz] called me the other day to tell me she appointed the first woman to that level on the bench that she appoints directly. She called because she was proud of having done it. That's how it starts to happen. You put women or minorities in positions where they can affect the hiring or appointment process, and they will then begin to open things up.

RM: Is it now more likely than it was three years ago that you don't have to send back a list of names because there is no mixture of people on it?

CTW: It's getting better. It's still not where I want it. For instance, I have not appointed a minority prosecutor. I just haven't gotten the names. We've got some women, and we'll be making some appointments of women. But I went to a prosecutors' meeting, and I was struck that they were all men except for one, and everyone was white. The criminal justice system is not that way. I really think the prosecutors should reflect some of that diversity.

Back to your question about whether the lists are improving, if you've made some appointments that outlast your term, those people will have made appointments of their own. The critical mass will be rolling. You may take four steps forward and then two back, but those two that you're left with represent quantum leaps ahead of where you were. Deborah Poritz is going to be there for a long time; they can't do anything about her. So she can continue to make those appointments. The more you spread the base, the more difficult it is to revert completely. People can't go back all the way.

MH: This is a natural segue into a question about younger women. If your daughter came to you with an interest in going into public life—as more people's daughters we're seeing at Rutgers and elsewhere are doing now—what advice would you give about taking that road today? The world seems to be somewhat out of synch in that there's a growing cynicism out there about politics and politicians just at the time when more young women are getting enthusiastic about these possibilities for themselves. Seeing exciting role models such as yourself, they are increasingly daring to say, "Hey, maybe I could try for something like that," even as these cynical messages hit them that little can be changed.

CTW: See, I don't have a lot of tolerance for that. That's an excuse. It's never been easy to get things done. It's never been easy to get where you are in politics. It's just not easy. Male, female, it's not easy. People always say that you have to compromise, and that's bad. But we all compromise every day. We don't all go straight through traffic lights, even though there's no traffic on either side. We recognize the rules and we stop; we make way for people. I'm reminded of our pediatrician, who was a wonderful woman, saying, "I don't understand why people talk about not bribing their children to do things." She said, "If you do a good job working, you get a raise. That's bribery. I mean, you want people to perform well, you tell them, 'If you do a good job, you'll get a raise.' So why not say, 'If you go to bed without crying, you'll get a prize?' " I don't understand this "purity of purpose" thing; and I think sometimes we use it as an excuse.

It's the same sort of thing as saying, "It's all because I'm a woman that x, y, and z happened." I believe, deep down, "Yeah, a lot of the tough stuff may be because I'm a woman, but I'm not going to spend my whole time thinking and complaining about it, because then I won't get anything done. All I will do is concentrate on the fact that the road's a little harder because I'm a woman." After all, there are lots of people for whom it's much harder than it is for me, and that's true of almost anybody. This is again something instilled in me by my parents. My father said, "If you bitch and you don't participate, you lose your right to bitch." It *does* mean long hours and it *does* mean giving up things you want to do and trying to find a balance that isn't easy to strike, especially with family and children. Yet you've got to believe that it's important, that the effort and the sacrifice matter. If you don't believe that, then fine, stay out of politics. But don't talk about how important it is to be involved and then refuse to make the needed sacrifices.

As for my daughter, she says she'll never run for elective office, but she's majoring in international government, and she interned in Washington a couple of years ago. I don't think my son, Taylor, has an interest in a political career, but I think Kate does. I think she's there, although she jokes about being warped by all the people trying to persuade her to be a lawyer and make millions off the misery of others.

RM: May we talk a little about your leadership style? It has been fun sitting here and talking with you today. I know you have an incredibly demanding schedule and that we're going to get thrown out of here by your staff before much longer, but I'm quite sincere about how relaxed this interview has felt. Another image of your unpressured style lingers from your participation in the Eagleton Campaign Forum last winter, when you sat all day long, listening to the program discussants debate how we conduct election campaigns in New Jersey. You asked questions and participated as a member of the audience. For months afterwards, people remarked to me, "The Governor stayed there all day!" Not long ago, Mary and I returned from a conference where we saw high-level government officials protected, surrounded, and completely controlled all the time. They arrived, made fast speeches, then left in a hurry. How typical of you was that Eagleton Campaign Forum day? Do you think your style is unusual? Does it have anything to do with being a woman?

CTW: I think a lot of it has to do with being a woman, just because we learn early on to balance a lot of demands. Women do have a different set of life experiences and expectations. We remain the primary caregivers, whether it's for our parents or a sibling or a husband or a child; and if something goes wrong, it's likely to be the woman who's expected to be there. So you learn to balance a lot of things and keep a lot of balls in the air; and I think you also learn to compromise. Because of those demands of keeping so many things going at the same time, you also learn you can't do it all.

One of the LPGA golfers, Alison Nicolas, who won the tournament recently, is only 5 feet tall, and she hits the ball 200 yards. The question was raised at the time in an interview about whether men should look more to women's style in that sport. Women don't have the physical strength, and they're not worried about outmuscling everybody. They're worried about getting the best score, and their sense of competition is somewhat different. It's very real, and they want to win, but they don't feel they have to prove themselves off every tee by hitting a bear of a drive. Instead what they are concerned about is putting things together right, having the right equipment, and practicing well. They get there, and they're very competitive, but the style seems to be different. Maybe men can learn something from it. You've got only one or two really good men, and everyone else is way below, whereas there are more good women clustered at the top, all playing very, very good golf, although they approach it in a different way.

So I think we women do have a different style. You can get out of touch, though, partly because you have to be more protected in jobs like this one. I get more death threats, for example, than the last couple of governors. There are a lot of them, and I think some of that comes because I'm female. There are people who just don't like women, or don't think a woman should be in this position—that kind of thing. They're not all serious or anything like that, but it means that there has to be a little more security. You have to keep pushing the security people away and saying, "No, it's okay, I want to be with people" because in an office like this, we have been getting around a thousand invitations a month. You try to attend as many things as possible, but that means you can't spend as much time at those things as you may want to.

For those events or meetings that really interest me, I'll say, "I'm staying." The others I will stay for as long as I can and try to be as loose and relaxed about it as I can, because I've got a lot to learn. I know that, and I'm not afraid to say, "I don't know everything, not by a long shot." I find I get very bored if I'm not going up a learning curve. So I like to have people around me, or be at events or participate in things where I'm learning too, and we can exchange ideas and strategize amongst ourselves.

Again, I have found that women generally go into politics for reasons different than men. This may be changing now as more women enter politics. More of them may see politics as a means to an end, or else see the prestige or the power of the office as the main attraction. But women generally go into politics because they want to accomplish something, because there's a particular issue that interests them or a problem that they want to solve, whether local or global.

RM: Often very close to home.

CTW: Yes, the school crossing guard—that kind of thing. That's how they get involved. More men get involved because they want to have the title of "The Mayor" or "The Councilperson" and make decisions about other people's lives. Women tend more to get into politics because we want to get something done. That carries through; it's a different way of looking at issues and problems. That's hardly to say we're all pure or anything like that. We're not and I'm not. But I'm not quite as cynical as Millicent Fenwick, who said that women were going to be just like men, once they had the numbers.

RM: She did! She used to say that all the time, and it drove me crazy.

CTW: I don't believe that; I honestly don't believe that. I think we still will be different, no matter what.

MH: I'd like to turn briefly to your role in the national party. For whatever detractors you have had for your so-called sins of moderation, you have had many more admirers. You have held to a consistent moderate position in the party from the time you were a teenager, and you have spoken out again and again for a party that is not captured by any one group, a party that is supportive—among other things—of women's rights and of abortion rights. How do you see this playing out in the next few years? Do you see the Republican party shifting its position?

CTW: I hope it's going to shift. I see more concern from those very conservatives about whether I win this election—and if so, how big I win it—because of the influence that I could have as a moderate. I'm not dogmatic, and I'm not quite the ogre they paint me to be. But neither am I quite as far off on some of their issues as they'd like to think, although I'm certainly not within their parameters on some of them. I try to call them as I see them, and I continue to be where I always was on those social issues that are important. I'm not a purist. On very few subject matters is there an all-right or an all-wrong approach. And the truth is, there are a lot of people who agree with me.

The Republican Leadership Council, which was the Committee for Responsible Government, has a very strong basis of people now who say, "We must, as Republicans, get the message out that there is variety in our party." I have always believed that we don't have to denigrate someone else in order to build ourselves up, and the other side's got to recognize that there's room for everybody in the party. It's going to be a hard-fought battle, though. There is going to be some bloody fighting, particularly in Washington, where it's much more ideological. I will say, though, that some of the leaders I expected to be the most hidebound are the least.

Newt Gingrich, for example, is someone I didn't know until I got into this office. I only knew what I'd read about him in the newspapers, and I thought, "We're pretty darned different in how we look at issues." I found him, however, to be extremely bright, very thoughtful, willing to compromise, and a man of his word. If I go to him with an issue, we may come at it from totally different philosophical perspectives, but he will listen to what I have to say. He's smart enough and practical enough to know that if I'm making some sense, he'd better listen. He's someone who will compromise, and that has put him at odds with the more radical members of Congress. There's a lot of them. That is part of why he did some stupid things to himself, hurt himself, and became a hindrance. But he also is very, very bright and someone who really held it together for Republicans in the 104th Congress. I don't think a lot of people appreciated how intense some of the pressures on him were and that if he looked extreme, it was nothing compared to what he was dealing with in many instances.

MH: Well, I'm very glad to hear that he's listening to you.

CTW: I don't say all the time, but when I have gone to him on several matters, he's been very moderate and he's listened.

RM: We can't end the interview without asking you the inevitable question about the future—not only because everyone wonders what your plans are but because even a quarter of a century into the new movement for women and politics, we can count on one hand the women who have even been mentioned as real contenders for the top of the national ticket.

CTW: I have no interest or focus on that.

RM: But everyone else does.

CTW: Yes, everyone else does. It happens every day, and it's flattering up to a point. It gets to be a problem, though.

To want to be president, that's what you've got to want to be. It's a little like when I wanted to be governor. I started in 1990 and I kept at it relentlessly. If I want to be president in 2000, I've got to be doing the same thing right now. I've got to be making the contacts, starting to raise the money, putting together the organization—it's got to be all-consuming. It's not. Sometime in the future might I want to do something more? I don't know. Maybe? Sure. I certainly didn't want to be vice president last go-round, when everybody said that was what I really wanted most in the world. No, I didn't. At some time in the future, is that a step to take? I don't know, but right now my focus is here.

Harkening back to my roots, I was taught that good government is the best politics. If you want to move up the ladder, you try to do a good job where you are. If you don't, you're not going to get anywhere. If you do, the results eventually will speak for themselves. Then you have to decide that you want to fight all the battles. I don't want to do that right now. The rest of them can do that. I'd like to stay here and do a good job here. If something happens and things fall that way, if I think I could make a difference, then maybe I'd think about it.

RM: Aside from the annoyance of having every reporter thrust that question at you, it's also almost breathtaking, isn't it?

CTW: I don't think of it as real. I just sort of laugh and dismiss it. I say, "Get real," to myself, because it just doesn't happen that way. For instance, the way everybody talked about it in the last election as part of a plan I had to be vice president made no sense. Nobody does that, and there's never ever going to be a great groundswell. The convention isn't going to rise up and say, "Please, Christie, come save us and be our candidate." That is just not going to happen.

It's a very pragmatic, practical world, and there is a lot of stuff that has to get done. If you're not doing it, you ain't going to get there. Maybe the vice presidency is somewhat more possible if you're doing a good job where you are. Then you become someone that they've at least got to look at, and they may come to you and offer you that. That's certainly one step because you can then say, "Okay, if you're vice president, you certainly would have to be looking at the next step up." But I still think that's not something you plan. I don't think you run for vice president. I know people say Dan Quayle did, but I can't. My thinking is convoluted, perhaps, but not that convoluted to be able to plan that kind of a thing out!

RM: So here it is—1997. One looks across this country, and if what it takes in advance planning is what you're saying—building ahead for years—we can't even talk about a woman at any time in the foreseeable future. Because if you're not doing it, who else is?

CTW: I'm not so sure about that at all. I think Kay Bailey Hutchison is, and I wouldn't put Susan Molinari out of it at all. I mean, it's not a dumb move for her to have left Congress now for national television. There are all kinds of routes for getting there. All I'm saying is you've got to be planning and working towards something, and she may have a strategy. Then there are lots of names that I may not even know, because it's awfully early for everybody's name to be out there. You can't peak too early either because, boy, if they get you in the crosshairs of the gun, they'll take you out pretty fast, particularly if you're a woman. It behooves you to be behind the scenes campaigning for others, using other ways to get attention and prepare yourself.

MH: What impresses me about the way that you're talking about your life as governor is that despite some frustrations and problems, you seem to be having a good time.

CTW: I'm having a ball. I love it. I'll be happy when the campaign's over, because what I resent now is that everything that I do governmentally is perceived as—quote unquote—"political." That drives me nuts, but again, that's the way things are. I'm having a great time, though. Among other things, I get to go do five-trap landings in an F-14 on a carrier.

RM: It's a valuable contribution to politics and government in this country for an unspoken message to be delivered that someone who is a governor, a high-ranking officeholder, is actually having fun at it. I think that's an important educational message.

CTW: I think what you find among the governors is a lot more of that than for almost any other kind of officeholder. One reason is that a governorship is a wonderful position from which to effect change. You can do more of it directly than from almost any other position. With the legislative branch, you've got to get through the subcommittees, and then the full committees, and then the full house. Talk about compromise—you're doing it every other second there. Executives get a lot more hands-on contact with people and issues. I have a ball when we go to National Governors Association, too, because the other governors are great fun. My husband, John, picked this up at those meetings and said to me once, "You guys really have a good time." It doesn't matter much if we're Republicans or Democrats, since we face so many of the same problems. And they're just a good group of people for the most part, although George Pataki said to me a while ago, "You told me it was going to be fun. I'm waiting."

MH: We're glad you haven't had to wait to have fun. Governor, thank you so much.

NOTES

■

1. Margaret Mead, *Continuities in Cultural Evolution* (New Haven: Yale University Press, 1964).

2. Helen S. Astin and Carole Leland, *Women of Influence, Women of Vision: A Cross-Generational Study of Leaders and Social Change* (San Francisco: Jossey-Bass, 1991), p. xi. A useful discussion for the biographical approach to women's leadership being presented here is set out in the introductory chapter, which uses interview data from the lives and achievements of three generations of women leaders, seventy-seven in all, who worked for educational reform in America from the 1960s through the 1980s. These women, drawn from the higher education community as well as from foundations and government agencies, created reentry programs for returning women, pioneered programs in women's studies, proposed legislation to combat sex discrimination in the workplace, and more. Their stories present a powerful collective portrait of how a group inspired by the wider social change that was embodied in the second wave of the women's movement— a "small group of thoughtful committed citizens," in Margaret Mead's phrase—worked to effect lasting educational and social reforms that have already benefited generations of women.

3. This figure is cited from the 1997 fact sheets published by the Center for the American Woman and Politics at the Eagleton Institute of Politics, Rutgers University. For fuller global statistics, see *The World's Women 1995: Trends and Statistics* (New York: United Nations Publications, 1995).

4. The figures cited here, aside from the U.S. congressional figure, were taken from "Men and Women in Politics: Democracy Still in the Making" (1997), a poster produced with support from the European Union and the Swedish International Development and Cooperation Agency (SIDA).

5. *Women in Corporate Leadership: Progress and Prospects* (New York: Catalyst, 1996), esp. chap. 3, "The Quest for Balance—Juggling Career and Personal Life."

6. Cited in *NGO Forum on Women: Beijing 1995*, Final Report (New York: NGO Forum on Women, Beijing '95 Inc., 1996), p. 6.

7. Remarks of Ambassador Madeleine K. Albright, U.S. Permanent Representative to the United Nations, concerning the Fourth World Conference on Women, Center for National Policy Breakfast, Washington D.C., August 2, 1995.

8. *Report of the Fourth World Conference on Women* (New York: United Nations Department for Policy Coordination and Sustainable Development, 1995).

9. See Astin and Leland, chap. 5, "Leadership for Change," pp. 84–106. Such programs include ACENIP (the American Council on Education National Identification Program for the Advancement of Women in Higher Education) founded in 1977 and, since 1997, the American Council on Education National Network for Women Leaders; Catalyst, an organization founded in 1962 whose mission is "working with business to effect change for women—through research, advisory services and communication"; and the Center for the American Woman and Politics at the Eagleton Institute of Politics at Rutgers University, a research, education, and public service center, founded in 1971, whose mission is to promote greater understanding and knowledge about women's influence and leadership in public life.

10. Anne Firth Murray, unpublished paper from a plenary speech at Mills College in June 1993, on the occasion of the founding there of an institute for women's leadership.

11. David C. Smith, "Ethics and Leadership: The 1990's," introduction to the Special Issue of *Business Ethics Quarterly* 5, no. 1 (1995): 1. A current project on general leadership studies that is producing exciting approaches to the theory and practice of leadership is the Kellogg Leadership Studies Project, based at the University of Maryland at College Park at the Academy of Leadership there. A series of working papers by affiliated scholars and practitioners is being published in three volumes on the topics "Ethics and Leadership" (1996), "Leadership and Followership" (1997), and "Transforming Leadership" (1998). These pamphlets are available from the Kellogg Leadership Studies Project, c/o Center for Political Leadership and Participation, University of Maryland at College Park, College Park, Md. 20742-7715.

12. Joseph Rost, *Leadership for the Twenty-First Century* (New York: Praeger, 1991).

13. See Rost, *Leadership for the Twenty-First Century*, esp. chap. 1, "The Problem with Leadership Studies," pp. 1–13. For a useful and comprehensive discussion of Rost and other recent leadership literature, see Joanne B. Ciulla, "Leadership Ethics: Mapping the Territory," *Business Ethics Quarterly* 5, no. 1 (1995). Rost's study is hailed in a foreword by James MacGregor Burns, himself the author of the Pulitzer Prize–winning book *Leadership* (1978), as "the most important critique of leadership studies in our times: and the future 'Bible' for the emerging post-industrial school of leadership" (Rost, pp. xi–xii). See also, in the same issue of *BEQ*, p. 143: Al Gini, "Too Much to Say about Something," a review of Rost's book.

14. See Rost, chap. 4, "Definitions: The 1980s," pp. 69–95.

15. Rost, p. 102.

16. Rost, p. 182.

17. Bernard M. Bass, *Bass & Stogdill's Handbook of Leadership* 3d ed. (New York: Free Press, 1990).

18. Noteworthy among such studies are N. Adler and D. Izraeli, *Competitive Frontiers: Women Managers in a Global Economy* (Cambridge, Mass.: Blackwell, 1994); Lotte Bailyn, *Breaking the Mold: Women, Men, and Time in the New Corporate World* (New York: Free Press, 1993); Constance H. Buchanan, *Choosing to Lead: Women and the Crisis of American Values* (Boston: Beacon, 1996); D. Cantor and T. Bearney, *Women in Power* (Boston: Houghton Mifflin, 1992); Cynthia Epstein, *Women in Law* (Champaign: University of Illinois Press, 1993); Sally Helgesen, *The Female Advantage: Women's Way of Leadership* (New York: Doubleday, 1990); Kathleen Hall Jamieson, *Beyond the Double Bind: Women and Leadership* (New York: Oxford University Press, 1995); Karin Klenke, *Women and Leadership: A Contextual Perspective* (New York: Springer, 1996); Jean Lipman-Blumen, *The Connective Edge: Leading in an Interdependent World* (San Francisco: Jossey-Bass, 1996); Larraine R. Matusak, *Finding Your Voice: Learning to Lead . . . Anywhere You Want to Make a Difference* (San Francisco: Jossey-Bass, 1997); Ann M. Morrison, *Breaking the Glass Ceiling: Can Women Reach the Top of America's Largest Corporations* (Reading, Mass.: Addison-Wesley, 1987) and *The New Leaders: Guidelines on Leadership Diversity in America* (San Francisco: Jossey-Bass, 1992); Judy B. Rosener, *America's Competitive Secret: Utilizing Women as a Management Strategy* (New York: Oxford University Press, 1995); and Margaret J. Wheatley, *Leadership and the New Science* (San Francisco: Berrett-Koehler, 1992).

19. *Quest, a Feminist Quarterly* (spring 1976); see esp. the lively and thought-provoking interview of Charlotte Bunch and Beverly Fisher, "What Future for Leadership?" pp. 2–13.

20. Rosabeth Moss Kanter, *Men and Women of the Corporation* (New York: Basic Books, 1977).

21. See the fuller discussion in Astin and Leland, *Women of Influence, Women of Vision,* pp. 2–7.

22. Carol Watson, "When a Woman Is the Boss: Dilemmas in Taking Charge," *Group and Organization Studies* 13, no. 2 (1988): 163–181.

23. For a good summary of this viewpoint, see Judy B. Rosener, "Ways Women Lead," *Harvard Business Review* (November–December 1990): 119–125.

24. Constance H. Buchanan, *Choosing to Lead: Women and the Crisis of American Values* (Boston: Beacon Press, 1996), pp. 213–214.

25. Anne Firth Murray, unpublished paper presented at Mills College symposium, 1993.

ABOUT THE
INTERVIEWERS

∎

CHARLOTTE BUNCH is the founder and executive director of the Center for Women's Global Leadership at Douglass College, the college for women at Rutgers, the State Univesity of New Jersey, and a professor in the Bloustein School of Planning and Public Policy at Rutgers. An activist, author, and organizer in the women's and civil rights movements for three decades, Bunch is known worldwide for her work on women's human rights, especially combating violence against women. She was inducted into the National Women's Hall of Fame in Seneca Falls in 1996. The center she directs coordinated the Global Campaign for Women's Human Rights at the 1993 United Nations World Conference on Human Rights in Vienna and organized the caucus on that topic at the United Nations World Conference on Women in Beijing. The center is coordinating the 1998 Global Campaign to celebrate and demand women's human rights as the world marks the fiftieth anniversary of the Universal Declaration of Human Rights.

DOROTHY SUE COBBLE is an associate professor at Rutgers University in the School for Management and Labor Relations, where she teaches labor studies, history, and women's studies. Her extensive publications in the field of women and work include an award-winning book on waitresses and unionizing in the twentieth century. Professor Cobble was the founding director of the Center for Women and Work (1993), which is a member of the consortium of the Institute for Women's Leadership. Under her direction, the center sponsored interdisciplinary conferences, launched curricular initiatives on women and work, and advised the special issue of the Institute for Women's Leaderships publication *N.J. Women Count*, a survey of the economic status of women in New Jersey.

ADRIENNE COLELLA is an assistant professor in the Department of Management in the Lowry Mays College and Graduate School of Business at Texas A&M University. Dr. Colella's research focuses on the socialization of organizational newcomers and disability issues in human resource management. She has served as a consultant to several organizations on projects concerning performance appraisal and organizational structure. She has been an investigator on grants and contracts from the Army Research Institute and the New Jersey Developmental Disability Council. A member of the American Psychological Association, the Society of Industrial/Organizational Psychology, and the Academy of Management, she serves on the editorial boards of the *Journal of Applied Psychology* and the *Academy of Management Journal.* In 1995–96, she was acting director of the Center for Women and Work.

MARTHA A. COTTER is a professor of chemistry at Rutgers University, where she also serves as vice chair for the graduate program of the Department of Chemistry. Professor Cotter is a theoretical physical chemist who uses the techniques of statistical mechanics to study the relationship between molecular structure and interactions and the usual macroscopic properties of liquid crystalline states of matter. In addition to teaching and research, Martha Cotter has long been involved in efforts to increase the number of women pursuing careers in science and related fields. She has participated in the Douglass Project for Rutgers Women in Math, Science, and Engineering since its inception in 1986. From January 1995 through June 1996, she served as acting dean of Douglass College, where she became involved in the activities of the Institute for Women's Leadership.

HARRIET DAVIDSON is the director of the Women's Studies Program at Rutgers and an associate professor of English and women's studies. Her teaching and research specialties include feminist theory, women poets, and twentieth-century literature. Her current scholarship focuses on the role of poetry in feminist movements, the social function of poetry, poetry and performance, and poetry and the politics of identity. As a co-organizer in 1997 of a major conference, "Poetry in the Public Sphere," Professor Davidson, with Rutgers colleagues, hosted poets including Adrienne Rich, Sonia Sanchez, Amiri Baraka, and Poet Laureate Robert Hass, who held exchanges with academics, activists, teachers, and students about the transformative possibilities of poetry.

MARIANNE DEKOVEN served as director of the Institute for Research on Women from 1995 to 1998. She is a professor of English and women's studies and cofounder of the Gender Group, an interdisciplinary feminist colloquium of the English and History Departments at Rutgers. Her scholarship is in the fields of twentieth-century literary and cultural studies and feminist theory and criticism. Professor DeKoven has served as chair of the Division of Late-Nineteenth- and Early-Twentieth-Century English Literature of the Modern Language Association and currently serves on the editorial boards of several journals in her field. As director of the Institute for Research on Women, she led the first annual interdisciplinary seminar, a joint activity with the Institute for Woman's Leadership units, whose theme for 1997–1999 is "Women in the Public Sphere: Practice, Power, and Agency."

MARY S. HARTMAN is University Professor and director of the Institute for Women's Leadership at Douglass College. A historian who has published widely in European social history and women's history, Dr. Hartman served as the dean of Douglass College from 1982 to 1994. In that role she initiated a number of nationally recognized programs for women, including the Douglass Project for Rutgers Women in Math, Science, and Engineering; the Center for Women's Global Leadership; the Laurie New Jersey Chair in Women's Studies, and the Institute for Women's Leadership. Since assuming the directorship of the institute in 1995, Mary Hartman has coordinated planning and support activities for the consortium and will be participating with colleagues in a new institute-sponsored leadership curriculum for undergraduates.

LISA HETFIELD is associate director/director of development for the Institute for Women's Leadership consortium at Douglass College. Former school development officer for Douglass in its seventy-fifth anniversary campaign, she has more than twenty years of experience in fund development and public relations for educational and nonprofit institutions. As associate director of the institute, Lisa Hetfield coordinated the planning of the Leadership Scholars Program for undergraduates as well as the Gender and Technology Project, which is bringing new dimensions to the research, teaching, and public service missions of the consortium member units through presence on the Worldwide Web.

CORA KAPLAN is a professor of English at the University of Southampton, England. Professor Kaplan was director of the Institute for Research on Women, a member unit of the Institute for Women's Leadership consortium supported through the New Brunswick Faculty of Arts and Sciences, from 1992 to 1995. In that capacity, she sponsored several interdisciplinary seminars for faculty and graduate students, ran an international conference in collaboration with scholars from Princeton University and the Institute for Advanced Studies, and coordinated annual conferences on gender research for scholars and practitioners in the New Jersey, New York, and Pennsylvania area. Her scholarly interests include modern culture and global feminism. Hers was the original idea for the collaborative project which became *Talking Leadership: Conversations with Powerful Women.*

ALICE KESSLER-HARRIS directed the Rutgers/New Brunswick Women's Studies Program from 1990 to 1995. A professor in the department of history at Rutgers, she has published extensively in the field of women's history, particularly the history of working women in the United States. Widely recognized as one of the foremost authorities in that field, she has lectured and consulted worldwide, served on numerous editorial boards, and held offices in several professional organizations. She holds honorary degrees from Goucher College and from Uppsala University in Sweden and is the recipient of major awards from the Ford, Fulbright, Rockefeller, and Guggenheim foundations.

RUTH B. MANDEL is director of the Eagleton Institute of Politics and Board of Governors Professor of Politics at Rutgers. From 1971 through 1994, she served as director of Eagleton's Center for the American Woman and Politics, where she remains affiliated as a senior scholar, writing and speaking widely on women and leadership with special emphasis on women candidates, women in office, women's political networks, and the gender gap. Since 1991, Professor Mandel has been a member of the U.S. Holocaust Memorial Council, the governing body of the U.S. Holocaust Memorial Museum in Washington, D.C. She was named vice chairperson of the board by President Clinton in 1993. Ruth Mandel holds numerous awards for her pioneering research, education, and public service activities with a focus on women officials, elected and appointed.

BARBARA A. SHAILOR became the eighth dean of Douglass College in 1996. Under her leadership, the college is expanding its nationally recognized programs in mathematics, science, engineering, and technology; increasing its emphsis on women's leadership; and promoting educational programs and opportunities for young women in professional fields. Before coming to Douglass, Dean Shailor was vice president of student services (1991–1996) and professor of classics at Bucknell University, where she taught Latin and Greek language and literature as well as courses in humanities and classical civilization. Her special areas of research include Latin manuscripts, classical texts of the Middle Ages, and classical mythology; and she is the winner of awards for excellence in teaching as well as research.

DEBORAH GRAY WHITE is professor of history and Africana studies at Rutgers and also codirector of the Black Atlantic project at Rutgers's Center for Historical Analysis from 1997 through 1999. She specializes in American history, American women's history, and African-American history. She is a former member of the executive board of the Organization of American Historians and a former academic director of the DeWitt Wallace Readers Digest Fund/Woodrow Wilson Foundation Summer Institute for Middle School Teachers. Dr. White is also a consultant on integrating women and minorities into public school curricula.